Dare To Dream

Matthew Dieumegard-Thornton

Second Edition Print

Copyright © Matthew Dieumegard-Thornton 2016

First published in Great Britain by Blurb, Inc. in 2013.

Discover more about the author:
www.matthewdthornton.com

The right of Matthew Dieumegard-Thornton to be identified as the author of this work has been asserted by him in accordance with the Copyright, Designs and Patents Act 1988.

All rights reserved. No part of this publication may be reproduced, stored in or introduced into a retrieval system, or transmitted, in any form, or by any means (electronic, mechanical, photocopying, recording or otherwise) without the prior written permission of the publisher. Any person who does any unauthorised act in relation to this publication may be liable to criminal prosecution and civil claims for damages.

Every effort has been made to contact the copyright holders of material included in this book, but if any have been overlooked the Publishers would be pleased to make restitution at the earliest possible opportunity.

This book is sold subject to the condition that it shall not, by way of trade or otherwise, be lent, re-sold, hired out, or otherwise circulated without the publisher's prior consent in any form of binding or cover other than that in which it is published and without a similar condition including this condition being imposed on the subsequent purchaser.

To Chhewang Dorjee, my Sherpa brother
Same thumbs, different mothers
&
To Mum
You gave me the inspiration to climb

This book is dedicated to Dawa Dorjee Sherpa who I summited Baruntse with at 11am on the 4th November 2011. He was tragically killed on Manaslu in 2012.

Table of Contents

Chapter I – Acknowledgements
Chapter 1 – Why We Climb
Chapter 2 – The Beginnings
Chapter 3 – Sir Isaac Newton & Abi Titmuss
Chapter 4 – University Life
Chapter 5 – Life in the Alps, a Realisation
Chapter 6 – The Plan
Chapter 7 – Back to University, Almost
Chapter 8 – A Decent Proposal
Chapter 9 – Year 3
Chapter 10 – The Scottish Winter
Chapter 11 – Graduating In Life
Chapter 12 – A Mountain Cometh
Chapter 13 – Kyrgyzstan: A Travellers Guide
Chapter 14 – Peak Lenin: The Climb
Chapter 15 – Home Bound
Chapter 16 – Where to Begin
Chapter 17 – Training for a Decision
Chapter 18 – Training without Oxygen
Chapter 19 – Progress and Preparations
Chapter 20 – Baruntse
Chapter 21 – The Ascent of Mera Peak
Chapter 22 – To Baruntse
Chapter 23 – Moving up the Mountain
Chapter 24 – The Ascent of Baruntse
Chapter 25 – The Base Camp Slumber
Chapter 26 – The Amphu Lapcha
Chapter 27 – The Aftermath
Chapter 28 – A Well Timed Break
Chapter 29 – Can You Yell Hibu?
Chapter 30 – Incomprehensible Ecstasy
Chapter 31 – Progression and Preparations
Chapter 32 – Final Checks, One More Run
Chapter 33 – The Jet Set to Everest
Chapter 34 – The Java Coffee House
Chapter 35 – Third Time Lucky
Chapter 36 – From Bengkar to Bengkar
Chapter 37 – Along the Lonely Road
Chapter 38 – In the Shadow of Everest

Chapter 39 – The Blessing
Chapter 40 – End of the Road
Chapter 41 – Base Camp Life
Chapter 42 – Recurrence
Chapter 43 – Another World
Chapter 44 – The Long Cwm
Chapter 45 – Too Close
Chapter 46 – Base Camp Routine
Chapter 47 – The Final Rotation
Chapter 48 – In the Search for Oxygen
Chapter 49 – A Matter of Numbers
Chapter 50 – The First Push
Chapter 51 – The Lhotse Face
Chapter 52 – Get In Line
Chapter 53 – The South Col
Chapter 54 – Reformation of the Line
Chapter 55 – Leading Into the Night
Chapter 56 – Technical Difficulties
Chapter 57 – The Pinnacle of a Dream
Chapter 58 – Rush Hour
Chapter 59 – To the Col
Chapter 60 – The Summit Aftermath
Chapter 61 – The Final Icefall
Chapter 62 – Dark Clouds
Chapter 63 – Clearing Skies
Chapter 64 – Blue Skies Part 1
Chapter 65 – Blue Skies Part 2
Glossary

Acknowledgements

I prefer to think that the author of this journey is really Dieumegard-Thornton et al. *Et al* meaning 'and others' is a Latin phrase which goes some way in describing that this metaphorical journey has been written by a multitude of people who have helped to make everything which follows possible. The climb of Everest was not a single person's effort, nor could it have been done without the help and dedication of the many people who are listed below.

It takes a strong person to deny all help, but always a stronger person to ask for it.

To the Sherpas of Everest and of the Himalayas, the mountain would not be possible if it wasn't for your strength, courage and laughter: Chewang Dorje Sherpa, Kame Nuru Sherpa, Chyang Jyabu Bhote, Lhakpa Tundu Sherpa, Lhakpa Wangchu Sherpa, Dorje Gyalzen Sherpa, Tapchen Lama Bhote, Padawa Sherpa, Nuru Sherpa, Dawa Dorjee Sherpa, Sonam Dorji Sherpa, Surendra Gurung Sherpa, Bhim, Khumar and Pasang Temba.

The people of Everest who made up the 2012 season on the world's highest mountain: Henry Todd, Kenton Cool, Mollie Hughes, Rick, Ryan, Paul Keleher, Roger Owen, Becky Bellworthy, Keith Partridge, Bonita Norris, Robert Jen, Valerie Boffy and Rob Casserley. Thank you too, to the unforgettable Iswari Paudel and your team for many unexpected helicopter evacuations and the contribution to an unforgettable experience each time I have ventured to Nepal.

To three of the finest guides in the mountains, ranging from Glen Coe to the Himalayas: Zac Poulton, Mark Scales and Paddy Cave.

To the team of Baruntse: Debbie Spencer, Roy "Baby" Baines, Nicky Tuer, Eoin Corcoran, Hannah Vickers, Gordon Brown, Ian Hobson, Mary Reape, Andrew Milne; the finest team to grace the Himalayas. To FO (soon to be Captain) James Morrison—for the hundreds of hours we have spent discussing the art of flight, David Wilson, Ian Ellis, Adam Osbirk-Jensen, Wesley Marks and Dave Pritt for that first crazed journey into the back of beyond.

To Dr Chris Bussell, Dr Graham Sharpe, Dr Michael Johnson, Dr Toni Minniti, Dr Caroline Sunderland and Jenn Bennett for the knowledge, a most precious commodity; and Dr Brian Saunders—clearly all those blood tests in the altitude chamber were worth it.

To Martin Lane for some wise advice in the Alps, Dom Cole for all those laughs with Terry and Brian, Martin Gibson for turning me from that little donkey into a squash player, James Knight, Simon Scott and Eddie Charlton for more laughs and occasionally excusing me from university. To all those from Sleaford SC who had the patience to help me learn, Steve Varney, Mad Mac Mackenzie, Ken Smith, Stan Wisdom and Dave Bailey.

Wempy Dyocta Koto, the man of mystery and just the business head I needed right up to the end.

To my expedition equipment sponsors, AMG Group (Vango, Force Ten, Asolo), Maximuscle, Osprey, Trekmates, and to partners present and past, NTU Hive, NTU Stars, Harrow Sports, Kentbridge Sports and Wardour And Oxford.

To Mike Pocock, Bob Wigley, Christian Wells, Kimberley Watts-Fitzsimmons, Julie McCallum, Sue Mitchell, Jon Salmon, Demelza Fryer-Saxby, Jin Gill and Sandra Holt—the team at Yell/hibu, thank you for taking that risk and believing in me, perhaps more than I often dared to myself.

And finally, to Mum for your endless love and guidance, and Dad for those first few tentative steps into the vertical world.

Chapter 1 – Why We Climb

"The first question which you will ask and which I must try to answer is this, 'What is the use of climbing Mount Everest?' and my answer must at once be, 'It is no use'. There is not the slightest prospect of any gain whatsoever. Oh, we may learn a little about the behaviour of the human body at high altitudes, and possibly medical men may turn our observation to some account for the purposes of aviation. But otherwise nothing will come of it. We shall not bring back a single bit of gold or silver, not a gem, nor any coal or iron. We shall not find a single foot of earth that can be planted with crops to raise food. It's no use. So, if you cannot understand that there is something in man which responds to the challenge of this mountain and goes out to meet it, that the struggle is the struggle of life itself upward and forever upward, then you won't see why we go. What we get from this adventure is just sheer joy. And joy is, after all, the end of life. We do not live to eat and make money. We eat and make money to be able to enjoy life. That is what life means and what life is for." George Leigh Mallory, 1922.

Loud, cold, ferocious and foreboding, how does anyone begin to contemplate a climb up the icy face of Mount Everest, let alone reach the summit and get down alive? This is the question I posed to my 14-year-old self standing in front of Doug Scott's bloodstained suit, and George Mallory's ice axe at the Everest Exhibition at Rheged in Cumbria.

Although it hadn't crossed my youthful mind which instantly got down to the task of working out whether this feat would be possible, there is another question which is far harder to answer than the question of possibility versus impossibility.

Why would you want to climb Everest? As Mallory himself said, there isn't really anything to be gained from climbing the mountain; except for the geological and physiological studies which occasionally take place on the mountain, you can't actually bring anything of worth back home.

So again, why would you want to climb it? There are so many obstacles to overcome which in all reality must outweigh any possible gains. Examples of the dangers you might happen to face on Everest include intense cold where your skin freezes in seconds leading to frostbite and possible limb amputation. Then there are the direct effects of altitude itself. Firstly altitude can kill in two main ways, either HAPE (High Altitude Pulmonary Oedema), or HACE (High Altitude Cerebral Oedema). If you're lucky, you may be able to treat one of these conditions and descend but if you are unlucky, you may develop both and face almost certain death above 8,000m. If you do happen survive the mountain, you will certainly have lost a large percentage of muscle mass since there is so little oxygen above 8,000m which means you are technically metabolising your own body through the process of atrophy—just one of altitude's little reminders of your own mortality.

Obviously the obstacles on Everest don't quite stop here. If you're not put off by the extreme cold, lack of oxygen, risk of HAPE, HACE, or the assured encounter with atrophy, you also need to prepare yourself for avalanches, serac falls, bottomless crevasses, hurricane force winds, living in a tent for 70 days, loss of appetite, loss of weight, loss of mental composure, potential loss of grasp on reality, potential loss of consciousness, and potential loss of life which may or may not be caused by a Yeti.

All this and we are still yet to consider the certain loss of brain cells, resulting in a decreased ability to engage in positive debate with armchair critics who enjoy nothing more than to lament over the floccinaucinihilipilification of any modern expedition to Everest or neighbouring peaks.

So clearly Everest isn't for everybody, but for me there was something magical about pitting yourself against the mountain, and asking the mountain *the* question: 'Am I good enough?'

Climbing at high altitude strips you of all the pretence and visage of the western world and leaves you with the essential ingredients such as determination and ability which are fundamental in surviving in this type of environment. Quite simply, to climb at high altitude, you have to be made of the right stuff.

But none of this really matters to a 14-year-old boy with the beauty of spontaneous adventure in his blood. The question of *why* you want to climb the mountain is irrelevant, the only thing that mattered was the *how,* and for a Taurus like me, the *when* was also quite a pressing issue.

Needless to say, after another thrilling adventure in the Lake District with the added excitement of adding Mount Everest to my to-do list, I went home, returned to my normal lifestyle in the flat county of Lincolnshire and the thoughts of Everest gradually faded away, on hold at the back of my mind with all my other dreams and aspirations until the right time came. At times I would review the to-do list in my mind and often thought that as much as I wanted to climb Everest, to stand on its fearsome shoulders, I doubted I would get the chance; it is Everest after all.

So I let Everest stay at the back of my mind just in case perhaps one day, fate called. Equally I tried not to worry about when I would get my chance to climb to the top of the world, and so my dream lay hidden but I never forgot my dream, just in case.

Chapter 2 - The Beginnings

This story, however, begins further back than Everest, for to climb the tallest mountain on earth it is usually good to have done a little preparation in the sport, perhaps even to have climbed a mountain or two just so you know what you're letting yourself in for.

My love of sport first grew when my mum started her trend of buying me a bicycle each year for my birthday. I remember my first bike vividly, a Jungle Book bike bought from the local bike shop, the owner of which was an exceptionally talented rider. My bike still remains the best present I have ever received simply because for me it was far more than just a bike. Metaphorically it was freedom and most importantly, it was my first introduction to sport which has since become an integral part of my life.

Ironically though I didn't appear to be blessed with the natural ability to excel at the sport of climbing, the main reason for this being an acute fear of heights which I had had from a young age. I didn't know it at the time but the fear of heights is quite a broad definition, and Catapedaphobia (the fear of jumping from height) is different from Acrophobia (the absolute fear of heights). Despite this fact I certainly did not display any climbing ability from a young age. On a trip to Australia at the tender age of eight, I struggled to jump from a two-metre springboard into a diving pool, and after five minutes of being told it was mind over matter, I promptly (and very tentatively) turned around and crawled back to the safety of the pool side.

My fear came back once again to haunt me on work experience at RAF Cranwell, when, after a successful training week, all the trainee officers including my school friend and I were asked to jump from a ten-metre diving platform. Standing at the pool side I couldn't see any problem with this; I had after all matured and clearly would now be able to put mind over matter. I carried on in this confident manner until the second set of steps to the top platform where I realised that this probably wasn't the best idea, and there was the potential to stand quivering at the top of the diving platform in front of 50 RAF officers until either someone pushed me off the edge or I fell. Walking back down the steps is certainly no option in the UK military where everyone has sworn to make the ultimate sacrifice to protect Queen and country if needed. Eventually, after all the trainee officers had jumped I stood at the top. As soon as my feet left the platform, that weightless feeling that is just as addictive as it is uncontrollable flooded through my body, and before I knew it I was under water.

That jump took more persuading than I care to admit but clearly these aren't promising signs of a high altitude mountaineer in the making.

I took with me the aversion to jumping from high places through most of my childhood and at the age of eight, embarked upon my first taste of the mountains with my dad. It wasn't the first time that he had ventured into the mountains of the English Lake District, but for me this was to be my first foray into a world of high places.

Everything seemed so impressive, especially to an impressionable young boy. The mountains were the biggest I had ever seen. The rain, thunder and lightning, the wind and the cold were more intense than I had ever experienced before. Here it seemed was the place that I would get my first taste of true adventure, a release from school life where rules no longer existed and you were just free to 'be'.

We spent the time backpacking around the well-known valleys of the Lakes and eventually when the time came to try and climb a mountain, we succeeded in climbing to the top of Scafell Pike, all 978 metres of it. Even more impressive was the fact that we had seemingly walked into a different world. From the green valley below, we now appeared to be surrounded by a moonscape environment with rocks and boulders the size of small cars all around us. This place was so far removed from home that you would be forgiven for thinking you had travelled to a different country.

Back at valley level, it seemed strange to think we had been standing at the top of that impressive massif of rock. It was majestic to see clouds roll over the summit of the mountain; we really had touched the sky.

Success and glory, however, cannot last forever, especially if you live only by your previous triumphs, so with that in mind and a hunger to try and climb just one more mountain, we left the base of Scafell in search of our next goal. We first headed over into Ennerdale, one of the Lake District's best kept secrets, and then into Buttermere. Although physically exhausting for my little legs, carrying a rucksack as an eight-year-old was made easier by the knowledge of the adventure to come and the option of a taxi for when the torrential rain turned the paths into rivers, and the rivers into lakes.

When we reached Buttermere, we saw our objective. Red Pike is only 755m tall, yet technically a bit more challenging than Scafell Pike with its loose scree paths, well eroded by years of travel. The following day we were ready, taking the first part of the walk in in our stride. The start of the climb didn't seem to be a problem either with nice and easy walking, but at three quarters of the way up a fellow walker said, "It's a bit of a scramble..." We listened to the advice, but then concluded that we had climbed the highest mountain in England, so Red Pike at some 223m lower should surely be within our capabilities.

After a matter of metres, the path suddenly got scarily steep and very loose. We had clearly come off the main path to the top of Red Pike, and were now traversing fairly close to what seemed like an almost vertical drop. At this point, both father and son were having a great deal of difficulty deciding the best course of action. I had decided that I couldn't possible descend and therefore must continue to go up until we reached the top, whilst Dad decided he just couldn't carry on upwards since realistically, there didn't seem to be anywhere left to go. We were both stuck between a rock and quite a hard place, where every minute that we waited, another strand would break from the clump of grass I was using to keep myself anchored to the mountain. Eventually we decided that going up was the only realistic option since that meant Dad had the least chance of losing his son given that I was going up no matter what.

After another hour of clinging to loose rock, then tentatively moving up to the next precarious piece, only to see it pull out and spiral down to the lake hundreds of metres below, we eventually saw our first piece of flat land, the first we had seen for hours. This was the summit of Red Pike but we didn't care. Both shaking from exhaustion and fright, we didn't hang around long before finding the easiest possible route for descent and getting away from the grasp of the mountain. Red Pike could be described as a relatively easy walk with a tricky section at the top, but to my four foot self, the mountain was as scary and foreboding as it gets; *this is probably what the north face of the Eiger is like*, I thought.

The rest of that trip into the heart of the Lake District was spent at a more manageable level closer to the ground, but unbeknown to me, the epic we had had on Red Pike had sparked a desire for further adventure which would eventually take me to the top of the world.

Chapter 3 – Sir Isaac Newton & Abi Titmuss

With such adventure at a young age, you would have thought it would become a day-to-day schedule; wake up, go to school, finish school as soon as possible and then hit the mountains. Apparently, however, whoever designed the UK clearly neglected to add any mountains to the county of Lincolnshire. Lincolnshire, known for having the two best beaches in the UK (Skegness and Cleethorpes), boasts only one main mountainous area, this being the Lincolnshire Wolds. Known for their outstanding natural beauty and proximity to the bustling market town of Louth, the Wolds tower an impressive 168 metres over England's second most interesting county.

Previous residents of Lincolnshire are the main reason for the county's fame. These include the Romans, Sir Isaac Newton, Margaret Thatcher, Samantha Cameron and Abi Titmuss. Even Nick Clegg PC MP has close ties to the county, having romantically proposed to his wife on the platform of Rauceby Station which sits beside the now derelict Rauceby Mental Hospital.

Despite its fame and notoriety, Lincolnshire lacked the mountainous area I craved, and still does. Given this fact, the only times I had chance to visit the mountains were during school holidays and on certain school trips. Even though I had taken up the Duke of Edinburgh Award half way through secondary school, this didn't help towards mountain experience since the first two awards were conducted in the Lincolnshire fens.

I didn't worry myself, however, with the missing Lincolnshire massif, because climbing mountains was only a small part of my sporting life as a child. Most of my time, including all my free periods whilst in sixth form, were spent on the squash court. It seems strange that while on one hand I loved everything the big open stage of the mountains had to offer, on the other I enjoyed an indoor sport contested between four incredibly close walls. So much so in fact that upon leaving school, I decided that I would take on the challenge of becoming a professional squash player with all the sacrifices and commitment it takes to compete in this demanding sport at the highest level.

There was one sacrifice I wasn't willing to make, however, and this was my education. It's funny that whilst in full time education, the only thing most adolescents want is to get out yet once you're out, you only then realise how much you miss learning in an effort to reach hallowed infallibility. I didn't completely share this view whilst slogging out revision and so I was quite glad to have finally finished sixth form in possession of a set of A-Levels. I did, however, recognise quickly that as much as I wanted to take up playing squash full time, I wasn't good enough to just leave school and sculpt my career by playing and training without a backup plan. The clear alternative for me was a degree but where, how, and what to study was something quite beyond my tunnel-visioned mind. This decision has since been made significantly easier with tuition fees increasing threefold meaning the only option for many is straight into employment (if you can find any), but if you are lucky enough to be able to afford further education, the competition for places is now so fierce, the prospective law student may have to settle for media studies after only gaining three A's instead of the triple A*'s and the £36,000 needed to mix it with the crème de la crème.

For me, as any potential athlete may be, I was tunnel-visioned and effectively blind to the choices I would make through the overwhelming desire to compete and win. It's quite hard to explain the drive where winning becomes everything but if you've had it, you know. I also happened to be the first person from my immediate family to go to university, so there was a real unknown about which choice to make. I decided to stay safe, and this meant sticking with sport, because after all that's what I was good at. Well not exactly; my best result at A-Level was geography, making me a certainty to choose that subject at degree level, but my sporting mind had other ideas and so I took to the *Times University Guide* to find the best university with the best squash court facilities. I had competed nationally at this point, and the obvious choice was clear to me even before delving into the book full of UCAS points and student quality surveys.

Nottingham is home to many Olympic quality arenas such as Holme Pierrepont National Watersports Centre, but it is also home to the NSRC, Nottingham Squash Rackets Club, which at the time was one of the finest squash clubs in the UK.

So, after two years of painfully going through sixth form, attempting to understand a fraction of what the physics teacher said and listening to a priceless speech by the head of the upper sixth on the subject of using bankruptcy to your advantage, I was accepted on my chosen course, and went on my way from the flat county of Lincolnshire to the flatter county of Nottinghamshire to study for the best part of the next three years. Well, that was the intention anyway.

Chapter 4 - University Life

Things didn't go too well on starting university, with my first problems arising before actually reaching the campus. Having come from a sleepy Lincolnshire town where a bus service is reserved for those over the age of 100, I encountered my first problem in Nottingham when trying to flag down the university bus. For the inexperienced bus traveller, there are three things that it takes to successfully travel from A to B. The first is knowing which bus to get on, the second is attempting to stop the bus once you've determined it's the correct one, and the third is having enough money, in the correct currency and in the exact amount to board the bus. The first two must be done with the desired bus travelling towards you at 40mph, the last one must be done with a full load of university students, especially when you have the embarrassment of dropping all your money, or counting out each individual 10p as it gradually creeps up to the £3 bus fare.

All this comes naturally to the city-wise, but for the uninitiated, it can be a frightful experience on your first day at university. I found this out first-hand when attempting to flag down three successive buses, the first by simply standing at the bus stop as you would a train station, the second by staring intently at the driver hoping he would read my anxious mind, and on the third attempt having previously lost the will to live, by practically throwing myself into the road in the hope that I would either be put out of my misery, or by some miracle I would get to my first day at university on time.

Fortunately the bus driver didn't kill me, otherwise you wouldn't have this tantalising story to enjoy on your lazy Sunday, but equally, it meant I could revel in this fascinating world of lectures, where finally you could fall asleep at will before waking up at any given opportunity to take in a ten minute pearl of wisdom, or eat whenever you felt hungry, or even just not turn up at all. University really was designed by students, for students.

So for the best part of two years, I stuck to my game plan: use my time at university to gain a high level of education to fall back upon, and at the same time, train as hard as possible so that on completion of my three years, I could turn professional and make a living from a sport that I lived for.

It was roughly at this point that I was fortunate enough to be sponsored by a US racket manufacturer, Harrow Sports, which buoyed my confidence in reaching my dream and provided a fantastic solution to my varied frustrations on the court. The longevity of a squash racket is a hotly debated topic and I somehow managed to adequately test most of my rackets to breaking point within two matches. Either disgusted at how I was playing, or more commonly how my racket was playing, I would hurl it into the wall and then look in disbelief as a crack magically appeared in the side of the frame. Fortunately this sponsorship deal came along just at the right time, and suddenly after trying every racket in the range, realised it may just be me rather than the racket. I could now proudly go to university knowing that I was a sponsored athlete of sorts, despite having chosen to play with a woman's racket with beautiful pink decals, which I never quite managed to live down.

I knew the first two years of university would be the best two years to succeed in gaining enough confidence, experience and fitness to turn professional after I graduated. Like many bachelor courses, the first year didn't count towards the overall degree, and it would only be the final year where the dissertation and final exam revision would prevent me from training as much as I needed to. To help me with my studies and performance, my university selected me for their talented athlete program which gave great benefits for students trying to juggle sport and education such as programme and nutrition advice, regular physiotherapy and massage sessions, plus an extra-extra-large hoodie that I could sleep in if I ever failed to make it back to my accommodation. I didn't realise it at the time, but my performance and training on the squash court would have a direct influence on how I performed in the mountains over four years later.

Once I had got into the rhythm and swing of university life, I started to add more and more hours to my training both on and off court. This reached a peak in my first three-month summer holiday where I committed to training full time and accepted that if I was going to become a professional athlete, I would need to do everything possible to achieve that goal. This meant training three times a day, six days a week, a gruelling regime by anyone's standard. On starting university, I hadn't let myself fully believe I had what it takes to turn professional, but after less than a year at NSRC, I knew this was what I wanted.

A typical day that summer would include a two-hour morning session on court with both ghost type exercises and solo practice. The second session would be either a practice match or fine technique work, which was then followed by an evening session of either weight training, a match or depending on the training period I was in, a five-mile run with the aim of maintaining a six minute mile pace for 30 minutes. Individually these would be tough training sessions, but put together, they made completing each day a mammoth task. I aimed to approach my training as professionally as possible, working with the best coaches in the game, and training with some of the top players in the world. Every day was a routine with a slightly different twist on training, and each individual session was planned to give the best possible results when I signed up to the PSA, the Professional Squash Association.

By far the hardest sessions were those without a ball and often without a racket. Speed training was a particular vomit-inducing session which was imperative to meet the demands of the modern game. Often this involved sprinting against an elastic bungee repetitively to simulate an effort far greater than you would encounter in a match. Another session just as hard and a club favourite was 22's. This meant sprinting 22 lengths of the court in under a minute, followed by varying rest periods, and then repeated for as long as you had the mental strength and muscular endurance to do so. The key to being good on a squash court, other than racket work and shot selection was the ability to move; to move well and to move quickly. Unfortunately, the compact nature of a squash court dictates that the movement is very explosive, with quick sprints followed by a sudden change in direction. To target this area of fitness is extremely demanding and places a lot of emphasis on the correct 'periodisation' of a training plan. What this means is that you have to train both for your base level of fitness to make sure you can cope with further demands of your training plan, then, after the base training has been completed, the speed and endurance training must be added on top. To periodise simply means correctly managing all aspects of your training, and putting it into an effective plan.

The first summer in Nottingham set the tone for the following academic year at university, and unfortunately, that plan didn't quite give the priority to my studies. Instead I continued to train as hard as possible with the extra pressure of lectures and coursework; however, I managed the two as best I could. It is often said that exercise is a key element for effective learning, but nevertheless the balance between effective learning and effective sports performance is such a fine line. Just as the line between winning and losing can be a matter of milliseconds, the measure between education and any extracurricular activity is delicate; education should never be overlooked in preference to sport, no matter how elite an athlete is.

Ignoring all of the above life advice, I was at times blissfully unaware that I was enrolled at university, and so kept sport as big a part of my life as possible. I had also begun to compete in the various leagues across the country, and at one point went on a three-day voyage with a training partner just to make my first paid league appearance where I went on to lose in emphatic style having spent the previous 12 hours travelling through the scenic north of England. During my first year in Nottingham, I also played my last competitive events in the junior U19 age category, playing both the British Open where I was cruelly seeded to play one of the top Pakistani players, and the British Nationals where I was seeded to play a 'nobody' who turned out to be quite good.

Despite there being little comparison between squash and mountaineering, it did teach me very important lessons that would become invaluable as I progressed through the high mountains. A key example is learning to lose. It may come as a surprise to hear that an athlete should train to lose as well as to win, but it is a fundamental part of competition as well as sport in general. Moving up through the rankings and forever playing better players, I had my fair share of defeats, but learning how to cope with a loss is imperative to improvement. An athlete who loses a match but is able to take key lessons from that defeat often gains far more than a player who wins but learns nothing. Equally if you can stare defeat in the face and still come up triumphant, the lessons learnt in this situation can be immeasurable, and as such the ability to be able to come back from the brink is often described as the mark of a great champion.

During my second year at university I carried on training and competing, anxious for the match where I would finally be able to make my mark, a mark I thought I deserved to make when I looked back through all the training I had done. Despite all this training, I felt I lacked something which was hindering my progress. I had all the fundamentals; great court speed, good shots, good fitness, and at times a good head for the right shots, but still, that little something was missing. A coach once said 'you have to be comfortable with dominating an opponent; to win vehemently'. However, my wins were always close and I was never able to quickly kill off an opponent. If I made it through the early rounds of a tournament, I would have been on court for twice as long as the best players. Clearly something needed to change.

My sport was getting stuffy and constricting, and I was consumed purely by winning which becomes an unhealthy way to live. I decided I needed a break to find the answer, as I had still not yet found an answer to the question of what I would do after university, I was still not good enough.

I didn't really need a break to work out why I could not bridge the gap to the best players. If you watch any elite sport, you can see it. There is a clear difference between those with, and those without. The commodity I am talking about is simply known as the X-factor. It is that thing, the thing that when you watch a successful athlete, it sets them apart from the rest. You can't quite put your finger on it, but the X-factor is what makes them good, and makes them win. Once you start to win, winning comes easily, and it becomes a habit.

Alas, I had decided that to reach my pinnacle, I would need to take a break, and now was the optimum time, at the end of Trinity term between my second and third year at university. I hadn't quite decided what I would do, but had by chance seen an opportunity for summer seasonal work in the French Alps. I had applied and then thought nothing of it, until I received first an interview, and then a job offer on my 20th birthday. This was the break I needed, and although sceptical at first of finding a squash court in a quiet alpine village, I decided that a few months away from the court would do me good. I still took a racket, just in case.

Chapter 5 - Life in the Alps, a Realisation

It may not seem like a big step at first, but for me this was on the large side. I hadn't thought before leaving the UK, but this would be the first time in seven years that I had spent more than a week away from the squash court. In those seven years I had spent almost every day training and playing a sport I simply loved, but when sport becomes an addiction, even the healthiest of past-times become dangerously obsessive.

So I relished this opportunity to work in the Alps. I had loved the mountains, but at home, they were just so far away. I had been to Chamonix twice before with Mum, and had fallen in love with the impressive alpine spires of Les Drus and Aiguille Verte and the impressive face of The Grandes Jorasses; however, before I had only been on holiday, now I was actually living it. There is something very special about the mountains, perhaps it is their grandeur, or the power they expel giving the feeling that no matter how hard or fast you climb, the mountains are in control. Most of all, in the mountains, there is no competition. When you climb, you only test yourself. You climb up, perhaps into the unknown and then pit yourself against the forces of nature with only the tools you carry plus your physical and mental strength and determination. When climbing, you are not fighting anybody else or even the mountain; you are only fighting yourself to be the best you can be.

For my summer posting, I was sent out to Les Gets in the Portes Du Soleil of the French and Swiss Alps. This charming little village is home to some of the best downhill mountain biking in the world, combining many resorts of the Portes Du Soleil in both France and Switzerland with a ski lift network covering around 400 square miles of pure terrain heaven. Working as a hotel assistant was a great way to truly enjoy the Alps. As soon as the guests had had breakfast at 10am, the morning work shift was finished, so between 10am and 5pm, I could be out all day with views out to Mont Blanc on the chair lifts before hitting the downhill as many times as possible in seven hours. This was as truly great way to spend the summer, and so different to what I was used to. Training was no longer a chore, I managed to run as often as I wanted and the difference was that in such breathtaking scenery I actually wanted to run.

It often takes a big change to shake up your routine, where you can finally look outside of the box, and see the little world you have been occupying. It's at times like this that you can ask yourself, is this really what you want from your life? Your life on planet earth is finite, and equally very short in comparison to the grand scheme of things, so it's worth making the most of each second you have and enjoying life as much as possible. Stepping aside from the usual routine is often quite revealing and often, the greatest adventures have been performed by people who were simply not content and wanted a break from the 9-5.

After my first month in the Alps, I realised that this was the first time I had ever not missed playing squash. There had been no competing, no big rivalries, no bravado of competition, just the fresh air of the mountains to wake up to, and the famous alpine glow to fall asleep to. Admittedly there was some work to be done in between, but I managed to bag some additional duties that were far more important than usual room cleaning and waiter service, such as hot tub and swimming pool maintenance which took up a surprising amount of my time.

Whilst in the Alps, I realised that I perhaps didn't want to confine the rest of my professional life, which could be shortened to 15 years, to a small windowless box playing squash. There are some sacrifices you have to make to become great at anything, and squash is no different, necessitating absolute devotion both on and off the court for any top player. I realised that whilst I wanted to excel in something, I didn't want my sense of adventure so confined, especially to an indoor sport. I also knew that I didn't have that x-factor, and since all the top professionals had started before the age of five compared to my age of 12, I would probably never reach the level I had so wanted; I hated admitting this to myself. Aside from the utter self-belief that is required to play sport at the elite level, occasionally a good grasp on reality is required before the tunnel vision becomes more detrimental than useful.

Having come to a conclusion that the sport I had devoted myself to just wouldn't quite cut it in the future, I spent another month in the Alps wondering whether I should carry on blindly with squash, or search for an alternative with which I could be more successful. I knew that I had one more year at university, but even spending the previous two years thinking, I still hadn't found my plan B if squash ever failed. It's never good to put all your eggs in one basket, and this is always the reason to take education as far as possible, no matter what you intend to do with the rest of your life.

The rest of the people who were working as seasonaires in the Alps had vastly differing wishes about where they wanted to take their lives next; most had degree level qualifications and most had worked more than one season. It is an easy life to get into; easy job, fantastic setting in the mountains, relatively like-minded people, and all the sport of varying kinds you could wish for. That said, it is also an easy lifestyle to get stuck in, especially if you haven't yet found your greater aspirations. I was keen to make my summer season a one-off, as on one hand, the learning experiences to be had are immense, however on the other, too many years can go by before you finally make crucial life decisions. With this knowledge, I tried to make a dream come true, and quickly.

Unfortunately for me, I didn't quite know what this dream was; however, it had been staring me in the face every time I went for a run, every time I went up on the chairlift and every time I tried and failed to hit a six foot drop in the bike park where I nearly always ended up in a concussed mess on the hard dirt floor. Mont Blanc was less than 25 miles away and although my sights were to be set on something far bigger, it was the perfect piece of inspiration.

I began to realise that I wanted to do something great in the mountains, but each time Mount Everest came to mind, I dismissed it as a dream that was almost unobtainable. It would take far too much time, money and experience which I lacked to even start to think about Everest. I couldn't piece together all the elements that would be needed to embark on such a journey, but to simply quench my thirst for this type of adventure, I started watching a series of Everest documentaries and films detailing previous expeditions and climbers. The more I watched, the more I wanted to achieve what these climbers were achieving; the seemingly impossible was becoming possible right in front of my eyes. One such climber, Bonita Norris who became the youngest ever Briton to climb Everest almost within two years of conceiving the idea was inspirational; this was clearly an achievable goal. Likewise it's hard to discount the inspiration I gained when reading *Facing Up* by Bear Grylls.

I went for another run, a great thing to do when searching for an answer clouded by different thoughts of both the rational and irrational. It's hard to then say whether my reaction was instantly clear, but within the same day I had made the decision; I would try to climb Mount Everest by any means possible. It's as simple as that. I had no idea how I would get the funding, I still lacked mountaineering experience, I had never been to altitude, and moreover, I simply didn't have a clue where to start. I had no training plan, and I didn't even know if such a plan existed for high altitude, so the likelihood of this dream even getting off the ground was slim by any standards.

I had harboured this dream of climbing Everest since seeing the exhibition in Cumbria at the age of 14. I had, however, never fully believed I would ever get the chance to even have an attempt on Everest, so to make such an important decision so quickly seemed quite rash. I have no explanation as to why I convinced myself that now was the optimum time but for some reason it felt right and ironically, against my better judgement, I started to believe that I could actually do it.

Chapter 6 – The Plan

So how do you go about planning for Everest? The perspective is on a scale like no other plan. You have to make sure you have done the correct preparation both physically, mentally and have obtained sufficient experience on other mountains. You then have to have the correct level of funding from the moment you start your preparation until the moment you step off Everest. You have to prepare for eventualities that you couldn't even imagine facing on home soil, let alone on an ice field over 4,500 miles away from home. How can you possibly prepare for the reality of fatalities in the Death Zone? Above 8,000m, no human can survive, and as you inch your way up the mountain, you metabolise your own muscle fibres and tissue just to survive. This is a very hard perspective to see, especially in the eyes of a potential Everest climber where there are so many obstacles to overcome, the ability to simply ignore many of the dangers to come, whilst unrealistic, helps you to not become too overwhelmed by the challenge ahead both on the mountain and before you even reach base camp.

You don't have to be a psychologist to know that approaching an Everest expedition as outlined above is an insurmountable task as a whole. I knew from the moment I started planning that this project had to be broken down in to bite-size blocks, which had to then be tackled piece by piece without causing the reality of what lay ahead to become unquestionably unobtainable.

I first started with questions, and lots of them. Still working in my little alpine hotel, The Christiania, I crafted email upon email to mountain guides, past climbers, future Everest hopefuls, and expedition organisations. Upon sending these emails, I received a wealth of information that would have been impossible to collect from one source. I now began sifting through all the information, building an encyclopaedia of information that I hoped would see me to the top of the world.

The initial emails, however, weren't as promising as I had been hoping. Frequent responses included 'you need lots of money', and 'you don't have the experience, you will need lots of money to gain the required confidence', and a personal favourite, 'you will need money-can't-buy-experience... this costs a lot'.

There were some more encouraging emails aside from the money orientated messages, and these included preparatory peaks to consider and training information specific to high altitude. I had clearly opened up a can of worms because the deeper I delved, the more avenues I found were opening up, each requiring further answers to a seemingly endless list of questions.

I had a journal with me for my time in the Alps. In this, I recorded everything. Every thought was recorded, even coming off the hill from a biking session to write a single line, before heading back to the chair lift. In my mind I was building a picture of what it would take, but the picture was still messy. I was struggling to answer the question of what side of Everest to attempt before I had even worked out the funding of my high altitude boots. There were so many unanswered questions, and so many ifs and buts to try and get past, the preparation felt like a mountain before I even reached the Himalaya.

After a week of constant thought on the subject, even 'tripping' into the pool during a work shift just to go back to my room and write down another potentially life changing thought, I had formulated a very basic and rough plan.

I had looked over all the information I had received and had worked out a schedule of preparation that would complement the experience I already had in the mountains and equally the fitness I had from my training. It was simple. I would go to Scotland for one week of intensive climbing, especially concentrating on mixed climbing to get used to crampons on rock that is common on both sides of Everest. I would then concentrate on my final few months at university and attempt to graduate. Next, I would go to Mont Blanc, followed by Cho Oyu in the same year (2011); and then finally make my attempt on Everest in spring 2012. I relished in my blissful naivety; here I was sitting in this dingy dark room, slouched on my badly sprung bunk bed, writing *the* plan for actual Everest.

I was pleased with my initial planning, so decided to celebrate with a midnight snack consisting of a non-microwavable *pain au chocolat* (cooked in the microwave for extra crunch) and a jam baguette. At this point I hadn't even contemplated how I would pay for any of this, but I didn't care, I had cleared what was in my eyes, a significant hurdle, and I could now start sharpening my crampons ready for the infamous Scottish winter. I could also write my 'to-get' list which would now include a pair of crampons and a metal file.

Over the next few days, I gradually pieced together more and more information. I counted my savings against expedition valuations from various expedition companies and against all the kit I would need. I managed to come to the conclusion that with my hard-earned savings which I had never touched, I could roughly afford two expeditions and most of the kit I would need; I would then promptly run out of money on the 31st December 2011. After the first day of accounting I had ever done in my life, I had worked out my money worries to the penny. Wouldn't Mum be pleased!

After weighing up many options, I calculated that the preparation to climb Everest wouldn't be as far out of reach as I thought. I needed to work my way up to as close to 8,000m as possible and then rely on luck and luck alone to secure the funding I would need and a coveted place on an Everest expedition. At this point I came to the one small snagging point; it had to be started in 2011 and no later. Whilst I was at university, I had the support of living in cheap accommodation and casual student work. Upon leaving university I would need to get a full time job to support myself and working 9-5 whilst training for an Everest expedition is both impractical and potentially a fatal mistake if I wasn't able to put in the training and the preparation needed to survive the extremely hypoxic (oxygen-deprived) environment found towards the top of Everest. I decided I wanted to keep the number of things potentially fatal to an absolute minimum and so it had to be started immediately.

With that realisation, I started increasing the intensity of the best training I knew; running. Running in the Alps is tough and I thought, if you can run up a mountain you can probably walk and climb up it too. Running also gave me the time to think about the next obstacle, a mountain so large it can feel like you have already climbed Everest if you succeed. That mountain of course is sponsorship. I couldn't worry whilst still in the Alps about where the money would come from, but I could start working on commercialising my expedition. How am I going to make my climb of Everest different from any other individual? How am I going to sell my idea, my dream of climbing Everest? These are questions that Everest throws at you, and you have to come up with an answer one way or the other. I remember being jealous when hearing about rich business men paying a company to take them to the top of Everest; did they deserve to step on the mountain? Did they put in the training to fully respect such a peak? I wasn't so fortunate. I didn't have money amounting to anywhere near that needed to climb Everest, yet here were people simply throwing money at companies to pull them up the mountain.

The above simply didn't matter. These people had obviously earned their money and so could spend it any way they choose. However jealous I was, it wouldn't find me any sponsorship and certainly wouldn't get me up Everest.

I tried to free my mind of an even more confusing picture and, using my journal, write a new plan incorporating everything I had newly learnt. Instead of money making schemes, I simply wrote down ways of marketing my expedition. I wrote my training plan and preparatory peak list. And finally I started to write a list of companies who might be interested in helping me to the top of the world; for a small fee of course.

Chapter 7 – Back to University, Almost

So as quickly as it had come round, my time in the Alps finished and Michaelmas blissfully arrived. I still maintain that my 2.5 months spent in the Portes Du Soleil were some of the most important months I had ever spent.

My mind was still awash with thoughts and ideas. I have tried my best to explain them over two years on but imagine the difficulty I faced when explaining them to Mum in the car on the way home from Dover. I had been piecing together a fantasy world that would take me to the summit of Everest and yet had told no one. Now was my chance to make a good first impression and try to explain how I envisaged the next two years of my life to unfold.

Surprisingly I didn't receive the response I was expecting, as apart from the inevitable 'how are you going to pay for this?' I received quite a positive reaction to the whole 'I'm going to climb Everest in two years' announcement. Perhaps Mum was slightly off guard since I don't think most seasonaires come home with such a statement of intent. But that was it, the cat was out of the bag and strangely it felt good to share it with someone as I now had a person with whom I could iron out all my worries and fears about a non-starting, life-risking monster of an expedition.

As with any large undertaking, I felt that it needed a proper beginning to kick start the expedition and warn my body that it was about to go through hell. Since the majority of my training had been running, I decided to do a marathon. A marathon is one of those things that should receive an element of respect and therefore should be trained for. Unfortunately I had no time to train for this marathon; I was instead using a marathon as training for Everest. So having never run for longer than 1 hour 10 minutes (which was in the Alps only weeks before), I decided the 5th September 2010 would be the day.

Waking up all confident with my past record of zero marathons and zero half-marathons, I set off to Rutland Water which conveniently had a perimeter of roughly 26.2 miles. After taping my feet up, there was nothing left to do but set off. So with Mum as my moral support on the bike, I plodded on at a surprisingly fast pace. I was running well, even passing cyclists on the hills around the picturesque lake. The alpine hills had certainly paid off as now all the English hills just felt flat. To my surprise, I wasn't getting tired and after the original surge of adrenalin on starting the run, I had fallen into a rhythm of three hour marathon pace. After running round the so-called 'peninsula' I was over half way having run the first 13.1 miles in 1.5 hours. I carried on running happy with the pace I was doing and the fact that I was over half way when gradually, things started to change. I started feeling my feet more acutely than before and I also started to feel my quads, slightly tight and starting to heat up. I carried on for a bit longer, then without any warning, clattered head first into the wall of pain. I hadn't just reached the wall; I had hit it at considerable force and now with every step, my body felt like it was falling to pieces as each individual limb ground to a gradual halt as I crawled my way towards Myseryville, each step more miserable than the last. Clearly I had run into the metaphorical wall that every long distance runner has met before, but I had a bigger problem in that I had never trained for this distance so had no way of dealing with the world of pain I was now in. The cramp started in my quads and then promptly moved into my hamstrings which were now spasm-ing uncontrollably. I could barely stand, let alone walk or continue running. I was three-quarters of the way round the marathon, but my pace had been gradually falling until the point of stopping. I had some fluids and jelly babies to keep the sugar levels up, and then tried to carry on. The final quarter was the most painful thing I had ever experienced as I literally hobbled the final miles. I wasn't even close to walking pace, but I could do no more. Close to being sick with the searing pain of lactic acid that was now pooling in my legs, there was nothing more I could do except for plod on as slowly as I could, often hanging over the fence at the side of the track just for a respite from the pain.

I'm not sure how I managed to carry on for the last few miles, but I did. I stumbled towards the car which I had left four hours previously. Still a good time for a first marathon, but the satisfaction might have been greater if it had been the six hour epic that it really felt like.

This was obviously not a good start to my Everest expedition preparation, but what mattered to me was not the time it took, but the fact I managed to finish and the subsequent lessons I could learn. These were obvious though; I hadn't trained hard enough, instead relying on my base fitness to get me round and then more specifically to the run, I paced the race terribly. I couldn't afford to make the same mistake in the high mountains; running out of energy above 8,000m could be a fatal error, so it was best I made the mistakes now whilst nestled safely in England's smallest county, arguably one of the most beautiful counties in the country.

I went back home after the marathon quite content that that ordeal was now over. In some ways I had proved to myself just what I could do even when everything seemed stacked against me. It hadn't been pretty but just to cross the finish line, that was good enough.

It was the humble beginnings of a long journey and now home, I had a short period of free time before returning to the final year at university and in this time there was only one thing I could think of that had to be done. That was of course the infamous proposal.

As a squash player I had been sponsored by a racket company; however, corporate sponsorship is a completely different kettle of fish. I knew I was able to control my training as best I could but to complete my goal and climb Everest, I would need a type of sponsorship which was completely out of my hands and based around luck. To get this, I needed to create a document of intent which would try to explain in non-mountaineering terms the aims of the Everest expedition and why it was a worthy investment; certainly a difficult product to sell.

Chapter 8 – A Decent Proposal

At this point I had a few problems, the first being my training plan. It is hard to train for long distance events such as marathon running in general but especially when previous training has revolved around strength and speed exercise of no more than 100 minutes. To rectify this, I would need both physical training and also psychological conditioning. This, however, could wait until I got back to university; for now I had a more pressing matter to confront.

A proposal in this sense is nothing more than a polite request for money which is much harder to write than I first thought.

My initial attempts at writing this document proved futile, so I decided I needed some expertise in the art of commercial language. I teamed up with Wardour And Oxford, a business development agency who had skills which would take a lifetime to learn; a length of time I didn't have if I was to climb Everest in the next 1.5 years.

From the team at W&O, I learnt the invaluable skills needed to construct the perfect proposal. The proposal had to be crafted, each word perfectly measured for its purpose with no excess, just the bare facts. The proposal was three pages long including the front cover, and in the two content pages, the words which could fit on half a page of A4 would stir the imagination of every CEO on the FTSE 100 and Fortune 1000; at least that was the aim.

Explaining the expedition on the first page was easy. This would be skim read so needed the minimum of detail. It was the final page that would pack in the most important information, the information a CEO wants to see. The numbers would be the heart of the proposal and quite simply after two minutes of previous skim reading, the whole proposal rested on one point; what can I do for you? I had to make an offer they could not refuse.

The whole proposal took a fortnight of painstaking work. All the details had to be checked and facts had to be collected. The numbers had to be believable and they had to add up.

Perhaps the most difficult part of the proposal process is creating the selling point. Unfortunately no matter how hard you try and how much effort you pour in, no one is going to buy into your idea if it isn't unique. For instance, defining the purpose of the expedition and having clear, original objectives is the key to success. Why are you different, what makes you so special from every other climber who wants their shot at the summit? And less scientifically, are you lucky?

Having produced the proposal, I had crossed the first hurdle, but what use is a proposal if you don't do anything with it? The next piece of effort is the single hardest thing to achieve before you set foot on Everest. You can run a marathon every single day for two years in preparation for Everest, but in many respects this would be far more pleasant than the agony, despair, stress and overwhelming rejection faced in the corporate world of sponsorship.

In the last 20 years, the game on Everest has changed. It is no longer enough to possess the ability of a climber; it is now about the rounded ability of a person. In the modern age of expeditions, on top of the fundamental climbing and personal admin skills you also need a degree of business acumen and the confidence to sell your expedition at the beginning and relive it vividly through talks at the end. It should come as no surprise that sponsorship of sports is a dominant market force, with sponsorship ranging from endorsement of sporting equipment such as a tennis racket or a golfer's shoe, to pure advertisement of other brands such as financial institutions and technology manufacturers. In fact, much of top level sport is funded through sponsorship; for example much of the GB team are Lottery funded, and as an example of when perhaps the value of sport is taken out of proportion, as of 2012 Wayne Rooney's annual salary stood at £17.2 million or £300,000 per week, which means he could singlehandedly fund an Everest expedition from six hours' work, or pay back the UK's national debt in 61,941 years. Ranging from athlete support to the funding of an entire sport, sponsorship is crucial for sport as a whole and much as I wished I didn't have to seek external help myself, for me, financial sponsorship was the only way forward.

The next chapter of my Everest life contained some of the hardest moments I faced along the whole journey. This chapter, the endless hunt for sponsorship, spanned over two years, seven days a week and for as many hours a day as I could find.

The top priority now that the proposal had been completed was to contact as many companies as I could. Many people have a figure which they think should suffice when seeking corporate sponsorship. The truth is there is no number, you just have to try, keep trying and whilst being realistic, never give up.

In the remaining days before university I gradually built up a list of companies. I used every trick I could think of to build a contact base, even writing down every single company name from the sides of vehicles on the A1. I scoured the internet every hour of the day to find companies who just might align to my expedition philosophies and aims. Eventually I had a list but getting this list was only one third of the battle. The next and final job before announcing your hopes and aspirations to the world is to find a name. Just a name. Because with this name, the name of the CEO, CSR or HR executive and a clever ability to deduce that individual's email address, you have the direct line, a contact with the highest authority of the organisation. Who else would be a better contact for the highest expedition on earth?

My list had grown out of all proportion; it had tested my organisation skills to the maximum, and my investigative skills beyond. In total, I had a list amounting to 3,000 entries. I had at my disposal the email address of every CEO in the FTSE 100, FTSE 250 and Fortune 1000 index, as well as many additional sources ranging from Saudi oil giants to the head of the Worcestershire County Council.

This was simply the mother of all lists and I felt quietly confident that it wouldn't be long before I secured the sponsorship I so desperately needed.

I spent the first few days after completing my own business directory sending out my proposal. Each email was individually crafted for the company, fine-tuning the expedition proposal to the ethos of the organisation. This took time, but I managed to send 100 emails per day, each one with my very own proposal set to go straight to the highest names in business. Clearly this sounds very much like a carpet bomb or cold calling strategy which isn't perhaps the most polite way to ask for financial assistance, however, I quickly realised that business at this level is usually cut-throat. I knew that no one was going to come and help me and so if this more aggressive tactic of asking for sponsorship was the only way, then I would have to be prepared to go along with it regardless of whether that was in my nature or not.

The most important work had been completed. Now it was simply a case of contacting the right people at the right time. I had the perfect proposal, the perfect contact list; I even had time to train for my fast up-and-coming Scottish winter. Nothing could go wrong.

Chapter 9 – Year 3

Upon going back to my little town flat in the picturesque Park of Nottingham where I was lucky enough to live on the same estate as Hugh Grant, I started to get into a routine, something I knew was important if my mission was to be successful.

Every day I sent out more proposals, attended my final lectures at university, managed to maintain a good level of training and even had some spare time to fit in my dissertation which was gradually becoming more and more abstract as my thoughts drifted away to the mountains each time I typed in standard deviation and a value of $p = \leq 0.05$, a thoroughly mind-numbing value.

Despite my best efforts at organisation, my time at university was flying by at a significant rate of knots which was proving difficult to keep up with. The final year is tough enough without having to contact and convince hundreds of CEO's of companies I'd never heard of. I did manage, however, to study hard as I knew this year would be the hardest, and equally the most important of my whole academic life. I started well, handing in many pieces of work to a good standard but these marks were drastically downgraded when I managed to deliver a full thirty-minute presentation on hyperplasia whilst unknowingly standing in front of the projector. This was an unexpected disappointment since the lecturers clearly looked like they were enjoying my monologue delivered in perfect monotone whilst undoubtedly holding back their desire to laugh.

Meanwhile back on planet corporate responsibility, rejection emails were coming in thick and fast. On average, for each ten emails I sent, I received one reply in the form of 'we took great care and attention in reading your letter, but we regret to inform you...' Almost all the responses were similarly written, each one giving a summary of why they were unable to support the expedition at that current time.

I brushed these responses off and carried on with my mass marketing campaign. A one-man spamming machine just waiting for the right company to realise the potential in the commodity I was selling them.

Working through Christmas and New Year to finish off my dissertation (now full of numbers that I felt had so little meaning, they could have been made up—and eventually were), I began to realise that my first real test was just around the corner. The marathon had been the spark that I hoped would ignite the Everest expedition process, but my first real test was to be in the depths of winter in the Scottish highlands.

I had read so much about the terrors of a Scottish winter. This was infamous climbing, notorious for its killer combination of cold temperatures and wet water. If you're not deterred by long sweaty walk-ins and hypothermia, you will eventually succumb to agonising 'hot aches', narrowly surviving these only to be finished off by a haggis. This was climbing at its most extreme.

Chapter 10- The Scottish Winter

Packing for the trip was easy. I had built up a collection of most of the kit from previous years, and everything went into place strangely well, my only problem being where to put my climbing boots. Climbing boot manufacturers, especially those who make mountaineering boots, rarely design a boot for use in public. My classic yellow boots which wouldn't fit in my luggage would have to be worn for the duration of the journey meaning an interesting trip through the exotic departure lounge of Luton airport.

For the journey to Scotland I had chosen the quickest route which was incidentally the least direct route available. I started from Lincolnshire, driving south (away from Scotland) before catching a flight back up to Glasgow to catch a connecting bus and finally after a long five-hour wait at Buchanan, the coldest and most uncomfortable bus station going, I caught a coach to Onich, Glen Coe. The average speed of my journey was 23mph which was incredibly slow given the 600mph ground speed of the airbus.

This was my very first time across the northern border and it came as quite a culture shock. This is a mysterious country, known only to a select few as Scotland. You may have heard many tales about the people from this land being kilt-wearing, deep fried Mars Bar eating, caber-tossing bagpipe players. And for the most part you would be right. However, there are a small minority who carry unwieldy axes and ironmongery to scale the most foreboding precipice.

That night after settling in at the Onich hotel, I finally met my course companion, James, a first officer for Ryanair and our guide, Zac. After discussing our hopes, aspirations and being generally philosophical about life, sleep soon followed after a thoroughly jet-lagging journey.

Over the course of the next five days, we climbed a variety of classic gullies and ridges on the North Face of Ben Nevis and in Glen Coe including a somewhat epic ascent of Dorsal Arête where on leading the final pitch, step-in guide Mark didn't hesitate in telling me that as I was leading, a fall now would equate to double the distance of the previous pitch since with no protection opportunities, I would fall all the way back to Mark, then that same distance again before the rope would even attempt to catch me. We then managed to somehow separate and lose each other in the aptly named Lost Valley, ending up somewhat disorientated after fifteen minutes of circle walking and arriving back at the van after dark.

Nights after each day on the hill were characterised by many glasses of water, supersized meals and three very sleepy people. As winter climbing has developed throughout Scotland, the number of possibilities of climbing routes has also increased. Unfortunately the road network through the highlands is still somewhat sparse, giving plenty of room for the infamous Scottish walk-in. Unlike parts of Northern America and Canada, Scottish winters aren't always the coldest meaning that on any walk-in taking longer than thirty minutes, you are usually soaked in sweat and given that it rains eight out of ten days, you also have a high probability of being wet regardless of the walk-in length.

After having given plenty of effort carrying a rope and most of the climbing equipment (as mountain guides are well known for travelling light), it is almost always necessary to change at least the top half of your clothing system before starting the climb and succumbing to hypothermia.

Over the five days I got particularly well acquainted with the walk-in to Stob Coire nan Lochan, a particularly cruel walk-in with a relatively steep path which gradually winds its way up and into the Coire. On more than one occasion, I saw raindrops falling down in front of me apparently from clear skies, only to find that it was in fact sweat dripping from my hair as I struggled upwards, hunched over with the weight of the pack.

Other highlights of the week included gearing-up every day as only two 'students' can, i.e. the students taking at least twice as long as the guide after putting the harness on back to front, and the crampons on the wrong feet. Also during a slightly easier walk-in to the base of Ben Nevis, I did develop a worrying method of passing the time in my head by counting the pattern of streams that crossed the path. Most were path, rock, stream, rock, path; however, double and triple rock crossings are also encountered leading to a path, rock, stream, rock, stream, rock, stream, rock, path pattern, though this was rare... moving swiftly on.

Aside from the various antics on the hill which on the most part were thoroughly enjoyable (except for when James dropped his glove into an icy stream and spent the next hour with hot aches), we were actually learning vital skills that would serve us well on future adventures into the mountains. Leadership, teamwork and various climbing skills were essential for progress and we picked these up well. I also had a chance to practise some important skills which I would need on Everest.

Scotland is not the first place you would think of for learning techniques to deal with the climbing high on Everest but it really is one of the best places in the world especially for the art of mixed climbing. To cling to steep icy slopes, climbers wear crampons which are spiky metal plates that literally clamp onto the bottom of the climbing boot. These work fine on snow and ice but when this runs out such as on many pitches of Everest, you have to be proficient in mixed climbing where for long periods you will be climbing on bare rock, scratching the surface for the smallest hold to gain another metre.

Mixed climbing is very technical and Scotland is one of the best places to hone the skills, very often in weather worse than you might face even on the highest slopes of Everest.

In the final few days I had the opportunity to ask Zac about the best routes into climbing Everest. Forgetting about the financial costs of the climb for a small period, it becomes an interesting subject with conflicting opinions from both the scientific and ethical points of view. Zac persuaded me to change my mind about the preparation I would need for Everest, insisting Cho Oyu was a step too far after the Alps. After a few days considering options, I decided the next chapter of my adventure would take me to Kyrgyzstan in search of the Pamirs Range of the Himalaya, followed by a second expedition to Baruntse, a mountain also in the Himalaya. Both these expeditions would be done in the same year, and compared to the prices of European guides, were extremely cost effective. I didn't even consider that these expeditions would push and test me to the limit and perhaps beyond.

Getting back home from Scotland was a dreamlike experience, with thoughts going through my mind of both the previous week where I had done some of the best climbs of my life and also of the future. Arriving at Glasgow Airport didn't help the strangeness. The place was surreal, there was no one to be seen; the whole of Glasgow International Airport was literally empty. I counted the flights on the board; there were seven flights for the whole night shown on a three-screen board that had the capacity for 60 flights. Perhaps this land called Scotland was not as well-known as I had first thought.

As James had predicted, the flight was short and smooth; my car journey, however, was a different story being six times as long as the flight itself.

I had certainly found the magic of Scottish winter climbing which easily kept the spark burning as my journey started to take me further afield and into the greater ranges.

Chapter 11 – Graduating In Life

Back from the rigours of the Scottish winter where I had been surprised by the excitement and enjoyment of climbing even in such a place, I casually trundled my way back to university for the final semester. Fortunately I hadn't missed any essential work as lectures the previous week had revolved around how the menstrual cycle affects sports performance; I would be very unlucky if I ever needed this in later life.

I quickly got back to my routine of training and studying and upped my quest for sponsorship by revising various pieces from my proposal and contemplating the levels of financing I would need in order to pull off the expedition. In any situation in life, especially when you are not fully in control, it is always prudent to be prepared for change and be ready to capitalise on it. It was at this time I also realised that the scheduled date when I planned to climb Everest also coincided with the Queen's Diamond Jubilee and in a roundabout way, the very first climb of Everest by Sir Edmund Hillary and Tenzing Norgay who gave their climb as a gift to the Queen on her coronation in 1953.

I decided that since no other expedition was using their platform to celebrate this milestone, there might be a chance that I could show my patriotic side from the highest point on earth which had such important historic royal connections. I wrote 'contact Buckingham Palace' on my to-do list, and carried on revising.

Alongside my work of planning expeditions, there was also the equally important task of working out how I was going to survive on little or no income once I had finished university. I had managed to save a small amount of extra money from part-time jobs ranging from bar work to racket restringing whilst I was at university, and this was set to keep me alive once I graduated. The problem with any training which is best done full time, however, is that it really is a 'full time' occupation, and so juggling too many things at once can only end one way. Training for Everest isn't just a case of climbing a few mountains in the summer holidays and then taking the plunge the week after. I knew that to be successful on Everest and to have the best chance of getting back home alive, I would have to continue training full time right up until I left for the expedition itself.

The two problems with this were obvious. Firstly, I had to somehow overcome the mental doubt that I may never actually get sponsorship for Everest, and therefore would be wasting my time trying to train for a year when I could be finding full time employment. The second problem was that if I committed to training full time I would have no time for any work especially when any remaining time was spent looking for sponsorship. I was in effect putting all my eggs in one basket with the theory that if plan A failed, I would revert back to plan A, and if I wasn't successful I would redefine success.

I did realise very early on in my planning that the whole concept of climbing Everest would be high risk. It was high risk whilst fundraising, whilst training on preparatory mountains, and eventually it would be Russian roulette on the slopes of Everest itself. I had to be prepared for that, and try to manage the risk as best I could; after all, who dares wins.

The key to my situation was planning. To plan well meant that I would be in control as much as I could be, and so with this in mind, I planned my way around finding full time employment after graduating by earning as much money as I could prior to leaving university; there wasn't really any alternative.

During my final few months studying, I also managed to persuade my lecturers to let me train in the environmental chamber on campus. This chamber was able to reproduce almost any condition experienced on earth, including the alteration of the simulated altitude. By replacing a percentage of the oxygen in the chamber with nitrogen, the simulated altitude (excluding barometric pressure) could be raised to around 6,000m. This wouldn't quite reach the heights of my lowest trekking peak (Mera Peak 6,476m), but would certainly elevate me above the flat plains of Nottinghamshire for a short period of time at least, and so I thought that the more experience of high altitude I could get, the better.

Unfortunately, using such a sophisticated piece of equipment comes at a cost, and being at a university, the cost would either be given in money or blood. As payment for my time in the chamber, I had to become a participant in a number of studies being conducted by the PhD researchers at the university. These were great in that they gave me time to experience varying levels of altitude whilst exercising, but they did cause a great deal of pain during 90-minute test protocols.

During one experiment, I calculated that during the course of the whole study, I had done 80 x six second maximal sprints to complete failure, ten x 45 minute variable speed sprint protocols; and had been given 120 x bicarb/placebo tablets, 250 x beta alanine/placebo tablets, 370 x tablets in total, and had given 37 x blood samples and 37 x blood gas samples. So to summarise, I had run a lot, ingested a lot of tablets, and given a fair amount of blood, all in a heady altitude somewhere between sea level and the stratosphere.

Opportunely, these studies were conducted prior to my revision for my final exams which were to be taken in May of my final year. After I had completed the final study, I went to a tutorial type lecture which gave information on how to revise three years' worth of work and use the knowledge effectively in a three hour exam. The lecture was extremely informative, but on looking around at everyone's faces, I knew they were all thinking the same thing. We had all been give sample answer sheets from previous years, with the focus being on one particular paper that had scored 90%, an outstanding first class. It was terrifying looking at this bundle of paper, wondering how the student had recalled so much information and in so much depth. As a small experiment, I took the paper home and copied it out word for word. This took me 3.5 hours, half an hour longer than the student who had recalled all this information straight from their revision. Worryingly, I couldn't physically write fast enough, let alone remember all the information required to achieve this grade.

At that moment, whilst surrounded by thoughts of exams, of failure, of Everest, and how long to cook my medium sized chicken from frozen, I decided to take a seemingly hard decision which came surprisingly easily. Everest was on hold.

To pass my exams, I had decided the only thing to do was, for the first time in three years, make university the priority above and beyond everything else. For the next six weeks, I sat in my room with a stunning view of the probation centre across the road, and revised. I was going to blitz these exams, and the only way was to revise harder and smarter than I had ever done before.

Having a great musical memory and being able to recall an unhealthy amount of song lyrics, I even recorded myself reading my notes into a Dictaphone where I then listened to them on repeat everywhere. I listened to them whilst washing up, whilst attempting to sleep, whilst doing an impromptu run, even whilst shopping. It had taken me twenty years to learn this technique, but just in the nick of time and for the most important exams of my life.

And it worked. Just like music that sticks in your head, my revision notes were stuck so much, that each time I practised an exam question, I wrote without thinking. I was writing the answers automatically, perhaps demonstrating the famed language teacher, Michel Thomas's sentiments, "what you know, you will not forget".

Not letting my confidence get the better of me, I carried on revising right up until my first exam. It was nice to finally have some peace away from Everest. Just as squash had consumed me in the past, I was now living Everest each and every day; although I thought of it as a healthy obsession. Leaving the world of Everest for a while was not made easy though, since it was the heat of the 2011 Everest season and so it was hard to escape news of summits and narrow escapes.

For my first exam I was nervous. I hadn't always done well at certain exams before, but this was different, I now had a method I could apparently rely upon. So after three hours of sitting in front of a blank paper at first, I managed to transform the bundle of blank pages into an almost book-like structure, just like that nameless student had in the example question. I was slightly stunned, as this had rarely happened before, but just as in practice, words were flowing from my pen before I had even finished reading the question. As a coach once said to me, practice makes permanent.

Prior to my third exam, I happened to be revising in the quantum physics aisle of the university library, and with a little time to kill, decided to peruse one or two books which I hoped would distract my mind which was consumed with nerves. As someone with a technical mind, I found the subject fascinating and was also able to relate very loosely the theory I was reading to my up and coming climbs. One such example stated that if all of the empty space in each atom of the human body was removed, the whole of the human race would fit inside an area no bigger than an apple. If you subsequently dropped this apple, it would have such mass that it would cut straight through the centre of the earth. This may seem completely irrelevant to Everest, but in some strange way, this gave a very unique perspective to my challenge. It showed just how tiny a single person is, and equally just how small Everest is in the grand scheme of things. In reality, Everest is just the same size as the diameter of the Large Hadron Collider and in terms of time, Everest for me would just be a small blip in my lifetime, assuming of course that I made it back home again in once piece.

My final four exams contained some of the best answers I had ever made which was reflected in my marks. At the end of the final exam, I felt a strange sense of achievement knowing that I had finished three years of education and had ended in some style. I vividly remember walking out of the exam hall feeling a considerable weight being lifted from my shoulders, something I am sure is commonplace when you achieve something that you have worked so hard to get. I am sure this pride came across when I graduated in front of my parents and Sir Michael Parkinson.

I never did manage to include the nonlinearities of the Schrödinger equation in my exam papers, however.

Chapter 12 – A Mountain Cometh

University was complete. My financial plan was organised. My training was recommencing. My kit was accumulating.

Since graduating, everything had been slowly coming together. The realisation was encroaching that I was soon to leave for a country I had never previously heard of. It seemed hardly real that I was about to go and climb my first true mountain, since I had booked the trip almost six months previously. I quickly racked up my training, perhaps a little too fast since I had spent the best part of the last two months in a seated position. My first training session was to cycle home from Nottingham which would mark a good end to my university life and a resumption of my training.

As was predictable for someone so sporty, I was keen to get straight back to my previous level of fitness after having been cooped up, but after overdoing the first few training sessions, combined with a bad reaction to a combined hepatitis B and tetanus vaccine required for my next adventure, I soon became ill.

I was aware of the risk of flu-like symptoms post immunisation of hepatitis B and tetanus, however, what worried me more was the reason for needing this vaccine. I wasn't going to be surrounded by rusty nails or bodily fluids, but equally, I wasn't going to be surrounded by a huge amount of infrastructure, let alone a hospital. Apparently where I was heading was so remote, a hospital could only be reached after two days, the first day to arrange a vehicle, and the second day to drive to the nearest city where there might be some chance of medical attention. In total, I would be a full five days travelling away from the UK, a sobering thought. Still, struck down with flu-like symptoms is not a good way to be less than a month before attempting the climb of your life.

I managed to rest from the symptoms and gradually began to pack for the fast upcoming adventure. I hadn't been able to squeeze in as much training as I would have liked, but I thought I could rely on my good level of base fitness which would hopefully get me through, and in any case, I would get fitter on the walk-in to the mountain. I really had no idea of the effects of high altitude, since I had only been to around 4,000m previously, and the difference between 4,000m and

7,134m, the altitude I was hoping to reach, is by all accounts a world apart.

Discussing the upcoming expedition with friends, I was also aware that the acclimatisation strategy would be fast. 23 days to climb a 7,134m peak does not allow for too many 'down days' so I would have to be on top of my game just to stay alive on this trip, let alone reach the summit. Thoughts and conversations like these were not great for morale, especially when I was resting up in bed, but all I could do was be excited for the adventure ahead.

After a week in bed, I had two weeks in which to prepare myself for the rigours of a country I still could not pronounce. I decided that it was best to do light exercise to keep myself mobile, and avoid any further exhaustion episodes which had finally calmed down after a blood test came back 'normal'. I put this period down to stress as while going through large changes in life, it is often easy to ignore how stress builds up, and finally releases when you least expect it.

The upshot of the enforced rest period was that I was packed for my next adventure rather ahead of schedule which is almost unheard of. On closing that final zip, I realised I had no idea what I was in store for, but knew it would be the trip of a lifetime.

A very emotional farewell ensued at the airport where I left Mum, both of us in tears as for the first time neither of us knew quite what would happen over the next 23 days, but I could guarantee it would be the most indescribable event of my life so far. In hindsight, neither of us knew what I was letting myself in for, I could never have imagined in my wildest dreams or deepest nightmares how the next month would unfold.

This was it. I took the plunge.

Chapter 13 – Kyrgyzstan: A Travellers Guide

I had been caught out for most of the 2011 'summer' in England which was mostly plagued by rain, but my luck changed during late July and early August as I ventured to Kyrgyzstan, a country famous for... What followed was the trip of a lifetime, consisting of a luckless yet indescribable expedition, a massive culture shock, and a brief stopover in Almaty, the former capital of Kazakhstan and the nation's largest city. Kazakhstan of course being most famous for Borat Sagdiyev and Johnny the Monkey.

After the most brief of stopovers where the plane toilets were out of order to prevent an explosion whilst re-fuelling, a four-man team comprised of Ian, Dave W., Wesley and me buckled up and prepared for take-off whilst airport staff from Almaty International airport cycled round the plane on 1960's push bikes, watching in amazement as a former USSR pushback tug managed to move the plane without breaking down.

Arriving into Bishkek Manas airport in the early hours of the 24th July, we were taken to the Alpinist hotel where we met up with Adam from Denmark, and Dave P., the leader of the expedition and owner of Adventure Peaks, the expedition organisers for the present escapade.

All six of us, Ian, Dave W., Wesley, Adam, Dave P. and I were to attempt a new mountain for the company, Peak Lenin. At 7,134m above sea level, the climb provides a significant challenge, and as some of our group pointed out, Lenin was known for two things. Firstly the extreme weather that can be experienced on the mountain, and secondly, being part Russian revolutionary and part Marxist dictator.

Bishkek was my first real culture shock of the expedition. Bishkek is an incredibly hot city during the summer months, and surprisingly eerily quiet. The former USSR city has been seemingly forgotten but left with all the hallmarks of the Soviet Union. Concrete blocks upon concrete blocks, everything built devoid of detail, emotion or any kind of scale. Bishkek is the collective collapse of gigantism and totalitarianism, a concrete jungle paying obeisance to the decayed thoughts of Comrade Stalin.

Notwithstanding the US military presence, Bishkek clearly gets very little in the way of western visitors. Constant smog fills the air which combined with high summer temperatures simply exaggerates the culture shock, however no words could do this city justice, it is in a completely different world, an historic but sadly forgotten corner of earth which truly has to be seen to be believed.

The first job of the expedition was getting to the mountain, Peak Lenin itself which meant leaving the city of Bishkek and attempting to reach the city of Osh. This was done simply by plane; an extremely old Antonov An-24 to be precise. Getting to the plane proved to be more comical than the flight itself. This centred on getting through security once again at Manas Airport, but to keep this part to the bare minimum and avoid infringing any safety secrets of Manas Airport, I ended up sitting in the plane with my ice axe, crampons, trekking poles, and large knife in my hand luggage. The most baffling thing is that my hand luggage went through two X-ray machines, and the only thing that was of concern to the security guards and police men were the size of my climbing boots which I was wearing in order to bypass any excess luggage fees. Later in the trip, I found out that the Avia Traffic Company, the airline we used to get to Osh was one of the air carriers banned in the European Union, as is every airline in Kyrgyzstan. This blacklist prevents any plane from banned airlines entering European airspace due to safety concerns from alleged poor maintenance and low safety standards. Thankfully I only found this information out after I had flown from Bishkek to Osh, and the return flight back to Bishkek wouldn't be a problem even with that knowledge since that would mean I was on the way home, a place which currently felt a million miles away.

Once in Osh, a place where time has been standing still since the evolution of man and a city which beats Bishkek hands down on the culture shock front, we got settled in to our hotel and then went shopping round the local bazaar (market). It was at this point that things started getting confusing, and the culture shock really took hold. Firstly, every second person had at least one gold tooth and every fifth person had a full mouth of gold teeth. Then, as we took to the streets, with no exaggeration, every second or third car was a nearly new Mercedes. This was in deep contrast to the infrastructure, where a sewer channel ran down the side of each street, and was used by the locals as drinking water and water to clean vegetables. This city is poverty personified; a place which simply does not have a connection to the western world and where the local people are only surviving.

It is hard to explain Osh, or even Bishkek, except for saying they are worlds apart from anything you can experience in the western world. No description would do these cities justice, and no picture could ever capture the life of these places.

After a night in Osh, we set off for Peak Lenin some six hours away by minibus, a Mercedes of course. The journey was as eventful as the previous three days. We started the drive by picking up some meat and bread for base camp. The bread was typical Kyrgyz round naan bread of which we had enough to feed us for weeks. The raw bloody meat on the other hand was basically stuffed for the entire journey in a big plastic bag by our feet. This meat slowly began to warm during the journey, and after several hours, began to exude a very pungent rancid smell as both the blood and meat began to cook as we journeyed through the impressive valleys of the Osh Provence. The way of life in these valleys can be described as nomadic with isolated groups of people living in yurts (traditional Kyrgyz tents) in uninhabited valleys. There are no forms of communication in these areas and the people simply travel with their horses and live off the land. This very simple way of existence was refreshing to see and was essentially like turning the clock back to the Ice Age across northern Europe. On one hand, the people living in this wilderness have nothing, and yet on the other they have everything.

Trundling along these ancient valleys, you would have thought the journey was relaxing, and maybe a little boring, however being in Kyrgyzstan, excitement is never too far away, and very quickly, the journey got more intense with the driver clearly intent on giving us the full tourist experience.

After about three hours on the incomplete Chinese road which was being built as we journeyed, we stopped off for 'lunch' at what can only be described as a building. Inside, our driver asked the lady in Kyrgyz to make us all a meal. When our food was cooked, we received what I can only describe as a plate of shit. The cooking recipe was simple:
1 Large frying pan,
21 Eggs,
2 Litres of cooking oil,

3 Tins of spam.
Serves 7.

Out of our group, three people ate their meals. One of these people was our morbidly obese, chain-smoking driver. The other two were Ian and Dave W. who also attempted, and successfully ate their meals. Ian suffered gastro-intestinal problems for the remainder of the three week trip whilst Dave W. was perfectly fine, leading to him aptly being renamed 'The Dustbin', the only place any normal human being would consider putting a plate of shit.

Before seeing what was for dessert, we set off for Peak Lenin base camp. The final hour of the drive was by far the dustiest part of the journey, and after about 15 minutes, we had a steady stream of dust coming through the windows, the holes in the windows, the open air vents, and the closed air vents. After 30 minutes, we reached hillier terrain where the vehicle promptly filled with engine smoke. All of a sudden, we left the A372 and headed straight for a rough track through desert-like terrain where the minibus really started having problems, firstly filling with even more smoke and dust than before, and then breaking down on one particularly steep incline where everybody had to get out to give the ancient machine a chance to heave just the kit and the obese driver to the top of the hill. We were now headed straight for Peak Lenin, the most direct route possible where no roads existed, just miles and miles of wilderness and the very distant sight of the snowy mountains of the Pamirs.

Finally, after about six hours on the 'road' (and I use road very loosely), we arrived at base camp. This is where I first noticed the altitude. At 3,600m, base camp is not the highest place in the world, however six hours previously we had been close to sea level, so it came as quite a shock when Ian and I attempted to unload the van, which included moving about ten of the biggest water melons I have ever seen, each one weighing in at between five to 10kgs. The first melon was an easy task, however once we progressed onto melon number three, I was already feeling the lack of oxygen. Describing what this feels like is extremely difficult, but initially, the feeling was like having a semi-permeable paper bag over your head, where after every five breaths, you need another half breath to compensate. Gradually as you spend more time at this altitude, you start to feel slightly weaker as your body is overcome by the altitude. You can't quite put your finger on exactly what or how you feel, but the most pressing matter is that you are no longer in control, and are governed completely by the unknown, i.e. what effect will the altitude eventually have on my body, and will I adapt and acclimatise, or be one of the unlucky few who cannot adapt and eventually come to the realisation that high altitude mountaineering is not for them? This is clearly a hard fact to face when you have spent your life savings to capture your dream.

Chapter 14 – Peak Lenin: The Climb

After waking up on the second day and attempting to eat some cold meat for breakfast, I knew the altitude was starting to take its toll already by suppressing my appetite. During this day, it became increasingly clear to me that I was struggling to acclimatise quickly enough after an acclimatisation climb on Petrovskogo Peak. Throughout the climb up this short peak, less than 500m higher than base camp, I was struggling to keep up with everyone else in the group. Eventually, I lost sight of the group and didn't see them again till the top of the day's climb. I knew at sea level I was one of the fittest in the group, but at altitude, this clearly counted for next to nothing as I struggled to maintain even a snail's pace. The feeling is hard to describe aptly in words, but it is sickening to be struck down with an overwhelming sense of weakness from some invisible force; altitude lassitude if you will.

Whilst descending the mountain, I found I was much faster, mainly because I was now still fighting altitude but with gravity on my side. But once back on the flat ground leading to base camp, I was soon exhausted, and getting back took all my energy and powers of visualisation that there really were endless tubes of Pringles sat at base camp just waiting for me. I was now starting to realise just how difficult the ascent of the actual mountain would be. We had only climbed to around 4,000m, however there was still over 3,000m left to get to the top of Peak Lenin which doesn't sound so bad at sea level, but when you are in a foreign country, with no obvious escape route from the pain, the prospect of the next phase of the expedition was daunting as I realised I was out of my depth.

Whilst Peak Lenin isn't one of the hardest mountains to climb in the technical sense (in fact it's one of the easiest), it is the altitude which creates the main problem. I could do all my technical training for Everest in Scotland, but to know how I would cope with the altitude, peaks like Lenin provided the perfect exposure to the lower level of oxygen not usually associated with the British Isles. The higher you are able to climb up a mountain, the lower the amount of available oxygen in the air. At the summit of Everest, there is roughly a third of the oxygen found at sea level, which means there is a high risk of uncontrollable hypoxia. Hypoxia is a normal state found in high altitude mountaineers where the body is starved of oxygen; however, if this isn't properly managed through the correct acclimatisation process, the hypoxic state can be lethal when climbers display low cognitive function such as sitting down and falling asleep in the snow. The aim of acclimatisation is to allow the body to adapt to low oxygen levels by producing more red blood cells, this in turn limits the severity of hypoxia and lowers the risk of other ailments such as HAPE (High Altitude Cerebral Oedema) and HACE (High Altitude Cerebral Oedema).

I hadn't intended to climb Peak Lenin to acclimatise for Everest though since acclimatisation typically only lasts for around three weeks after returning to sea level. The main focus for Peak Lenin and indeed future expeditions was to assess how my body reacted to altitude, and to get used to the feelings high altitude brings about. By repeating this prior to Everest, I hoped to be able to climb on Everest and have a good idea of how my body was coping with the extreme environment, and then determine whether I would be able to safely push on, or whether I need time to rest and recover. This was the intention of the pre Everest expeditions, though on Peak Lenin, I was struggling to even reach the altitude of Everest base camp, let alone an altitude where I could assess how I was really coping.

On day three of the Peak Lenin climb, I was reassured by Dave P. that I was just in the acclimatisation stage, and that everything was normal. This is where experience on big mountains pays off, where you can not only deal with your condition and assess how you are coping, but also see and understand the effects altitude has on other team members, especially when they are less experienced; after all, everyone has to start somewhere. With this news, I set off again with the group to climb up to ABC (Advanced Base Camp) at 4,400m. I was feeling tired in the morning, but was quickly woken up by the 25-minute journey in an old Soviet war van which had done more miles than the clock could keep account of. After disembarking the engine smoke-filled van, we bade the old but deceptively skilful driver farewell.

The start of the walk went well, and unlike the previous day, I was not only keeping up, but was with Ian at the front of the group for the first half of the walk. Unfortunately, exhaustion was never far behind me, and the higher I got, the more I felt it creep up upon me like inescapable jaws. All of a sudden with no real warning signs, I hit the wall. This wasn't like the wall on the marathon, this was an altitude wall which sapped me of all energy and I suddenly found I no longer had the strength to stand, let alone keep climb up the hill to ABC. I knew I had to make it to camp since being left out under the stars wasn't exactly an option with the -15 night time temperatures, and in any case, my group wouldn't leave me so I had to try as hard as I possibly could so that everybody could get into camp as soon as possible and have the greatest time to rest and recover. I sat for a minute to regain some form of energy. Eating was out of the question with even a tiny piece of chocolate from a Mars Bar causing me to gag. I dragged myself up, and started to stumble in the rough direction of ABC. The plan was walk for a minute, then have 30 seconds hunched pathetically over my walking poles to regain some form of control over my racing heart. Eventually, after four hours of walking, physically and mentally exhausted, I stumbled drunkenly into ABC.

It was a feeling like no other; Dave P. had to take my bag from me just so I could collapse onto the nearest rock. The place I was now in felt so alien and so hostile yet little did I know I would be spending a significantly higher amount of time here than most climbers intend. The other members of the team were also tired by the walk, but all seemed to have escaped the effects of the altitude as I collapsed into the tent, breathing but unable to control my body which was screaming for a release from this pain, a release that didn't exist.

At this altitude, things started to happen extremely slowly. Unzip the kit bag. Five minute rest. Take out sleeping bag. Five minute rest. Blow up Thermarest. Five minute rest.

By this point, the altitude had almost completely shut down my body. All I could think to do was sleep. I lost my appetite for at least three days, I had a constant splitting headache regardless of the water intake; but worst of all, there was the overwhelming feeling of weakness. An indescribable, but tireless adversary.

The next day, instead of getting the rest I desperately needed, the acclimatisation programme continued. This was a painful introduction to the world of high altitude mountaineering with muscles screaming out at every step. The plan for the day was to move up from ABC and recce the route up to camp two, with the aim of getting practice on the fixed ropes which spanned a steep section, and part of a crevasse field between the two camps.

The day started reasonably well. Despite the lack of rest, I felt I was beginning to acclimatise, if very slowly, but perhaps I was adapting after all. We walked over tough terrain across the moraine field at the bottom of the glacier for an hour, before reaching the bottom of the crevasse field, where we geared and roped up. In spite of feeling better than the previous days, I was physically and mentally unprepared for the stress of moving together on a rope at high altitude. The terrain was technically very easy, with a few bottomless crevasses, but being at the back of the rope, my concern lay with keeping up with five other very fast team members who were obviously much more acclimatised than myself. Gritting my teeth, however, I somehow managed to keep pace with the team. We climbed up to the base of the fixed ropes, and eventually I began to start enjoying the experience, the first time since we had arrived at the mountain. I love the technical elements of climbing and this was no exception. It was something I could excel at, which felt great considering how slowly I was moving on the non-technical ground. Reaching the top of the fixed ropes at about 4,700m, we turned round and headed back. Abbing down the fixed ropes first, I was starting to feel slightly more human again as my body continued the endless acclimatisation process. Adam even commented how well I was moving now in comparison to the morning which was a great confidence boost; especially considering that the night before in the mess tent, everyone had said how bad I was looking after the exhausting trek up to ABC, whilst I stared sickeningly at my bowl of soup.

On the way back down to ABC, I somehow managed just to keep up with the group, and eventually saw our tents; home. Perhaps despite the pain, something was working, something was happening that would make this gradually easier and more bearable.

Strangely, sleep that night wasn't easy. In fact, perhaps due to the next day's planned climb, it became an unnerving and restless night. The next day, we had planned to climb all the way to camp two. We would be waking at 4am, and setting off in the dark. We had done a portion of the walk, but even though we didn't have an accurate description of what still lay ahead, we knew it would be one of the toughest climbs on the mountain.

This knowledge filled me with an uncontrollable anxiety. After no rest days, I was beginning to doubt myself, and how much longer I could last at this pace. When I was completely honest with myself, I knew I wouldn't be able to make the distance the next day, I simply didn't have the strength to tell myself otherwise; weak but still unable to rest.

The next 14 days of the expedition are a complete blur, mostly indescribable even in my own mind, and I expect it will stay that way for some time.

In the very early hours of the next day, the day I was meant to be going up to camp two with the team, I woke up to perhaps the one feeling and sound I wasn't expecting, and equally the one set of symptoms that I was dreading. At four in the morning, I had to ask Ian to get Dave P. I knew something was wrong, and instantly, HAPE came to mind. HAPE (high altitude pulmonary oedema) is essentially fluid on the lungs. The main hypothesis to explain the cause of HAPE surrounds the mechanisms of lung capillary pressure, where high pressure due to hypoxia (oxygen starvation) and a spontaneous change in the permeability of vascular endothelium leads to fluid entering the lungs. Dave P. agreed with my diagnosis, that there was at least some obstruction, and advised I stayed at ABC. I subsequently missed the most important day of acclimatisation.

Over the next week, an abstract world unfolded. During the three days post diagnosis, I spent most of my time in my tent, unable to comprehend this bewildering situation I was now in. I wanted more than anything to be home, but the ever optimistic side of me, the never say die attitude, kept me at ABC longing for both an answer to my question, and an opportunity, just one chance. In two days of sitting in my tent, I read a 530-page book which Ian had left for me. Ironically, *The Death Instinct* turned out to be one of the best books I had ever read; but equally ironically was that it contained references to both mountaineering, and Lenin, the dictator from Russia. On the third day of confinement, and having done two long walks previously, I realised that my symptoms had almost miraculously abated. This was unexpected since HAPE, the original diagnosis, rarely behaves in this way when the climber neither rests nor descends. So perhaps this was the chance I needed, the one opportunity where I could turn my expedition around. As my guide was somewhere high on the mountain, above a crevasse field, I needed to find another guide. Fortunately I was in luck, and found a young 22-year-old, extremely tall Yaroslav. This was the fourth day after the HAPE diagnosis, and I was feeling fit. We woke at 4:30am in darkness, and after an extremely cold breakfast of spam and cheese, we left at 5am. We had a turnaround deadline of 12 noon, giving us seven hours to reach camp two. Fortunately, I was feeling great and we were moving extremely quickly. We overtook every other team on the mountain, and after an exhausting ascent of a particularly steep section above the fixed ropes, we reached the so called Skovorodka, or 'frying pan'. The area is essentially a long flat traverse; however the sun and heat which are reflected at you from all directions make it almost unbearable. At this point, camp two was in sight, and gradually we inched our way towards it. After the final notorious snow slope which is purely energy sapping, we reached camp two in five hours, one of the fastest times for the climb. After some chocolate, soup, and a precarious toilet break on an open scree slope, we geared up once again for the descent. This, however, was going to be a descent with a difference, and proved to be the most exhilarating part of the expedition. We set off at 12 after making the midday radio call to ABC, and after reaching the end of the flat plateau traverse, we ran down. Overtaking every team on the mountain once again, we essentially skied down the now sugary soft snow with our crampons. We reached the bottom of the climb in 1.5 hours, and could only think to laugh at how quickly we had moved, as we looked up at the route where an endless stream of climbers moved, as small ants hundreds of meters above us. A long chat and multiple bags of peanuts and chocolate bars later, we resumed the long trudge through the glacial moraine back to ABC, just in time for a huge four-course lunch of soup, potatoes, salad and meat.

I had taken my opportunity to move higher, and it had gone perfectly unlike any other day on the mountain. From this point on however, my expedition had finished. Unknown to me, I would not use my crampons or ice axe on Lenin again.

I spent the next two days resting, and speaking on the radio to Dave P., helping to coordinate any requirements back to the ABC and BC managers. In my head, I knew I was back to full fitness. My vitals were back at acceptable measures, and I consequently began to plan how I was going to reach the summit. I could no longer afford any more guiding, so would have to rely on my team after they came down. I scrutinised the itinerary, and eventually came to the conclusion that the summit was a real possibility. The rest of the team was running almost five days early in their summit bid, and that gave me five days to make a summit push which was not out of the question. The timing was tight, but all I had to do was wait.

The next day was the summit day for the rest of the team. They started at 5am, high on the mountain. I was in radio contact with them at 9am, and they were making great progress. Adam and Wesley were at the front, only a few hundred vertical meters from the summit. I then waited for the planned midday radio call, a call which never came. Likewise, the 3pm call never came. Finally at 5pm, the radio came to life, and a rough copy of the transcript follows:

Matthew: Matt at ABC to Dave, do you copy over?
Dave W: Copy you over.
Matthew: Where are you over?
Dave W: We are back at camp four, Dave P is guiding Wesley down, he has lost a crampon, over.
Matthew: Congratulations on the summit, I will pass on to ABC, radio when Wesley is back, and take care on the descent, over.
Dave W: No, we never reached the summit. None of us. Exhausted, just exhausting. Wesley struggling.
-Out-

From this point, events happened rapidly. My first thought was to keep in radio contact, to make sure the team came down safely. My thoughts then turned to a second summit attempt. *Surely, we have enough time to try again, Dave P. especially will want a summit to get the new addition of Peak Lenin off to a good start for the company.* The next day came a call at 9am which took me by surprise, and confirmed all my doubts I had in reaching the summit.

Dave P: Matt, this is Dave P, I need you to arrange porterage down from camp four, arrange porters for our kit back to BC, and set up our transport from BC to Osh; for two days' time.

That was it. There was no coming back from this situation. Still, as much as I tried, I could not think of the reason why Dave P. wanted to leave the mountain so quickly. There was still enough time for a second attempt, and surely some of the other guys wanted to try. I sat in my tent for the rest of the day, thoughts of the mountain, home, friends and a few words of encouragement flying round in my mind. I listened to my iPod for the whole day in an effort to switch off. The same pattern followed during the next day; however, at midday my iPod ran out of battery, and I was left in my tent surrounded by Spanish and Russians, just waiting for the rest of the team to come back. I had not seen another English person for almost a week.

Finally, at around 4pm, I saw a familiar face, it was my tent partner Ian, and almost instantly, the thought came into my head... 'The English are coming! As soon as I saw the team, it struck me why they wanted to leave so quickly. They all looked so differently, so worn out and battered. They looked exhausted, gaunt, and lifeless. So different from the healthy people I had been surrounded by for the past five days.

Chapter 15 – Home Bound

We were now back as a team, slowly but surely readjusting to each other with tales of a mountain that refused to be beaten. Part of me was glad I didn't have to endure the blatant hardships faced high on the mountain, but the rest of me was disappointed that I never had my chance to ask the mountain, am I worthy of a place on the summit?

The following day, we descended back to BC which after days on end spent at ABC, seemed like a new journey in itself. A few eventualities occurred which included throwing 15 loaves of traditional round Kyrgyz bread like frisbees into the glacier below. We had no real idea why we were doing this except for ridding us of everything Kyrgyz that reminded us of Lenin, and if that reason wasn't sufficient for the locals, then they were clearly for the marmots. We also ended up crossing a river by horseback after it had swollen significantly since the last time we crossed it. This brought us swiftly back to the bribe and barter culture of Kyrgyzstan where everything has to be paid for, even a 20-second ride on a horse. The Kyrgyzs take their culture so seriously, they would be prepared to leave us stranded on the other side, however as soon as they caught a glimpse of a Kyrgyz note, they couldn't have been more attentive to their new clients. A final thrill saw Adam slip over, subsequently injuring his knee, but narrowly missing hitting his head on a sharp rock behind him which made everyone understandably extremely nervous. We all knew the possibility of hospital treatment in this area; the simple answer was that there wasn't any treatment to be found for days. This would be worst case scenario during a trip where almost everyone faced their own near-death experience.

The events of the next four days summed up the expedition quite well. We transferred from BC to Osh in the same minibus as the one we arrived at BC in, but this time instead of the meat on the floor, we had to contend with spilt diesel and the laziest child we had all observed in a very long time who point blank stubbornly refused to clean the van which contained an overly toxic atmosphere which only added to our hypoxic daze.

Our early departure meant flights, connections and hotels had to be changed, including our international flights. As this was my first trip to the extremes of the world, I hadn't quite prepared for this little eventuality and knew my bank balance would subsequently suffer, but quite frankly we were all just happy to have an opportunity to get back home in the quickest and safest manner. We were yet to learn that London was in the process of being heavily rioted, and that we would be far safer staying in Kyrgyzstan which has very close border connections to Afghanistan amongst other countries.

Back in Osh, we had a bit more chance to walk about, where Ian and I decided to climb the famous hill, Sulaiman-Too, in the centre of the city giving a great panorama. We also had a chance to meet the second team who were fresh-faced and prepared to give the mountain a go after some encouragement and words of advice/experience from our team. We were all still trying to work out what went wrong from our own trip, so advice was hard to give, but by all accounts, the summit camp from where the final push to the summit would be made needed to be higher in order to shorten the summit day which had forced other teams to climb for up to 16 hours, an unacceptably long time to be at such altitudes. The next day, we boarded the internal flight back to Bishkek with more fascinating security procedures, such as the ticket desk getting extremely confused when my passport photo apparently didn't match my appearance which was put down to our experience on the mountain by our Kyrgyz guide. It turned out that they were in fact looking at the passport of the 6ft 6in Wesley by accident which somehow resulted in me narrowly escaping excess baggage fees in what could be described as inconsistently loose security procedures.

Once in the plane, Adam and I discussed the existence of divine light, the omnipresence of God, religious pluralism, and scientology, which seemed appropriate for the flight ahead. We then read a Russian 'ladies' magazine, which was highly educating, and to some extent proved the existence of the divine light.

During the flight where it is advisable to keep mobile phones on in order to relay the flight status to loved ones, Dave P. had a call from the agent and decided it was best that he pay the £500 to try to get home that night which included an indefinite stay at Istanbul airport. Adam also chose to leave that night, so after arriving at a gothic style B&B along a backstreet of Bishkek next to the 'nearly new' Mercedes dealership, we waited up until midnight for their taxi back to the airport. It was at this point that I began to show symptoms of what can only be described as chronic and explosive diarrhoea. This lasted for the rest of the expedition, and even after taking 12 Imodium tablets over the course of 48 hours (well over twice the stated dose), my body was still having a crisis. The day before the nine-hour flight home there was only one thing for it, to start taking a seven day course of ciprofloxacin. Fortunately, 12 Imodium tablets and a course of antibiotics stemmed the flow, and I was able to enjoy a final meal debate with Dave W., Ian, and Wesley; where topics included the state of the Euro and IMF, the war on terror, the London riots, and a quick stint on the undervalued factory workers of Great Britain.

Alas, nine hours after leaving Kyrgyzstan, we landed at Heathrow. All alive. Ten fingers, ten toes.

Chapter 16 – Where to Begin

The expedition and the month after perhaps understandably became an emotional rollercoaster. Why was the expedition so unsuccessful, why did it all end so quickly and why could I not make it above camp one? These were all questions that flew around my mind. During the expedition, despite prolonged stays in a tent, there was no time to truly think. I still struggle to fully comprehend and digest what happened during the expedition, and perhaps never will quite know how and why my body reacted to altitude in the manner it did. However I do know that I gained so much from the expedition to climb Peak Lenin and subsequently had the opportunity to learn from my triumphs and mistakes, and equally, I had an experience which I could draw upon whenever the time arose. After all, people in the western world quite often find themselves needing the experience from a failed high altitude mountaineering expedition in a third world country.

The lessons I learnt on this expeditions were hard, and it was never going to be easy to bounce back, I would have to think long and hard about my next move. My first and most immediate question I had to try and answer was whether the Peak Lenin expedition was an indication that I simply didn't go well at altitude, or whether, with the correct acclimatisation programme and a longer time spent at altitude, I could overcome the illness I faced on Lenin and climb to higher altitudes in the future.

I knew that the most likely reason for my illness was simply the lack of time acclimatising; however, my thoughts were fogged by disappointment, what-ifs, and thoughts of worse happening if I tried to go to altitude again. Perhaps this was just a gentle warning from my body that I am just not designed to go high altitude, after all, there are many people in the world who simply don't adjust to these types of changes, and unfortunately I might be one of them.

I consulted the advice of a high altitude doctor and various climbers and came to a rough conclusion that I could try again once more, but this time, the shock of reaching over 5,000m had to be reduced to a gentle exposure rather than day after day of relentless pushing onwards, forever upwards.

However disappointed I was with the relative failure on Peak Lenin though, I do not want to convey the message that the mountain was easy, instead, perhaps unfortunately it was underestimated. Whilst we were at ABC, we were surrounded by approximately 300 other climbers. Only six made the summit whilst we were there.

Whilst the one chance I needed during the expedition never came in the way I expected, the expedition gave me another, more subtle opportunity away from the artificial desire to progress towards Everest. Expeditions like these give a rare glimpse to see the true character of both your team mates, and yourself. In this respect, I had the opportunity to learn about myself in a way many others never get the chance. For this reason, in my eyes, the expedition was a success. It gave me valuable preparation and experience, and taught me lessons that are not always found in everyday life. By the same token, just as in Scotland, I found great friendship in my team mates, with bonds forged over an unforgettable experience; perhaps this, no matter what the result on the mountain, is the most special and rewarding of outcomes.

Once back on UK soil, I had less than two months to make one of the hardest decisions I have had to make. Do I carry on risking everything in blind hope, or do I quit, losing everything I had been working so hard towards, and never reaching my dream? The next expedition was to Baruntse, a 7,129m mountain in Nepal. I would be lying if I said I wasn't nervous or didn't feel the pressure of the next expedition given the circumstances on Peak Lenin. I had to think of a plan, and I had to do so quickly, otherwise there would be no reason to continue and risk everything on another 7000m+ mountain which was much more technically difficult than Peak Lenin.

For a day or so, I allowed myself to forget the confusion I seemed to be surrounded by, and tried to remember the most prominent points of the Lenin expedition. There were both good and bad memories which I knew I could use to my advantage if I did try the high altitude thing just once more. I realised that through naivety and lack of experience, I had failed on the expedition over and over again. I wrote everything down and knew the next time I tried, I would be prepared, and it would be better; as they say, experience is a hard teacher because she gives the test first, the lesson afterward.

There was one thing I knew I had done well, however. This was taking something that reminded me of home and of loved ones. Kyrgyzstan is a place that is so far removed from home that it is all too easy to forget that there are people thousands of miles away thinking of you as you inch your way up a cold and isolated snow slope. Even though they can't feel the pain directly, they are thinking and willing you to the top. I took a letter from Mum to the mountain, which I read and found comfort in during the hardest and loneliest times. At the end was a quote that will forever stay with me:

"Dedication and commitment has got you to this stage. Determination and vision will drive you on. Realization and love will bring you home."

Chapter 17 – Training for a Decision

Within a few days of being back home and strangely missing the feeling of being absolutely alive on an expedition (incidentally on an expedition, the closer to death you are, the more alive you feel), I had made the decision that with the go-ahead from various doctors, I would continue as planned on my second expedition to climb Baruntse in Nepal so long as I was able to rectify the problems I faced on Lenin. The name Lenin gained almost swearword status at home since Mum thought the mountain had almost killed me, and I thought it had nearly destroyed my dreams, so wherever possible, discussion over Lenin was kept to a minimum.

I had been able to rationalise that the failure on the previous expedition was due to a few main factors. The first was simply an underestimation of the mountain which was compounded by lack of experience. I had already gone a fair way to overcome this problem by gaining experience on Lenin itself. The lessons I learnt on the mountain would stay with me, and I would be much better for them when I was be forced to be as self-sufficient as possible on Baruntse.

The second factor was the altitude. This is an inescapable force that turns every small task into a herculean effort, and generally makes life quite miserable, especially if you don't respect the environment and continue to neglect your body. The key to this would be to ensure my next trip to the mountains allowed for sufficient time to acclimatise at each stage of the journey. The expedition to Lenin had been a 23 day scramble; however, I was sure that I would require more time than this to gradually increase the altitude exposure. The shock to altitude on Lenin had also been exaggerated since we arrived straight from sea level, and after a day of driving, we were situated at 3,600m which is a significant gain in altitude with no subsequent rest days to recover. The main lesson I received from Lenin was simply knowing how my body reacts to altitude, and when it is being pushed too far. This was certainly the single greatest lesson I took from Kyrgyzstan.

I also changed many smaller factors such as personal medicine and items from home which I felt would be more appropriate now I knew what being part of an expedition away from home felt like. There was one last major thing, however, which I knew I had to change. This was my training.

I had learnt many lessons from Lenin, and one happened to be that the notion that you will get fitter as you walk in to a mountain at high altitude is false, because to walk in at high altitude means you have to be fit before you even start, only then will you adapt to the lower amounts of oxygen. I also knew that I could not simply rely on my base level of fitness because in truth, whilst I could run a marathon at a moment's notice, whilst I could cycle hundreds of miles, and whilst I could play a very brutal sport in the confines of an overly large box, I couldn't do any of these things if they were more than 1,000m off the ground. I could run up Scafell Pike which is classed as a mountain, however it is a mountain less than 1,000m above sea level. All of the training which I had done previously counted for almost nothing because in the simplest possible terms, it wasn't specific to the task I wanted to do. You could then equally say that I was unfit to climb at altitude because fitness is defined as the ability to comfortably perform a given task. So therefore, it could be true that you are fit to complete an Ironman, or walk to the North Pole, or even ride the Tour de France, but even with all these accolades, this does not guarantee you the automatic ability to exercise at high altitudes.

So my mission for two months lay in quickly designing a programme which would allow me to train specifically for work at high altitude where I would be benefiting from each session I did. This was crucial since much of climbing at altitude is about confidence in your ability, your team mates and the countless hours of training you have done at home in preparation for the climb of your life. Knowing that you have prepared well and put in the effort at home when you are climbing up a mountain doubting how much longer you can keep going is often the only thing saving you from the dreaded surrender.

I set about searching for the training regime which would really make the difference, and I used some common sense to narrow down the options. The most obvious need was to make the lungs more efficient since you have to work on much lower concentrations of oxygen the higher you go. I knew this much, but didn't know quite how to effect this adaptation. The second thing I needed to do was to become stronger without bulking up with muscle, since a working muscle is very hungry for oxygen so the smaller and stronger it is, the better it would be for altitude. In any case, it would be a waste of time bulking up because if I managed to go above 6,000m this time, I would start metabolising all the muscle I had built up due to the decrease in levels of oxygen.

I also had to be realistic. I only had two months to train, so the results were never going to be massive, I just had to do the most efficient training I possibly could which would give me the best results in the time I had.

As I casually flicked through my university notes during a break from the endless search for sponsorship (which I had still not found which clearly meant I was still not going to Everest), I came across a piece of research and almost immediately put two and two together, then squared the answer and got 16. Just by chance I had stumbled upon the answer to my training worries that would be my key to success for not just Baruntse, but for when I had my chance, Everest.

Chapter 18 – Training without Oxygen

What follows is the single most important method of preparing for high altitude which is both crude in its simplicity, and smart in its complexity with applications at the cutting edge of sports science and physiology.

Apnea training, or more precisely dynamic apnea training became my focus immediately prior to my expedition on Baruntse. It takes a little background reading though to understand the mechanisms and effects of apnea training, so I will start at the beginning.

In the beginning God created the heavens and the earth et cetera et cetera. Approximately 13.75 billion years after this point, God realised all was not well in the land of human physiology, so created Ewald Weibel who together with Richard Taylor in 1981, conceived the symmorphosis hypothesis. This concept instigated a paradigm shift, forever changing the way we view biological structure, function and adaptations in humans. In short, this hypothesis states that the biological systems adhere to an economy of design, matching structure with function. Hence, no single parameter in the system has unnecessary excess capacity, beyond the requirements of the system. After testing this hypothesis, it was found that every part of the mammalian respiratory system such as the heart and mitochondria are well matched to the functional capacity of the system; with the exception of the lungs.

It has been well documented in many studies that the capacity of the lungs, i.e. the size of the lungs does not change once a person is fully grown. There is very little excess space for any growth to take place, so when a training method is said to increase fitness and create efficiency, it is other parts of the respiratory system, such as the blood, which are adapting rather than the capacity of the lungs.

Many sports and many athletes have been tested and no evidence has been found to suggest that lung size can change, that is until they tested swimming. Out of every sport, including high lung capacity sports such as rowing, it has been well documented that lung size remains the same throughout training, except for when athletes swim.

Swimming is the only sport which breaks the rule, and the hypothesis states that this is the case because swimming is a restrictive breathing sport. In sports like running, cycling and rowing; an athlete is able to breathe when and as often as they need to. With swimming, athletes clearly have to wait until their stroke is at a set point before they can raise their head and breathe. This is even more important in competitive swimming where to breathe on every stroke would slow the swimmer down, therefore the fewer times the swimmer needs to take their head out of the water to breathe, the faster they will be able to swim. This restrictive breathing is said to increase lung size due to the inability to breathe freely and when observing swimmers, findings show a 15-20% increase in lung volume when other sports including weight training show little or no significant changes.

Apnea training takes the restrictive breathing of swimming to the extreme, and accentuates the effects, allowing for large gains in lung capacity to cope with the extreme hypoxic state; incidentally, extreme hypoxia is also found in climbers near the summit of Mount Everest.

The aim with my apnea training programme was to firstly increase my lung capacity as much as I was able, in order that when I was at high altitude, I would be able to cope better with the reduction in oxygen. Secondly, exercising with low oxygen at sea level is a good way to mimic the short term effects of altitude on performance, without having to travel to the Alps or the Himalaya. My training programme was at first very simple, and only after the expedition to Baruntse did I elaborate on the design. In the lead up to Baruntse, the programme was as simple as it gets. I would swim one length under water, then one length over water, repeating this for an hour at a time. This is not only extremely difficult, but also quite dangerous since I came all too close to blacking out on a number of occasions, and was only comforted by the knowledge that my friend happened to be the pool life guard.

This programme of apnea training was designed to gradually build up tolerances to low oxygen levels, and like every training regime, it required a way of measuring progress. This just happens to be the most dangerous exercise in apnea training and also the most stressful on the body, so much so that I was only able to test my progress with this method once prior to Baruntse.

The methodology is simple. On making sure that I was the only person left in the pool with the sole attention of the lifeguard, the first process is to hyperventilate. This ensures that the blood is oxygenated as much as possible. This level of ventilation is maintained until the feeling of light headedness ensues, at which point it is time for one last breath, and the swim of your life. The test stops when you can physically hold your breath no longer, at which point it is time to take the first of many deep breaths of oxygen rich air. This is an exceptionally dangerous method when done alone, and should only be done under supervision with the correct techniques.

Using apnea training in this way for high altitude travel is not new; however it is poorly researched, and seldom used. After two months of this type of underwater dynamic training, I saw significant gains in the distance I could cover under water which I knew would put me in the best physical shape to climb to new heights.

I later discovered a whole variety of techniques and routines which made apnea training much safer and more controlled, and most importantly, increased the capacity of my pulmonary system which is a critical step in being successful at high altitude.

In the two months lead up to the Baruntse expedition, I realised that this meticulous preparation of leaving no stone unturned was what I missed from my training for Peak Lenin. Climbing big mountains is not simply a case of turning up at the base of the mountain and slowly adapting and getting better. It is the ability to train for months on end for a goal which whilst at the time may seem farfetched, once you actually start climbing your way to the summit, you realise exactly what all those months of training in dark hours has given you in the ability to climb high. At altitude, you realise that nothing which is ill prepared will survive, because up high, there really is nowhere to hide. I also realised that perhaps the epic on Peak Lenin was the best thing that could have possibly happened to me. It hadn't quite killed me, but it had taught me many lessons, one of which was the clearly urgent need to improve my capacity for performing in a hypoxic state.

I created and maintained an apnea training programme which I used for each successive expedition to high altitude, and I maintain that it was one of the most beneficial methods I have ever used with applications not just in high altitude sports, but in any sport where this level of preparation means everything.

Chapter 19 – Progress and Preparations

It's fair to say that I hadn't been making a great deal of progress with my sponsorship aims and therefore my Everest aspirations. In the two month period between Peak Lenin and Baruntse, I had to somehow fit in my training, my preparations for the upcoming expedition, and the continuation of my search for sponsorship.

It was weighing quite heavily on my mind the fact that with just over six months until I was meant to be on Everest, I still hadn't had even the slightest bite from the corporate world. With the team at Wardour And Oxford, I trawled the internet and every magazine I could find in order to find just one potential investor; this was torture in its finest.

There is a famous saying when it comes to expeditions and time consuming objectives such as this, and it is largely true; people either have the money but not the time, or they have the time but not the money, people rarely have both. Unfortunately I didn't have the money, and I was fast running out of time to make this Everest dream a reality. It is a very harsh reality of life that sometimes, things simply aren't to be, like the sportsmen with all the talent in the world who never quite make it, or the businessmen with big ambitions, who never quite fulfil them. I started to feel that even if I somehow managed to speak to every company in existence, I still wouldn't receive an offer of partnership.

Having a generally positive outlook on life, it wasn't my own thoughts that were provoking this negativity; unfortunately it was my email account. I was still sending out hundreds of emails to prospective companies, all personalised, slowly and meticulously working through a list of thousands. This meant that I was distributing my aims far and wide amongst the corporate world, but the downside was that no one was interested. Just as before Peak Lenin, I was receiving hundreds of rejection emails and letters each week. From the largest companies, to the smallest local businesses, all of their letters, no matter how fancy and articulate, came to the same blunt response; no.

I became very glad that I had managed to save enough money whilst at university to survive, because very simply, I had no time for a job. My expedition was my work and it was a 9-9 job seven days a week. The only way my job differed from hard labour was that I wasn't being paid for it. I very quickly realised that for my expedition to be successful in receiving sponsorship, it needed to be as high profile as possible; however this meant my workload doubled, and I eventually ended up with a never ending list, comprising of media contacts, press releases, articles to write for local and national newspapers, and on top of everything else, I had to somehow fit in my training sessions which included the daily drowning in the swimming pool.

The key was firstly to be organised which is certainly easier said than done, and secondly, not to let the rejections from prospective companies get in the way of ambitions. It is, however, important to take note of any advice received which again isn't easy when 100 rejection letters are all telling you different things, and as with many things, persistence is key and will eventually pay off, no matter how impossible it may seem.

I felt like many times I had insurmountable odds against me, both by way of sponsorship, and the physical mountain I had to climb in Nepal after the failure in Kyrgyzstan. I tried to remember that if I gave up, I would never know, and that whilst others may see the idea as destined for failure, that doesn't mean it's the case, as demonstrated by the rejection Colonel Sanders received over 1,000 times in his quest to start the KFC food chain.

So whilst progress wasn't being made on the subject of sponsorship at the rapid pace I had hoped for, the preparations for Baruntse were going exceptionally well. I had, with a perhaps unhealthy amount of drowning, and many hours running and cycling as hard as I possibly could in the beauty of Lincolnshire, become as fit as I had ever been, and more importantly, ready to climb a mountain. My apnea sessions were drawing to a close as I tried to eke out the final millimetres of growth from my stretched lungs, and I was getting ready for a final challenge I had set myself to try to assess roughly and very unscientifically whether I was ready.

I had chosen to use a bike as I would be able to cycle for much longer than I could run, and therefore would be able to assess my endurance over the day, for a similar period to that which I would be exercising on the upcoming expedition. Being exceptionally imaginative, I knew I could come up with a great route which I would aim to cover in my allotted eight hour time allowance. This test was more than just a physical challenge; it was a psychological test where I would know at the finish line that I was confident enough in my ability to once again tackle the Himalaya. I scrawled for hours over maps of the Lincolnshire countryside which is a known tropical paradise and area of outstanding natural beauty, especially the coastal town of Boston which is famed for its aesthetically pleasing outlook and somewhat unfortunately, for having the highest obesity rate of any town in the United Kingdom. I decided to steer clear of Boston, and just when I thought my imagination knew no bounds, I completed the route.

The route was simple, a 26 mile circuit which I would complete as many times as possible. Although being a little disappointed that I had only been able to conceive this tiny route instead of the 100 mile monster I was hoping for, I knew that the character of the route meant the quality far outweighed the quantity. Travelling through fantastic fen roads and stunning patchwork fields for as far as the eye could see, this route was simply a masterpiece, but just when you thought you had reached the climax of the journey, the route turned south and headed straight through the RAF base at Cranwell; this had to be a thrill for a civilian, I thought.

As luck would have it, I picked one of the windiest days of the year for my cycle, and, after eight hours of hard pedalling, somehow managing to get past the checkpoint posts of RAF Cranwell at least half a dozen times, I staggered back home having completed 150 miles; and with this, I knew I was ready, for an attempt at least, on Baruntse.

Over the past two months, I had trained twice a day for six days a week, and had somehow fitted in hours upon hours of corporate bombardment. With one week left before I once again flew out of London Heathrow, I started getting down to the unenviable and inevitable task of packing. Having packed for Peak Lenin, I knew almost exactly what I needed to take, and except for the desperate need to wash my clothes, I could have left everything in the kit bag after the eventful trip to Kyrgyzstan, ready for Nepal. The process of packing was very low on the list of priorities since I had a million and one things to organise. An expedition, no matter whom you go with or where you go, is an expedition, and amongst other things, it helps to be prepared. So along with visas, foreign currency, a healthy knowledge *and* experience of AMS (Acute Mountain Sickness), and a complex transport arrangement which involved waking up at 2am to arrive at the airport before 6am, I decided that I would pack as and when I could face the agonising decision of which shoes to use on the walk-in, and whether a sponsor's sleeping bag would be best on the mountain, or on eBay.

So as fast as the end of school or the New Year comes around, it was time to get out of the car and haul my bags into Terminal 4 of London Heathrow where I would have to get through another emotional departure with Mum, before waiting on my own for an unknown of a different kind.

I had met two of the team previously who both happened to be the guides for the trip. Mark, I had had the pleasure of climbing with in Scotland earlier in the year, and I met Paddy in Bishkek whilst waiting for the flight to Osh prior to Peak Lenin where Paddy went off to the Tien Shan in Kyrgyzstan to make several first ascents of a variety of mountains in the area.

The unknown happened to be all the climbing members on the expedition who I had never met before, and apart from a list of names, I knew relatively little about the people I was going to be spending the next 35 days with. This risky strategy can often have nightmare consequences, but on a rare occasion, something magical unfolds; however, you only find out whether this is the case at the conclusion of the expedition.

Upon checking in, we all went for a morning coffee in the departure lounge prior to the flight. All strangers surrounded by unfamiliar faces. It is both strange and intriguing to be in this situation, all starting as outsiders in your own group, but knowing that these people whose names still escape you after 30 minutes of conversation will be your closest companions for a true adventure up and into the unknown.

Chapter 20 – Baruntse

The expedition to Baruntse began on the 14th October. It was even before I had met those unknown travellers, however, that the adventure really started, especially after a quick scout of Terminal 4 when I subsequently endeavoured to check in for the flight. The Indian lady sitting at the desk for the airline Jet Airways seemed baffled when I handed her my ticket and after scanning the computer, she simply asked "Where is Roy?" She clearly thought I looked a bit too young to be taking a flight on my own, which perhaps explained why she made a quick phone call after looking over my passport, although that could have equally been to check where and who Roy was. Was he the pilot?

I somehow managed to check my bags in without being accompanied by this mysterious Roy character, and then proceeded to wait for anyone who vaguely looked like they might be on an expedition to climb a 7,000m Himalayan peak. Most people in the airport either wore suits or dressed very casually in tee-shirt and shorts, exposing their legs which looked far too skinny for the epic climb to come. After waiting some time, I gradually started to see potential expeditioners. They wore light trekking trousers and the obligatory North Face fleece. Some even wore their high altitude boots, a common trick to bypass the strict baggage allowance which is often a necessity by virtue of the fact that the standard high altitude boots weigh around 5kg. The one extra tell-tale sign of an expeditioner is their luggage which tends to be an exceptionally heavy, wheel-less duffel bag which is slowly dragged across the smooth airport flooring to the nearest check in desk where the member of staff on duty promptly asks for the bag to be lifted just to check that there are no bodies inside.

Eventually, everyone with the common purpose of climbing Baruntse managed to gather round our little area in the airport, and excitedly and nervously, people began introducing themselves; and from this moment on, the group began to form. There were the two guides, Mark and Paddy (or Max and Paddy as they later became known), then the climbing members, Debbie, Nicky, Eoin, Gordon, Ian, Roy (expedition engineer, telecoms expert, and electrical generator supervisor) and myself. We would meet three other intrepid climbers, Hannah, Mary and Andrew in Kathmandu, the capital of Nepal and the historic starting place for most expeditions in the vicinity of the Everest region.

After the departure lounge coffee, the first part of this adventure began with the flight to Mumbai, where I had the pleasure of sitting next to none other than Roy who was fortunately not the pilot since we were roughly 25 rows from the front. I learned many things about Roy on the nine hour flight, such as his home town of Wigan, his dislike of accountants, his telecommunications background, and his ambition to build a shed. After a strange set of circumstances a few days later, Roy became my expedition dad.

On arriving in Mumbai where 99% of the population look like Freddie Mercury and spit on the floor at regular intervals, we searched for somewhere to stay for the night. We had a nine hour stopover in Mumbai which is the worst length of time to spend in an airport; too short to find a hotel and the perfect length to sleep through the connecting flight the following morning. Given this fact, most of the group stayed together for the night in the airport, as we gathered it was safety in numbers, and if one of us missed the flight, then at least all of us would be left in a similar position. After passing through security with more spitting guards and metal detection machines which bleep regardless of whether someone is standing under them or not, we slowly filed into the main international departures lounge. Mumbai is perhaps the perfect airport to help you through the culture shock of South Asia since the airport is lacking many western features such as sit down toilets and remotely clean surfaces on any part of the departure lounge; however, it still possesses just enough homely features such as duty free and a western restaurant to help you slowly ease into the role of a very culturally shocked visitor.

Eventually after a bit of scouting and finding only seats with annoyingly narrow arms which prevent even a comfy rest, let alone a lie down, five of us found chaise longue type seats which were a slight bonus for the nine hour overnight wait. A combination of excitement, nervousness and exchanging of life stories meant none of us got much sleep. Unbeknown to most of us, it was also Paddy's birthday, which was rather unceremoniously spent in Chatrapati Shivaji International Airport.

The following day as we slowly crawled off the reclining beds and with jetlag rapidly encroaching, we got underway for the remainder of the journey which after a relatively short flight, terminated in the sprawling city of Kathmandu.

This dense smog-covered city was a sight to behold from the skies. There seemed to be no order to any of the buildings, and straight streets seemed very few and far between. Looking very much like a big shanty town with all the hallmarks such as temporary corrugated roofing, temporary sheeting covering temporary holes, and clearly temporary brick work considering the amount of fallen buildings, it made me very much dread the prospect of setting foot into this world which, from the air at least, seemed all too similar to the sights of Kyrgyzstan.

After a quick kit explosion in the Hotel Manaslu where Ian's, Roy's and my room quickly started to resemble a shanty town of its own, we ventured out into the city for the evening meal. The next two days sent me very much back into culture shock 101. This city was crazy, so fast and chaotic, yet the chaos seemed to be controlled. There may be ten motor cycles hurtling towards you, and a further 50 behind, but by some miracle they seemed to just miss each other, perhaps due to the incessant horns that blare out. There are also the street sellers who approach you literally every 30 seconds to sell amongst other things, full sets of ukuleles, Ghurkha knives, chessboards, and a complete orchestra of flutes, perhaps to go with the ukuleles. Apart from the street sellers and towering buildings which seemed to lean towards each other at disconcerting angles, one of the most noticeable features was the city wiring which had no discernible function except to aid the third world look with multiple bundles of cables and exposed wiring hanging precariously upon lamp posts above the bustling streets. Kathmandu seemed in some ways very similar to Bishkek and Osh, yet in many ways is completely different, with Kathmandu seeming to have an endless buzz of life which after some getting used to, had an addictive and refreshing quality. The people of Kathmandu are clearly used to their western visitors and even the odd westerner who has settled in the city, by their use of English and their politeness towards complete strangers.

Following a stop at Shonas the famous gear store, and a quick browse through the endless streets of fake gear where you could buy anything from a fake down suit at 5% of the RRP, and a pair of Armani jeans for 10% of the RRP, it was time for the flight to Lukla. So far all I had heard about this airport were people's horror stories from 'the most dangerous airport in the world', but this part of the journey was one of the bits I was most looking forward to. The flight was relatively straightforward; we took off, the pilots did some adjusting, we possibly saw Everest, the pilots did some more adjusting, we landed, we departed. As flights to Lukla go, it was pretty smooth. You could, however, see the potential for disaster once you saw Lukla airport from the outside. Its sheer cliff face at the end of the runway, and brick wall at the other end were some of the main obstacles pilots had to overcome. Additionally to these obstructions, there were the locals who frequently used the runway as a passage from one side of Lukla to the other, and also the weather which blinds the pilots to the airport, and without any form of landing navigations such as ILS or even a PAPI, once the runway becomes shrouded in mist and cloud, it's usually a hairy flight back to Kathmandu providing the pilot hasn't already reached one of the many cliffs surrounding the village.

We arrived to find some of the bags weren't quite yet at Lukla which meant we had the whole day to look round instead of starting the walk-in. I was still feeling the effects of jetlag from the previous four days of travelling quite heavily by now, so this came as quite a relief. In an effort to recoup and enjoy the last place of real civilisation before the trek commenced, Gordon and I spent the rest of the day in Lukla's very own fake Starbucks, drinking hot chocolate and eating as many brownies as possible. Even at this relatively low altitude of 2,860m, the effects of the thinning air could be felt whenever you climbed a set of stairs, or did any form of exercise. This combined with the lower temperatures and airy feel meant this was the real deal, and therefore the start of the Baruntse trek was about to commence very shortly.

That night we stayed in the Paradise Lodge which has a prime location next to Lukla airport and hence is one of the main lodges that expeditioners use prior to commencing on expeditions and treks in the Khumbu and surrounding valleys. That night, the famous British climber Kenton Cool, who at this point had nine summits of Everest to his name just happened to be staying in Paradise Lodge. The highlight, apart from simply seeing Kenton in the flesh, was watching Andrew summon Kenton over to our table in order that he may have a chat with some of the girls on the expedition. Once seated, he subsequently sent the girls (but mainly Debbie who had a front row seat), slightly crazy thanks to his Gloucestershire charm, although in fairness according to the girls, he did have unbelievably good legs.

So on the 18th October we left Lukla and headed for Poyan, the first stop on the long trek to Mera Peak which went by the longer Surke La route rather than the shorter Zatrwa La. The expedition we were all undertaking had its primary goal in making an ascent of Baruntse; however the expedition was well planned and focused on the acclimatisation for the first half of the trip. This meant that we would all make an attempted ascent of Mera Peak prior to reaching Baruntse itself. This methodology had many benefits including better acclimatisation, good experience for the hard times to come on Baruntse, and a chance to test our systems and bond firmly as a team before being allowed to descend off Mera Peak with time to recover and recuperate before moving on to Baruntse. I for one was grateful for this extra time as it gave me so much more confidence, especially after the rushed attempt on Peak Lenin where acclimatisation was certainly a problem.

The first day's walk went well, and took away any apprehension I had prior to starting the walk-in. It was clear from where the route went on the map that the acclimatisation was extremely steady, not going above 3,600m for the first seven days. These initial trekking days gave us a great chance to get to know each other, and also get to know the Sherpas, the unsung heroes of the Himalaya. We had a great team including Nuru (Sardar/Head Sherpa), Sonam, Dawa, Surendra (cook), and Mungalae. In the initial days, Sonam and Dawa spent the most time with the group, and given their youth and enthusiasm were great people to be around. A favourite saying of Sonams in particular was 'zoom zoom' each time we set off. This was translated by Roy as 'Jum Jum' and for the rest of the trip Sonam was known as Jum Jum, hence the phrase 'Jum Jum, zoom zoom'. The gesture was repaid soon after however, as Roy tried to explain the phenomenon of 'bingo wings' to Sonam. This led to Roy being known as 'Bingo Wings' by 99% of the Nepalese Sherpa population.

From Poyan we continued the trek to Pangkongma, and from there to Nashing Dingma. This day was particularly tough, reaching the pass of Pangkonngma La (3173m), before dropping down to the valley below, then climbing the steeply through the forest to Nashing Dingma. Here we could buy small bottles of Coca-Cola for the bargain price of 3,000 NPR, approx. £3. It was also here that Hannah decided her hair was too long, so the afternoon was taken up watching Nicky rather skilfully cut her hair with the smallest pair of Leatherman scissors available. But the excitement didn't stop here, as soon as this entertainment had finished, the next piece started with a neighbouring group practising mountain yoga. Later that evening, we ate dinner which was a huge pizza in a rather smoky tea house. As Roy was keen to point out, the Sherpas were definitely trying to smoke us out as soon as possible so they could go to sleep whilst we retired to our tents.

The next day we woke up to drizzle and mist; weather typical of a good summer's day in the UK so we all felt a little more at home, especially Debbie who came from Scotland; however, I later found out that although Scotland is a notoriously wet place certain places such as Aberdeen have never seen the rain since their human colonisation. The walk on this day involved climbing over the Surke La pass to Chalem Kharka. I was becoming slightly lost with all these names as I didn't have a map of the area, so took each place, as strange as it sounded, as it came. It was at the beginning of this day's walk that due to the conditions, Paddy demonstrated the best way to wear a coat in the humid Himalayas and most importantly, stay bang on trend with the climbing world. Wearing the coat only by the hood with the rest of the coat over the rucksack allowed plenty of venting and kept the bag contents dry. This was a vital part since I had brought along my phone, an Earnest Shackleton book, and my wallet complete with national insurance number, student card and driving licence, just in case. Most importantly with this newfound way of wearing the coat, you really do look cool and almost blend in with the locals; although when it rains heavily, the locals just wear jumpers combined with jeans, flip flops, the obligatory westernised baseball cap and carry the biggest basket possible in which they put multiple kit bags and necessities for the expedition, which is all slung from their forehead.

Along the way due to the humidity, Eoin had a close and personal encounter with nature after a leech took a liking to his neck which explained why Mark suddenly asked for a knife and told him to hold still. The evening meal at Chalem Kharka was a particularly cold affair, which perhaps somewhat affected our communication skills since the post dinner conversation revolved heavily around stories of, for want of a better word, getting caught short in the most inconvenient places, vis-à-vis on the north ridge of Everest and various other tight spots.

The next day, we headed for Chanbu Kharka, which had it not sounded subtly different from the previous day, would have led me to the conclusion that we would be walking in a big circle. The initial climb led us into the coldest weather we had yet experienced, and once at the summit of the climb, a thunderstorm started overhead. For the final few hours of the walk, a huge graupel storm engulfed us as tiny avalanches slid down the sheer slopes all around us. This was incidentally the only day we experienced any snow-like precipitation on the whole expedition. Once we reached Chanbu Kharka, the conditions were taken advantage of as best as possible, and a snowball fight ensued. Having previously had a snowball fight at Nottingham University with the Chinese who are utterly abysmal snowballers, I thought this would be straightforward. Unfortunately, the super fit porters and Sherpas clearly had more experienced knocking people out with snowballs than us Brits and it resulted in many injured and out of breath climbers, and many happy smiling Sherpas.

The evening at Chanbu Kharka was spent in a small hut with one small door, which when closed with 12 bodies inside almost warmed up to the point where you could think about taking off the expedition mitts, and possibly taking off the woolly hat from under the down-filled hood of our expedition jackets. This setting gave a good opportunity for Roy to read out extracts from his diary on the back of a map from a previous attempt on Mera Peak. It wasn't the first time we had heard Roy's comical matter of fact excerpts, and definitely wasn't the last. An extract included "Now at Chanbu Kharka. Very cold. Warmer in Wigan. Pen froz.."

The following six days passed without too much occurrence. A few of the more notable incidents, however, included having a post walk river bath at Kote and subsequently paying £5 for a pack of Pringles, washing my boxers after the river bath which promptly froze solid whilst drying, and having a puja by a monk who was in an almost drunken dream-like state in a rock side monastery on the way to Tangnang. A puja is a sacred ceremony performed to ask the mountain gods for permission to climb on their mountain which is a requirement of the Sherpas before they set foot on hallowed snow. To perfectly contrast the hallowed ceremony with our drunk monk, there was also the story of Debbie who dropped her sunglasses into the Tangnang toilet which were subsequently retrieved by Paddy and Mark, washed in a river, and worn again for the rest of the trip. This is a good point to mention the state of not only Nepalese mountain toilets, but mountain toilets in general, including those in Kyrgyzstan. They are essentially a hole in the ground filled with excrement and a good floor if you're lucky; that's it. There is also a negative correlation which states the higher you travel, the less infrastructure there is; so whilst you may have a wooden box in a valley village, once on the mountain, you are usually on your own, peeing into the wind whilst attempting to avoid standing on both everyone else's excrement and your own. This, however, is not taking into account the need to go to the toilet during a white-out, the -30 degree Celsius temperatures that freeze skin relatively quickly, or the stress of going to the toilet at high altitude where just to maintain a squat position for a long enough period of time surpasses any previous level of exhaustion you've ever felt.

The final incident on our walk-in to Mera Peak was pure comic genius, and one which most of the climbing members remember above all else. Picture the scene; everyone is sitting down for dinner in a freezing tea house in Kote; that is everyone except for Ian who was tending to his kit explosion in his tent. The next minute, Ian walks in to the tea house and everyone just stares. Wearing his boxer shorts on his head, with his head torch over the top, he perplexes everyone by his choice of dinner attire and wondering whether the retired school teacher is more down with the kids than he lets on. It seems whilst sorting his stuff out, he hung his boxers up in the tent, which somehow ended up on his head. Not being able to find them, he gave up the search, put his head torch on and wandered off for dinner. Definitely a 'you had to be there' moment, but comic genius nonetheless which left most of the climbing members gasping for breath, and most of the Sherpas confused about the new lows to which western climbers would stoop.

Chapter 21 – The Ascent of Mera Peak

From Khare, a village after Kote, we got onto the Mera La glacier and for the first time, we stepped on snow. Khare is a 'last post' and considered the base camp of Mera Peak where the last remnants of human civilisation end before you step foot on the glacier. Amazingly, despite its remoteness, you can purchase a whole manner of things in Khare such as western food, western drinks, and even treatment in a full spar and massage parlour. Despite a few headaches in the group and the desire to stay and fully enjoy the luxuries of Khare, we had to move on and so found ourselves on the glacier with the opportunity to don the crampons and ice axes for the first time on the expedition.

A steady climb took us to camp one on Mera Peak, just below the Mera La. The climbing was roped up to avoid mishaps in any crevasses which might be lurking under the icy surface. This roping up technique makes the climbing difficult, since it is important to move as a group at the same speed, so the general tendency is to keep moving quicker to keep up with the person in front of you, which creates a chain reaction, and all of a sudden, ten minutes after starting, everyone is at their limit, gasping for oxygen in the ever thinning atmosphere. This urgency soon settles down once the team settle into a good rhythm, and you finally get an opportunity to enjoy the magnificent surroundings and environment which you are truly privileged to be in. Many crevasse, ridges and false horizons went by, and eventually, after a few hours climbing up increasingly warm snow, we reached the ridge above camp one. We all unroped and skied down on our crampons in the slushy snow in the rough direction of the camp. The aim of getting to the camp proved harder than it looked though with a few rocky steps to negotiate, which even at only a few metres above the camp caused some difficulties in actually reaching the safety of our tents; a slight inconvenience when you are very near the point of exhaustion.

Camp one was at 5,400m and was the first time I really felt the altitude. Although we had been gradually working our way up and acclimatising effectively, there are always tell-tale signs that you are ascending such as the drop in temperature and the obvious sights around you. Despite these signs, provided the acclimatisation programme is correct, it is hard to actually feel the true effects of the altitude until above 5,000m. From this point, altitude brings a whole manner of difficulties from trouble moving at any great speed, to trouble actually breathing; and if the trip up to 5,000m has been too quick, you can quite quickly find yourself in a world of problems and pain. The group considered a rest day at this point to give us extra time to recover, but even with our relatively long expedition, the time we had wouldn't allow for excess rest days, and so whilst we all wished for a small release from the ever increasing pain of altitude, we were all resigned to the fact that we would move on and upwards the following day. Fortunately, no one in the group was physically ill, only tiredness hung over us, but there was no guarantee that a rest day would fix this, so an early night ensued as a hot glacier day turned into a freezing arctic night.

We woke up to 'bed tea' from the amazing Sherpas. They are always awake very early which could be explained by the fact that they spend the night huddled together in the mess tent despite all being offered sleeping bags. Slowly, everyone started the slow process of getting dressed, putting inner boots on, and then stuffing these as best as possible into the high altitude outer boots. Getting the tents down with crampons on was a slight issue, and extra care had to be taken to avoid ripping a hole into our mountain homes. Once everyone had had some food and was ready to set off, we all slowly climbed up the same rocks that we had struggled down the day before, and eventually reached the ridge above camp one where we started tying ourselves into the ropes as with further crevassed terrain ahead, we would once again be roped together. Fortunately, I just happened to be standing in the right spot to be given the end of the rope that would be at the front. This was great news since I was able to go at my own slow pace and not worry about being dragged along and up to camp two. This time, perhaps due to the mental boost of being at the front, the going was much easier, and within a few minutes, our rope of four people was moving well as a team.

When moving well over gradual terrain like this, the distance and time seems to fly by, and in what felt like only a couple of hours, we were walking into camp two, the summit camp on Mera Peak.

On reaching the camp, the only thing I could think to do was sit down on the nearest rock, and gaze in amazement at the placement of the camp which was situated on a high ledge with impressive drops 1000's of feet into the valleys below. This was also the only thing I was able to do as the exhaustion from the altitude was catching up with me and quickly sapping any energy I had left. Most of the climbers from our team did the same, no one really wanting to get round to the task of unpacking the bags and laboriously blowing up our thin mats. That was everyone, except for Roy of course, who in his wisdom had spotted that not all the tents had the same enticing features. The main group of tents were happily sat on the snow in the middle of the ledge safe from any harm; however, there was one tent which was precariously situated on the edge of the cliff, where any attempt at exiting from the wrong door had the potential to send the occupant into the long space between the clouds and a very hard place on the valley floor. I wanted the strength at this point to go and select a good tent with Roy, but up at 5,750m the effects felt at camp one were exaggerated, and everything from eating to using the 'toilet' was a mission. Thankfully Roy had reserved me a spot in a relatively safe tent which didn't show too much signs of slippage into the abyss.

One of the most immediate problems I encountered once I had slightly recovered from my post climb coma was finding and then operating the toilet. When I say toilet, I actually mean snow ledge under a rock, exposed to the coldest wind, littered with years of human excrement; unfortunately the reality of life at high altitude camps. All my previous experience of mountain toilet craft had been wiped out; this was by far the coldest, remote, and hardest toilet to operate in more ways than one.

Once my toilet operation was completed, I sat in the tent with Ian and Roy, all of us in an almost dream like state, trying to take in just the enormity of where we were, and attempting to rest and recover as best we could. We knew the next day would be incredibly tough, although no one really had too much of an idea what lay ahead. All we knew for sure was that tomorrow, it was on. There would be no rest day; we would be waking up at 3am and launching an attempt for the summit at 4am, so we needed all the rest we could get. After a dinner of sorts, we took the opportunity for a spot of timely singing. Classics belted out from our tent included *Silent Night* and the theme tune to *Dad's Army*, whilst from the girl's tent, more upbeat, modern hits were being sung at a rather impressive quality considering the altitude. Lady Gaga's *Edge of Glory* was clearly the only song the girls knew all the words to, but a fine choice nonetheless considering that we were on the cusp of summiting the second highest trekking peak in Nepal.

None of us had much sleep. The three-man tent that we were staying in was never really designed for three fully grown men, especially when they were all cocooned in bulky down sleeping bags. We spent much of the night kicking each other in the head which although accidental, caused the hours to tick down very slowly, whilst each minute I cursed my inability to sleep. Eventually, after all those hours had gone by, 3am felt all too soon, and what we were about to do felt all too real. We took it in turns to slowly get into our summit gear. We all had heavily insulated trousers and bulky down jackets that would be used on Baruntse after Mera Peak. It is a definite art to get into these without exposing too much skin to the freezing cold air in the tent, or brushing across the frozen tent fabric which wetted everything that it came into contact with. The worse items of clothing to put on, however, are the high altitude boots. They were hard to put on at camp one with only two people in a tent and no real rush, but at camp two, booting-up was a completely different story. The first thing to do is to put on the inner boots, which provided they have been stored inside the tent overnight should be soft enough to slide into. The first difficulty to overcome is actually tying the laces with cold hands, an effort which required heavy breathing which is not particularly easy at 3:30am. The second part of the process is to put both feet out of the tent, and get the inner boots inside the outer boots and now, fully exposed to the cold, begin the fiddly task of strapping your feet into the outer boots and close the zips before frostbite sets in.

At this altitude, and with the low levels of oxygen, cold temperatures can rapidly induce frostbite as oxygenated blood fails to reach the extremities where vulnerable cells freeze and burst open, eventually turning whole areas of skin into the stereotypical black colour. Frostnip is a precursor to frostbite, and I encountered this first hand even before setting off whilst I fumbled about trying to attach my metal crampons onto my clumsy boots. I got ready as quickly as possible whilst trying to avoid any further contact of bare skin onto various items of metal which dangled off my harness such as my jumar ascender and figure of eight descender.

Not knowing what to expect with regards to the temperature en route, I set off wearing my liner gloves and my Scottish winter gloves which may have been a mistake given that the combined temperature with wind chill was below -15 degrees Celsius. At 4am, we set off in the dark with Sonam leading my rope and Gordon, Andrew and Ian behind me. Head torches shining, we headed off into the darkness. Even with the rope joining us which let you know you were not alone, the constant climbing sent you into your own personal realm where you were truly alone in a cold and dark world, just staring down at your feet. The pace was very high, and we soon found ourselves at the front of the three ropes in our group. Distancing ourselves from others climbing the mountain, I stopped to take in the view, but around me was only blackness. There were flickers from distant head torches, a quiet reminder that there was life outside my little zone, but they all seemed so far away as another strong gust picked up some more loose snow, and hurled it across the mountain.

The route was well defined into the snow, however it was deceptively narrow. At one point in the darkness, I stepped off the side and sank up to my waist in deep snow. Thoroughly weak from the altitude, I was barely able to lift myself out without the assistance of Sonam.

In the darkness, the cold and biting wind whipped across our route, and very quickly my hands got extremely cold. I didn't know before setting off, but quickly realised that I should have had my mitts on, but I had neither foreseen this intensity of cold, nor had I the strength to ask Sonam to stop so I could change my mitts, but in the process allow everyone else to get cold. For an hour I desperately tried to keep my hands warm, constantly keeping them moving, keeping one at all times in my pocket which emanated a trickle of body heat that was just enough to unfreeze my numb fingers, all the while trying to hang on till sunrise. Fortunately, Sonam called a rest stop after what seemed like an eternity since leaving the summit camp. I quickly took my bag off, and fumbled inside to try and find my mitts. I didn't have much at all inside my rucksack, but with my fingers absolutely frozen solid, I struggled to feel any of the contents. Eventually I saw the mitts as they flapped in the light of my head torch. I grasped for them and managed to hold them between my teeth, whilst I slid my useless hands inside, desperate for some rest from the intense pain of fast approaching frostbite. Not realising how much of a difference they would make, I almost instantly started getting hot aches, an agonising pain as your hands re-warm. At this point I could barely hold my ice axe, so balanced it precariously on my shoulder and carried onwards and upwards into the dark abyss.

Sunrise in mountain ranges is undoubtedly the most spectacular time to see nature at its best, and just like the famed alpine glow of the European Alps, the Himalayas have their own stunning sunrise which far surpasses any misty morning in the East Midlands. The morning glow is made even more special because you have been waiting for that sun to finally rise for the past many hours as you trudge up a frozen ice slope. The warmth that the morning glow brings is the most sought after effect of sunrise simply because the previous hours have been indescribably cold; however it is the view that takes everyone's breath away.

As we climbed, the snow ahead and around us turned from a black grey colour to a vivid blue, as the sky started to light up ahead and reflected off the snow in front of us. Then came the fire. The sun started to rise in the far distance, and for as far as the eye could see, towering Himalayan peaks started to glisten and glow in the deep red and orange of the eagerly awaited sunrise. The sky was a deep blue and black colour, almost space like, and as the sun gently rose, shards of light glistened over the clouds far below.

Everyone on the mountain, indeed everyone climbing in the Himalaya at that one moment stopped. It is true because there is nothing else you can do except to stare in amazement as the towering, imposing, dark world around you is lit up before your very eyes.

The sunrise was a relief since it took the worst of the cold away. Once the novelty of this new world had worn off, and the mind refocused on the pain and exhaustion, the climbing continued. Towards the top of the climb, the new pain came from the desperate lack of oxygen which is such a crippling force, movement is restricted to only a few steps before rest. This slow movement considerably slowed our pace; however, we were so close to the summit. Eventually we reached the bottom of the fixed ropes, and we knew we could make it. Almost at the summit of Mera Peak, there is a steep ice cliff which is both imposing and mighty impressive for a technically easy mountain. During each season, Sherpas fix ropes to this section so that is may be climbed by mere mortals who do not possess the supposed 'third lung'. I was incredibly exhausted at this moment, and staring up at this ice cliff, I still held out little hope of summiting even though I had climbed 99% of the way up. We slowly untied from the rope, and then sat on the flat plateau of snow and ice so that we could all regain some of our energy before this final push to the summit. This was like the sprint at the end of a marathon, and it was best to not think about the pain of the doing, rather the glory in success which hurt just a little less.

I took from my harness my jumar; a metal device which only slides one way, up a rope when locked in place, so that steep, or even vertical sections of mountain can be climbed. I jumared up the final section as quickly as I could, knowing that the quicker I reached the summit, the most rest I could afford to have as the rest of the group clambered up. As I crested the lip of the summit ridge, I could see the summit with prayer flags fluttering gracefully in the wind. Some of the group had already made the summit, so I attempted to join them little more than ten metres away. Those last little ten metres of climbing were by far the hardest ten metres I had ever done. I could barely do one step before stopping to breathe, but I could see the summit, and it was now literally in touching distance. I reached the summit with Nicky, and after four hours of climbing, it was just total elation. On the summit, the concentration of oxygen was around 44% that of sea level which perhaps explains the slight fatigue that the whole group felt.

As we were all talking on the summit, an unexpected person joined us in celebration. Mark had had to go back to high camp after leaving; however in an effort to join us on the summit, he raced up to the summit in around two hours, an incredible show of fitness and a very demoralising achievement for the rest of the group who had given their all to simply collapse on the top, but as soon as he had reached us, he was ready to begin the long walk back to the valley below.

Getting down was simply the reverse but much quicker, reaching high camp in around an hour. Along the way Hannah, who was on my rope, managed to drop her water bottle which rolled gracefully down the snow slope before coming to a rest on the lip of a crevasse. Thinking it was a lost cause, we resumed our descent. Once we were parallel with the bottle, however, it became clear that Paddy had other ideas, and on a tight rope, managed to edge over and rescue the bottle from certain death. I was unsure what to think as Paddy gradually edged over, since I was tied to the end of his rope and didn't want to end up being eaten by a crevasse. As the bottle rescue was successful though, my thoughts along with the rest of the rope quickly changed; Paddy was clearly a hero and we could only dream of the lengths he would go to if one of us was to fall into a bottomless chasm.

Reaching high camp, we were treated to some more of Surendra's cooking with a quick bowl of soup before we started the remainder of the descent to camp one. Surendra's job was to be at the least, a competent cook, however as the expedition drew on and we had the chance to sample a selection of his dishes, eating his food turned into a privilege since it was as good, if not better than any top restaurant food, and was always prepared in a cold tent, at altitude, with only a few petrol stoves and a pressure cooker. Eoin who also happened to be a top chef in London was full of praise for Surendra's tent-based culinary excellence, which only added to the Sherpa's smile and passion for his art.

The rest of the descent from high camp on Mera Peak was enveloped in thick cloud which gave a slight challenge to navigation with many weary bodies playing follow the leader in a complete whiteout. Fortunately for the group, there were old tracks to follow which had they have been covered in, would have made navigation almost impossible without the use of a GPS.

We did manage to safely descend though, and after a quick stop at camp one to change boots, we headed down the mountain into the valley below. As we had gone into the valley on the other side to the valley that we had ascended from, we were into new territory, and uninhabited terrain which gave peaceful solitude as we marched on to the camp so that we could rest our weary bodies from the morning's unnatural effort.

The whole team was exhausted as we arrived in Kongme Dingma, a well-known party town in the desolate Hinku Valley which was to be our campsite. In this little hamlet, there were two uninhabited stone buildings and one massive boulder. The only thing that was keeping me awake was staring in amazement at the size of this boulder which was an all-consuming presence in the valley. It had seemingly been placed in its resting spot with extreme care, and blocked out the view of the whole valley including Mera Peak. This boulder was so large, it could be considered to have hyperbolic geometry, and quite honestly, it was more massive than any boulder I have ever seen before in the whole of Lincolnshire. Indeed I have yet to see a boulder appear in this large county that matches the scale of the Kongme Dingma boulder. As I stared from the base of this impressive geological find, regardless of the prayer flags strung from the summit, I doubted that there would ever be an ascent of this ancient monolith that could almost certainly be seen from space.

That night, even after every other awesome meal we had received, we were all shocked at what the cooks brought out. Popcorn and soup for starter, a main that just flew off the plates and for dessert, an absolutely massive chocolate cake that rivalled the size of the boulder. The cake was complete with candles and icing. It's truly amazing what the Sherpas and porters can create in a tent with a pressure cooker and steamer, and the fact that no member of the climbing team became ill during the whole expedition due to food poisoning is testament to the Sherpas' skill.

After without question the hardest physical day of my life, sleep came very easily as my head sunk into a pillow of feathers and two weeks' worth of washing.

Chapter 22 – To Baruntse

As a group, we had bonded further over our hard fought ascent of Mera Peak which had tested everyone, except for Mark and Paddy, to their very limit. We all struggled to wake up the following morning because we knew that even after the exertion of the previous day, we would not be getting any form of rest; in fact it would be quite the opposite. We still had to keep to our schedule and arrive at Baruntse base camp as soon as possible so that we had the best possible chance of seeing blue skies and calm winds for at least three days high on the mountain.

Despite our lethargy, we all knew that the day ahead would not be a tough one since we were already acclimatised, and at around 4,000m, this walk was not going anywhere near our previous altitude record. We left Kongme Dingma, home of the boulder, and started the trek further up the Hinku Valley where we caught our first glimpse of Baruntse. We thought that we may have seen the summit from Mera Peak, but we couldn't be sure. This time, however, we were positive as we squinted up at its impressive southwest face. It was a beautiful sight, a mountain which stood out against neighbouring peaks due to its sheer size and grandeur. The thought of climbing the mountain at that point was still slightly stomach churning considering it looked so much larger than Mera Peak, and even that had been a relentless struggle.

We had one final night out on the valley floor before we would reach Baruntse base camp, and after trekking around its shores, we camped by a beautiful unnamed lake which had picturesque sandy beaches and a stunning outlook over the valley. This was by far one of the coldest camps that we had stayed in, and as we all piled into our mess tent which we were using for the first time, the cold refused to lift as the tent fabric was quickly covered in a film of ice. Most of the group were feeling the cold which explained why they wore their summit sleeping bags for dinner. Icicles grew quickly on the inside of the tent from the moisture in our breath as we ate. It was bitterly cold.

Perhaps not surprisingly, I woke up the following day feeling rough. Many of the group members had colds after the Mera climb, and reluctantly, I joined the club which made the walk to base camp significantly harder than it really should have been. As much of the group were suffering from a variety of ailments, Roy managed to save the day with a pack of Fisherman's Friends which he had brought as his 'luxury food item'. To the best of my knowledge, the purpose of Fisherman's Friends is to help you breathe better, however after eating the first one I was struggling to even see through the tears, let alone breathe. The only way I can describe Fisherman's Friends is like eating an extremely hot, mint flavoured chili; nevertheless, surprisingly addictive once the initial paralysis is overcome.

The terrain immediately prior to Baruntse base camp is best described as a moonscape with rocks and ice strewn as far as I could see. Towering peaks hung all around us, and there was not a single sign of life, animal or human. The sun-baked route that lay ahead of us crossed one final ridge and then descended steeply across treacherous snow and ice, before reaching a plateau. The whole group managed to safely cross this area without too much incident, and then we all stood overlooking the plateau with a glacial lake beyond. Baruntse base camp was situated on the plateau, and a number of tents were pitched including some of our own. This camp was a tiny concentration of life in an otherwise desolate place. But the desolation was beautiful, we practically had the whole mountain to ourselves, and the nearest village, as we would eventually find out, was an exceptionally long day's walk away which crossed a high and technical pass.

This arrival at Baruntse was impressive, as base camp, the moraine, and the towering south-west face of Baruntse opened out in front of us. This was our beautiful, isolated home for the next ten days.

Chapter 23 – Moving up the Mountain

During our first full day at base camp, we enjoyed our first rest day on the whole trip which was now 17 days long of constant movement. Unfortunately, the rest day probably wasn't quite what we had expected, and instead of resting back in the beating sun to recoup just some of our strength, we got straight down to business. We only had ten days scheduled on the mountain so every day had to count if we were to make a successful bid for the summit of Baruntse which stood thousands of metres above us up in the stratosphere, or as qualified meteorologists and geography teachers might say, up in the troposphere. The rest day was spent organising large piles and many barrels of food, equipment for high on the mountain, and our own itineraries. We were given free range with respect to how we would tackle the mountain, and it was eventually agreed by everyone that we would climb to camp one the following day and use an upwards itinerary with one rest day and three climbing days. On this day, we also had our puja, the aforementioned blessing ceremony which this time was a slightly cold but somewhat ethereal experience.

On the morning of the 1st November, we started the long haul up to camp one. I was blissfully unaware of what lay ahead of me. Simply, the next ten hours were utter hell, the hardest day I had ever had on a mountain. Everyone gets a bad day during an expedition, and this was mine.

The Sherpas had taken a lot of our kit, but we were still left with heavy packs. My 70L pack was full to the brim, as I was aiming to take six days of food for the full time up on the mountain, with a few spare days; just as everyone was. As soon as we set off, I knew I was struggling under the weight of the bag. I couldn't understand this, as at sea level I was fine even carrying my own body weight, however at altitude, I was just crippled. I couldn't keep up with anyone, and it was just me in my own little world, closely followed by Mark who was the only thing that was keeping me going and pushing onwards. Eventually after countless hours of agony, Mark went ahead of me and sat on a rock just in front, I climbed on for 40 minutes. Three minutes later, Mark caught me up having been sitting on the rock for the full 40 minutes. I was simply crawling along, a step and then two breaths. It was clear to see I wasn't going to make the camp at this pace, so on the advice of my guide, I took out all my food and left it in the snow for the Sherpas to bring up the next day, provided they had enough space in their already heavy rucksacks. Mark carried on and soon caught up the others guys, whilst I plodded on, this time easily at double the pace I had been previously doing. I knew that everyone else was finding the going equally tough, but they just seemed to cope better with the added weight than I did. Eventually though, I did manage to reach the bottom of the fixed ropes which was the last step before reaching camp one. The fixed ropes spanned a section of steep mixed climbing which was vertical in places, before crossing over and spanning the length of a steep ice wall of between 150 and 200 metres in length. This ice wall was the final stepping stone to the West Col which was the site for camp one, but these final few hundred meters turned out to be some of the hardest of the whole expedition.

When I reached the base of the mixed section, I was surprised to find that I had caught up the tail end of our team who were waiting for their turn on the ropes. Even though they had arrived at least an hour before me, I realised that with only two ropes spanning the full section and a limited number of anchor points, the climbers in front had to wait until the next rope was free before starting upwards again. This was a good tactic to limit the pressure placed on the worn ropes, but meant that the waiting process was a lengthy one. This didn't particularly bother me too much since I was utterly exhausted and could do with all the rest I could get. The wait also gave me a chance to have a bite to eat, the first real food I was able to have since leaving over five hours earlier from base camp. I still had no idea why I was struggling, and it certainly wasn't due to carrying too much kit, since when I (attempted to) lift Mark's bag, I realised his was at least twice the weight of mine, and that was before I had dumped the majority of my food. Clearly this was a testament to Mark's fitness. I didn't think too much more about the inability to lift heavy bags, I was just hoping that I wouldn't have to do the journey again which would be pure torture. I then forgot about this, and began to look forward to the opportunity of testing myself on the fixed ropes. I love technical climbing because at high altitude, it often means using brain before brawn, and gives plenty of time to rest, and as this was as technical as the day would get, I tried to get excited about the prospect of hanging off the end of a rope which after considering the cliff below, gave the potential of a 300m fall into a bottomless crevasse below, the beckoning bergschrund.

I continued to wait patiently in the queue. I had my bag off, and for the first time, I was enjoying the day. The views were simply spectacular, and rivalled any view, not just in Lincolnshire or the East Midlands, but in the world. After waiting for at least 30 minutes, I was given the all clear, and was able to start on the rock section, the most technical part of the climb with constant tenuous contact between crampons and exceptionally loose rock. At this point the sun was already getting low in the sky, so I put my head torch on and just hoped I wouldn't need it.

Once on the fixed ropes, I had a chance to see the route ahead properly for the first time. There were two very long ropes up the snow gully, and this explained the long waits with even fewer anchors than I had thought. Mark climbed up ahead on a second rope to help people up ahead, and I was once again at the back. Roughly halfway up the fixed ropes which would eventually take two hours to climb, it got dark. As soon as the sun went down, the temperature dropped and it became unbearably cold. I was only wearing a helmet, a thin pair of gloves and a fleece. It was dark and everyone had finished the climb and was presumably already at camp one. I felt very small and insignificant hanging on the end of a rope halfway up a steep snow gully with no concept of time, or confidence that I could actually make it up to the top which I could still not see; the ropes just shot out into the darkness and this played awful tricks in my mind. I had to get warm just to continue, and I now had to be fully reliant on my own ability, so found a tiny ledge and managed to put my warm kit on without dropping my bag into the black abyss below which considering the thought of what lay ahead of me, was an achievement in itself.

Even with my gloves on, my fingers felt the cold, and were much more susceptible after their recent brush with frostbite on Mera Peak. As I had let my hands succumb to frostnip on Mera, they now reacted much worse to a cold environment, and any contact with a cold surface led to instant agonising pain where I was unable to maintain my grasp, not a great thought when I was partly relying on my hands to pull me up the snow slope. When not in contact with something cold, the feeling in my fingers disappeared and became relatively numb, especially at the tips which meant my hands quickly became useless when trying to undo fiddly screwgate karabiners at the end of a rope.

I tried to climb on as best as I could since this was the only way I was going to keep warm. I was once again plunged into my own little personal climbing world, just as on Mera, there was darkness all around me, where the only difference was, this time I really was on my own. The lack of oxygen continued to slow down proceedings to a vertical plod where I would take one step, then five breaths as a minimum. I tried to keep a rhythm which would ensure I would eventually get to the top at some point. Jumar up, step up, five breaths, repeat. This process became slower and slower as I played a game with myself to see how many steps I could do before gasping uncontrollably. The answer was always not many. I began to realise that I might have another problem too. I knew that the camp was somewhere over the lip of the climb, but I had no idea how far or in what direction. I would hope to see the lights in the tents which would guide me, but what if there was a whiteout on top? I doubted this as I could see the stars, and then decided that I would work out that part of the puzzle once I had actually reached the top.

It was slow, painful work, but eventually by some miracle I reached the top of the gully where to my surprise, I saw Paddy just sitting on a rock waiting for me. It was pitch black and freezing cold, but there he was, just waiting like a guardian angel at the top of a brutal climb. I gladly gave him my bag at his first offer, and then proceeded to run to the tents over in the distance over fluffy powder snow behind Paddy. I then very quickly woke up from this dream, and slowly trudged in the wake of Paddy's full strides, struggling to keep up with his pace even with no load at all. I could see the tents ahead, not far now, only 20 metres at the most. Slowly but surely, I edged over to them through deep snow, and then looked up at Paddy as he pointed to my tent.

The tents were strung out in a line under a perfect night sky, although I took little notice of the perfect stargazing opportunity. All I cared about was getting into the tent, and then collapsing into my sleeping bag before finding the energy to cook myself some food. It was at this point I realised that I had left all my food down in the valley, but I was fortunate enough to be sharing with Hannah who clearly had managed to haul up plenty of food, putting my efforts of hauling up two squashed Mars Bars to shame. Hannah kindly donated a meal, and even cooked it for me which was a great relief since as I was struggling to even take my boots off, I couldn't quite conjure up the energy to delicately light a match and then cook my boil-in-the-bag meal al dente.

A very heavy sleep soon followed which was fitting after the effort that had been put in during the climb from base camp to camp one. As we had already decided and as the whole group had made the climb, we would now have a rest day at camp one before making the push to camp two the following day. This would be by far the longest that I had ever spent continuously in a tent, especially at this altitude, so it would take some getting used to. We awoke to a very frosty tent and after breakfast, proceeded to spend the rest of the day essentially lying in the tent and melting snow. One of the keys to successful high altitude life is to make sure you are well hydrated, which means you have to source clean water somewhere. At this altitude, there is snow everywhere which is easy to collect, however snow has too many air gaps, and so creates very little water when melted. The best source comes from ice which is dense and so gives much more water than the same volume of snow, but is much harder to find and acquire. Once the best source has been collected, often very compressed snow, the boiling process begins which can take up to an hour to produce a few cups of liquid which is safe to drink.

In between the technical process of producing drinking water and because I had been suffering with what seemed like an encroaching throat or chest infection, I decided the best course of action was to self-prescribe a course of amoxicillin in order to prevent a flare-up high on the mountain. I had previously taken drastic action with a self-prescription of ciprofloxacin on the Lenin expedition which had been a successful self-administration, and this gave me confidence to look after myself when over three days away from the nearest medical attention. With both these administrations in mind, I began to think that the only obvious next step is to learn to share my apparent gift with others by taking on a Master's Degree in pharmacology, (just joking, Mum).

The main use of a rest day on the mountain is to gain strength for the challenges to come. Many people find it incredibly difficult to rest effectively on a mountain, however I quickly learnt to very effectively waste time, and so a day in the tent becomes less of a chore, and something to look forward to, especially after the effort I had given on the previous day. I knew that I must have used a lot of energy and lost a lot of fluids, so both Hannah and I were constantly eating and melting snow for drinking water. The only problem is that when a healthy amount of fluids have been drunk, as some point you will need to get rid of any excess which is where the pee bottle comes in handy. Unfortunately for women, there are two main options which aren't very attractive no matter which way you look. The first is a 'device' which gives women a similar performance to a man, which can often be messy and isn't the easiest to use when in a social setting or when sharing a tent with someone of the opposite sex. The second option is to simply go outside. Whilst most women on expeditions prefer this option, it proves quite a faff when you have to get all dressed up in down gear and boots before venturing outside the tent in often hostile conditions. If bladder size is also a problem, this option quickly reduces morale, and importantly reduces the desire to drink which can quickly lead to a vicious circle.

For men, the solution to the problem 'where to pee' is much easier. A wide mouth pee bottle is usually compatible with most men and indeed some willing women, and is the method of choice at all times in tent life. Using this solution can be tricky however, especially when in female company where stage fright can be quickly induced. There are two methods which aim to solve any such problem as they both involve the cover of a sleeping bag. The first method is for the pros only. It involves urinating whilst lying down which is an amazing feat, especially at altitude, though this can lead to disastrous consequences in the case of bad aim and an overflow. The second method, the swivel and kneel is certainly the safest, and most practical of all methods, however even the most famous faces in mountaineering have fallen prey to the bottle drop which can leave you in a soggy, frozen mess for the remainder of the expedition.

Joking aside, this is a fundamental skill for the happy climber, especially when on more extreme terrain, and all part of the personal admin of an expeditioner, not that Hannah agreed.

After a very uneventful day, it was time for another sleep, and even after the full rest day, sleep came easily. Once again we awoke to a frosty tent; however, this time we would be leaving for camp two which meant we hadn't enough time to wait for the ice to melt before having a lazy breakfast. I made every effort to lighten my bag this time, including leaving most of my clothes in the tent and even removing the rucksack lid.

The Sherpas who were meant to be coming the previous day turned up just before we left. I naturally asked for my food, and was slightly bewildered when the response came back that it had been eaten. The best part was it had been eaten by huge black crow-like birds, who had even managed to get through the strong aluminium packaging of seven days' worth of freeze-dried food, leaving only scattered remnants strewn across the snow which I would find four days later.

Fortunately the Sherpas had brought up some more spare food, which I took on board before starting the climb to camp two. With a much lighter bag, I was able to keep up with everyone and even managed to perfect a pace which I could use on the summit climb. The aim was to walk quickly enough so ground was covered, but slowly enough that the pace was maintainable, and no stops were needed. On the whole climb to camp two, I stopped for breath roughly three times. It was a miracle that I hadn't worked this out previously, but I had found a pace that was perfect for me just when it mattered.

Strangely, after over 20 days of living with the same people, the previous day whilst resting was the only day where nobody saw each other or really spoke. It was great to hear how everyone else had managed to keep sane during the rest day, and that during the course of the whole day, no one had really gotten out of their tents except to collect snow before quickly getting back to the warmth.

As the climb to camp two continued, it was amazing just how fast the distance went by, and all of a sudden, we were standing there, on the plateau of snow where camp two would be. I just sat with Gordon and a few of the girls in an effort to recover from the climb before attempting to put a tent up. Eventually and reluctantly, I managed to get up and move into my new home with my tent buddies Roy and Ian. That night proved to be much more exciting than any of us had planned though, when I set fire not only to the cooker, but also the gas canister itself. After painstakingly melting snow for the previous two hours, I essentially threw the whole contraption, including the pan of water into a wall of snow in front of the tent, which subsequently melted my gloves. At this point, Ian was preparing to escape via the back door, and after I shouted a few expletives, Roy dived through the tent and rather heroically switched off the gas and prevented an explosion at camp two. Unfortunately, when we put the cooker back together, it wouldn't relight, so we called for Mark and told him the cooker had mysteriously packed up all of a sudden.

Apparently some ice had become trapped on the gas tube; although how this had happened we hadn't a clue.

Chapter 24 – The Ascent of Baruntse

Sleep wasn't easy to come by that night, with three in a tent all kicking and pushing each other into the side walls which were completely saturated. Before leaving for our abodes after the climb to camp two, we all had a brief word about what the plan would be on the following day. Essentially, the summit was on, and in order to make the distance, we would need to be ready to leave by 2am. This seemed like a daunting prospect considering our location and the fact that we felt woefully small in comparison to the mighty mountain which loomed overhead.

We woke at 1am for the summit attempt and tried our best to get as ready as possible, which took 45 minutes to simply put on a coat, trousers, and a pair of boots. I also remembered to put on my summit mitts this time and pack everything that I had needed on Mera Peak but had left at camp. We were still set to leave at 2am so I piled out of the tent first, followed by Roy and then Ian, and then attempted to gear up with crampons, ice axes and harnesses. This was it, the start of everything we had been training for. It's hard to describe the anticipation of what lay ahead of us. As everybody got ready, Roy and I who had been first out the tent stood and waited in the freezing cold. As we looked across, we saw some movement in the Sherpa tent. Then all of a sudden three Sherpas emerged kitted out in full Rab Everest suits, it was an awesome sight to behold as these spacemen made their way towards us.

Leaving slightly before the rest of the group to avoid getting cold, Roy led the way and I followed at the plodding pace I had perfected the previous day. It was slow going; however, we had to keep moving to keep out the freezing cold that surrounded us in the pitch blackness of 2am. As I looked round, a trail of head torches pointed in our direction was beginning to form.

I took my turn to lead after about 30 minutes, and that was the last time I would see Roy until base camp. I led for around another five hours with Paddy, Nicky, Debbie, Andrew and Dawa right behind. The darkness once again became an oppressing entity which shrouded everything but a small patch of snow in front of my feet which was dimly lit by my head torch. Despite the climbers behind being so close, we were all alone, alone in our own bubble trying to overcome a mountain of physical and psychological pain which was continually hurled towards us. Multiple fixed lines came and went as we kicked into the icy face, each one requiring a level of brain power just below that which we could muster in order to clip in and ascend. In the darkness, everything was running on autopilot and despite the route having many distinct and individual features, each section of the route blended into one long snowy ramp in our minds which were being deceived by the cloak of night.

As the sun came up, a similar view appeared as on Mera Peak summit day, although this time I was too tired to stop and take in a quite frankly stunning view. I was going well, despite the extreme altitude, but slowly, as my pace began to wane, Andrew and Paddy overtook and disappeared into the distance. Climbing up with Nicky, we ascended countless fixed ropes and ice steps, and on summiting the main ridge, had dramatic 3,500ft drops on either side. At one point, Dawa told us we still had a further six hours to go for the summit, having already climbed for seven hours. This took us way beyond the ten hour limit to reach the summit, and I began to have doubts whether I would actually make the summit at all. We carried on regardless, but hearing this news just seemed to make the climbing even harder, and I regularly found myself falling to my knees in sheer exhaustion. As I continued slowing Dawa, who was behind me on the fixed rope, started walking in front of me literally hauling me up. This wasn't the most gracious take on mountaineering, but I understood Dawa's desire for me to move faster and summit, but there was nothing more I could give except for the plod which I had been giving for the previous eight hours; fortunately though, Dawa soon went ahead to help Nicky who was nearing the top of a particularly steep ice field. Just after this, Paddy came down towards me and to my sheer elation, told me that I was nearly there and the summit was in fact just at the top of the snow slope I was on, only 15 minutes away. This news was indescribable; I just stood there and hugged him. With this in mind I carried on to the top of the snow slope and to a final step bridging a crevasse. Nicky had already reached the summit with Dawa at this point, and so I met her on her way down where after more hugs were exchanged, she told me to watch out for the crevasse having just fallen in it herself.

Dawa came up with me to the summit, and the euphoria was simply overwhelming, as was the exhaustion. At this point Eoin, Mary, Sonam and Nuru caught up and we all summitted together, nine hours after leaving camp two, at 11am on the 4th November 2011. It was an indescribable feeling walking up to the summit that will stay with me forever.

We didn't have long on the summit, only enough time for a few photos and congratulations, but I didn't need any longer, I just stared in amazement but could barely take in the view which was from another world. When it came time to start the descent, I left the summit with Eoin just behind. As I abbed over the summit step, one leg managed to reach the other side of the crevasse, but the other refused to move. Gracefully I did the splits at 7,129m, and then found myself stuck, wedged over a crevasse that I hadn't the courage to look down. Dawa, breathing heavily after Nicky's close shave, hauled me up and over to the other side, and I expect was quite thankful not to lose anyone to the crevasse that day, which was cruelly positioned on the cusp of glory.

I was into uncharted territory now as the exhaustion showed no signs of letting up, even on the descent. This time, I was much more aware of the amount of fixed ropes, and was shocked at the distance we covered on the ascent. At this point I was just surviving, making steady ground down to camp two, but it never seemed to come any closer. The weather came in above our heads, and as luck would have it, we were just low enough to avoid being caught in a whiteout which would have been a scary prospect with buried fixed ropes and lack of tracks. After around two hours, we abbed down a particularly large ice step, one of the most prominent features of the route, and at the base stopped for the first time of the day for some fluids and food. After a quick drink, I was too tired to open my stash of food, so took out some Lucozade dextrose tablets, and promptly ate the whole pack. This gave no noticeable effects, so with Sonam leading, I stumbled down to camp two. I wasn't sure where we would be staying for the night, as in the event of a storm, camp one was in a better position for getting off the mountain quickly, but I didn't really know if I had the strength to make the distance. Fortunately, Paddy had stopped at camp two for the night after also having had a relatively tough day out on the hill, so we all collapsed into the tents, thankful that we didn't have to face an extra descent to the camp. Without even taking my huge down coat off, I got into my sleeping bag and slept for 16 hours.

The following day, we all set off for base camp at different times. Nicky, Mary and Andrew left, and then Paddy went with Eoin who had badly frostbitten hands from the previous day's efforts. I left camp last and walked down to camp one, then base camp alone. It was spectacular as for the first time I could really appreciate the beauty of the place I found myself in. I abbed down the fixed lines which were even more impressive in the light and attempted to spot significant sections on the face which I recognised from my previous escapade three days before. After descending, I then walked past my pile of crow-eaten food which was now only a few scattered crumbs and packets.

Still exhausted from the previous days, I stopped and ate another whole packet of Lucozade dextrose tablets, before carrying on and meeting a young cook boy who had dragged up one of the large thermos flasks full of orange tea. With the tea and dextrose tablets, I quickly found myself absolutely wired, so thought it would be a good time to make use of the sudden energy rush and make haste to base camp. The whole descent from camp two to base camp had taken five hours, compared to the 14 hour climb from base camp to camp two which had been spread over two lengthy and exhausting days.

I met Mark, Paddy and the Sherpas as I entered camp and after a few hugs and handshakes, headed for the mess tent and collapsed into the nearest available seat. Over dinner Mark mention that he almost turned me around on the climb from base camp to camp one because had I not offloaded my food. I would never have made the camp in a safe enough time which I presumed was the next morning; a night out on the fixed ropes simply wasn't an option. I clearly owed him a lot for his trust and perseverance.

Sleep came oh so easily that night, as the summit replayed over and over in my weary mind.

Chapter 25 – The Base Camp Slumber

The following five days were taken up with a few random incidents, a lot of sleeping, eating and not much else. The night after reaching base camp, I called Mum on the sat phone which was the first contact I had had with anyone since leaving Lukla. The two minute phone call cost £12 on the sat phone, but it was so worth it.

After battling Baruntse in a pair of thin liner gloves, Eoin with his frostbitten hands needed to be evacuated from base camp as soon as possible so a helicopter was called for which finally came after a few days of waiting. At the same time, the team members who didn't quite make the summit the first time including Roy left for a second attempt on the mountain, whilst the members who did waited behind at base camp for them so we could all leave the mountain together.

During the days which followed, everyone left at base camp stuck to the same routine which went roughly as follows: wake up, have breakfast, go back to sleep, wake up for lunch, back in the thoroughly roasting tent, back to the mess tent for afternoon tea, back to sleep, mess tent again for dinner, then back for the longest sleep of the day.

This routine lasted five days, and was great at the start whilst there were After Eight Mints, Pringles, Galaxy hot chocolate and Lindt chocolate on the table. Eoin also left a few packets of truffle chocolate which were essentially devoured by a few greedy people, maybe or maybe not including myself, in a matter of minutes. Once these mountain luxuries were gone though, there was nothing left to do except lie in the tent and listen to the iPod. Once this finally gave up the ghost, reading a book was the only thing left to do. Of course this may make the team seem very unsociable, but there really is only a certain length of time to talk before every single avenue of conversation has been talked to death. However a few banterous evenings followed naturally, with Paddy, Nicky, Debbie, Gordon, Mary and Andrew, and I'm pretty sure it was only thanks to the other team members that I stayed as sane as I did.

As the days started blending into one, I decided I needed to do a walk to get the blood pumping. Everyone had been getting quite stagnant and I for one was even getting out of breath just walking to the toilet tent, not a particularly good place to be panting. So I picked a route up a near hill and set off with my big boots, crampons and an ice axe.

After two hours of falling into snow-covered holes, I came to a relatively secluded mini valley out of the sight of base camp. Here, I saw a few animal tracks in the snow, and convinced myself they were that of a snow leopard. Feeling a little silly, I retreated back to the safety of base camp, looking over my shoulder for much of the way. Having subsequently done a little research into these elusive creatures, I may have not been so silly after all since snow leopards can kill prey up to three times their size which undoubtedly would include a medium-sized human given the opportunity. In hindsight, there may have just been the tiniest possibility that the prints came from a mountain hare, but personally, I prefer the snow leopard theory.

During one of the base camp days (I lost track after the third day), the climbers high on the mountain started out on their summit attempt, and we were happy to hear that Mark and Roy of Wigan made the summit. Roy is perhaps the first person from Wigan to ever make the summit, a fine achievement for his little country.

To use up these rest days as wisely as possible, I decided to learn some history by reading Shackleton's remarkable account of the Endurance expedition, but at this point, my most significant finding was realising that Andrew, a team member on the expedition for over 20 days, preferred to go by the name of Andrew, and not Alan as I had been calling him for most of the trip.

Chapter 26 – The Amphu Lapcha

On Roy's return, we were glad to finally have the group back together and ready for the final voyage to Lukla. The journey took us over the Amphu Lapcha pass, around Island Peak and down onto the main Everest trail. We were initially told to wake up at 4am for this quest as we were planning to do the two-day climb of the Amphu Lapcha and down to Chukhung in a single day, however as the whole group were utterly horrified by this prospect, the guides bartered with the Sherpas who reluctantly changed the time to 6am. This was great news for me, since I would be doing all of the walk up to the Amphu Lapcha in trainers, just as I had for the whole walk-in, so a 4am start may have just been the final nail in the coffin for my already battered feet.

6am soon came round the following day, and a quick and cold farewell was given to Baruntse base camp before getting underway for Chukhung. This was expected to be a 12 hour day which would be a shock to the system after trekking for six hours at most on the walk-in.

Walking most of the way with Debbie and Gordon, we all doubted our ability to get over the Amphu Lapcha; however, the prospect of failing wasn't too great as the Amphu Lapcha was the only reasonable way out of the valley other than a helicopter which at this height would have been at huge expense if we were unable to conjure up a valid insurance claim.

Around six hours of trekking through undoubtedly stunning scenery led us to the base of the Amphu Lapcha pass where once more, we geared up and set off around the maze of snow slopes and crevasses, which as Nicky had quite aptly stated earlier in the trip, were like slices of Viennetta. It was a hard place to describe, but because of the lower altitude than that which we were now acclimatised to, we were all able to fully take in and appreciate the sheer beauty of the place. A friend had told me that this part of the expedition was simply unforgettable, just indescribably beautiful. They were right, a perfectly preserved hidden gem in one of the most remote valleys of the area, truly stunning.

Along the way, I attempted to show Mark my Ueli Steck moves, a modern hero of speed climbing at altitude; however he remained unimpressed given my apparent lack of ability to run up slopes at almost 6,000m.

The summit was an awe-inspiring place with breathtaking views of Everest, Lhotse, Nuptse, Baruntse and an unnamed peak which was the most perfect pyramidal mountain I've ever seen, rivalling both Ama Dablam and the Matterhorn for its perfect representation of the stereotypical mountain. For the first time in the mountains everyone in the team was able to just stop and stare, taking in views which were made even more spectacular because they were so unexpected. This time, instead of wanting to make a hasty retreat back to the safety of the valley, we actually wanted to stay longer just to appreciate the place we found ourselves. There were perhaps more photographs taken here than on the summits of the two previous mountains we had climbed which goes some way in explaining just how beautiful the place really was.

Unfortunately the descent had to be made at some point, and even this was a spectacular affair, abseiling down steep mixed ground until we reached a steep unprotected gully. Gordon made a spectacular ice axe arrest after slipping, which was both impressive and thought-provoking as I stood below him watching his crampons and a plume of snow shoot towards me. We also caught up with Nuru, who was leaving our expedition to meet another team at Baruntse base camp. We thanked him for all his hard work, since without him and the dedication of his Sherpas, the success of the expedition would have most likely been a very different story.

At the base of the descent, we de-geared and left our kit with Dawa's yak driving brother, and then set off on the long march for Chukhung. Walking with Roy, Mary and Debbie, we made good progress and thought things were going well, but after walking for a number of hours, we realised this was going to be a brutal descent to Chukhung and much longer than we had anticipated. We were already ten hours into the day and hadn't really eaten since 11am which made every little rise in the terrain much harder, but then, just as we had managed to eat some chocolate and recuperate for a moment, it started getting noticeably darker. The path was obvious, so this was of no concern, but no one really had any idea of how far we were progressing, or importantly, how far we still had to travel since the Sherpas who knew the area inside out were at the back of the group helping to make sure no one was left behind.

Paddy and Sonam caught up with our little group and went ahead with Roy and Mary, leaving Debbie and me to have a lunch of sorts at 6pm and continue the rest of the walk along a high ridge eventually resorting to head torches without sign of another person along the whole valley. Over 12 hours had passed when we eventually saw some lights and knew that since Chukhung was the very last outpost at the end of the valley, this just had to be our rest stop for the night. Thankfully this was confirmed when we were met by Sonam who had climbed back up the nearby hill from the warmth of the tea house to help the rest of the group find the resting place for the evening. We were taken into a real building, with real lights, and a real, non-smoking fire, it was simply bliss. It was also the first time in weeks we had been surrounded by relative civilisation, and everybody clearly took some time to get used to other humans as we all sat huddled close together in the corner of the lodge.

Sleeping on an actual bed for that night was almost too comfy, though we kept the exposure to civilisation as gradual as possible by using our sleeping bags over the top of what was most probably lice-infested bedding.

The next day's trek led us to Sonam's house in the quaint town of Pangboche. I think for everyone on the expedition, we had all experienced a trip of a lifetime which we'd never forget, and in some shape or form, had all been successful. With this mind, the festivities and celebrations commenced, and lasted from this night, all the way through to the flight from Kathmandu, and rightly so.

A few pots of *chang* (rice beer), a lot of beer and a few bottles of whisky later, we all went to sleep in Sonam's tea house relatively happy after some unforgettable teachings from Roy on the current state of world telecommunications, his antics in Saudi Arabia, a few electric generator tales, and at least ten reasons every man needs his own shed.

The next morning, I felt slightly worried that I might be getting an episode of diarrhoea which is neither funny nor easy to cure at altitude. I soon decided that evasive action was called for to try and prevent any further complications, especially with a long walk ahead. I didn't want to resort to antibiotics just yet, so called on all my medical knowledge and, in-keeping with the theme of self-prescriptive medicine and just to be on the safe side, I took a whole pack of

Imodium. This was the last time I would go to the toilet whilst in Nepal.

A deceptively long walk to Namche Bazaar followed; however, it was certainly worth it since this would prove to be one of the more eventful nights of the expedition. A quick look around, and a few purchases of fake feathery clothes later, we headed back for a huge meal at the hotel. Following on from the previous night, we agreed it would be rude not to experience all that Namche had to offer, so set off into the night. We reached the local night club at around 9pm, but found this was shut for the night after being open for seemingly most of the day. We then tried the deserted Irish bar, whilst we waited for the guides to arrive. On their arrival, a few hotly contested table football games followed before we headed for the busier bar across the street. It's worth pointing out at this point that the only Irish features of the Namche Irish bar were its green walls and its shot of the day – The Irish Car Bomb.

The celebrations and many a game of pool continued in the next bar. It was truly good to be able to completely de-stress from the mountains, where for days at a time, life was hanging in the balance through a multitude of threats. Now we could just enjoy ourselves and revel in what we had all achieved. Eventually, at 2:30am with the six-hour walk to Lukla the next day, Debbie, Nicky and I staggered back to the hotel, and I wouldn't be lying if I said we literally crawled up the stairs; well, one of us did anyway.

The final few days turned into a bit of chaos to get back home, and need little elaboration. As we woke in Namche, we had time for a quick last explore. In this time, Roy (as any great expedition dad would do) bailed me out with Sherpa tip money after I ran out of money the day previously and struggled to find anywhere in this mountain village that would accept a credit or debit card. We also visited the Namche market, where Roy was harassed to such an extent by a particularly good salesman, that he ended up spending 2,000 NPR (£16) on a piece of amber which supposedly contained a scorpion. We later found out to our utter amazement that both the amber and the plastic scorpion were fake. We were all astounded by these findings, although none more so than poor Roy. Subsequently before leaving and still concussed from the previous evening, Debbie was left temporarily blinded after applying far too many contact lenses, and Ian was nursing a blister on his hand after a champions run on the football table. It was true that the group suffered more injuries in Namche than on any remote mountain top. The walk to Lukla was tough and was made decidedly worse by the fact I had mistakenly eaten my walk-out chocolate, a four day supply, during the first day. Fortunately I still had a full pack of Lucozade dextrose tablets which I didn't envisage needing after Lukla, so ate the full pack as standard and found myself bouncing off the walls for the rest of the walk, as I'm sure the other group members would testify. The final slopes to Lukla felt never ending as time after time we were deceived into thinking we had reached the end. On reaching Lukla however, we were disheartened to see that the visibility was down to a few meters, certainly no flights would be running today and evidently we would be here for a long time. The first port of call for most of us, even before going to the tea house was to call in at Starbucks. After refilling on hot chocolate and brownies, we were ushered out by the guides who had been waiting patiently in the Paradise Lodge, and went off to find our rooms. As I was with Ian and Roy, we very quickly made a final kit explosion. All credit to Roy though, he spent the next 40 hours continuously packing for the flight, such an organised man. We also noticed the irony in the naming of the lodge we were staying in. We had stayed in Paradise Lodge at the beginning of the expedition, but now that we had time to see our surroundings, especially the proximity and severity of the incline of the runway, we realised that with any flight into Lukla, you were guaranteed to get to Paradise one way or the other. That night we spent some time eating with our Sherpas, where we thanked them for their hard work and commitment, and also handed out their tip money, a customary tradition in Nepal, and deservedly so, since without the help of the Sherpas, expeditions like these would certainly not be possible.

The following day, we were told to be ready at 6am for a flight if the weather was good. Unfortunately the weather was not good, and was arguably a little worse than the previous day. We spent the day in a café and using as much free Wi-Fi as possible, browsing all the news channels for everything we had missed from around the world in the last month. Such is the remoteness of where we had been, even the start of a new world war would have gone largely unnoticed. At around 4pm, the long day was starting to drag on, so we all headed for the Irish bar. This was distinctly more Irish than the Namche Irish bar, as this time a pint of Guinness was painted onto the a green wall with a shamrock. Searching for some phone reception so I could make contact with friends and family and let them know I was alive and well, I headed to the Scottish bar with Debbie where we met a Scottish man and his wife who had fallen off a horse. After hearing the trials and tribulations of equestrianism in Nepal, we headed back to the Paradise Lodge for dinner. At this point I had a rather fateful encounter with Rob Casserley, although not that I had any inkling that I would be climbing a big mountain with him the following year.

Not wanting to waste the day, we all headed back to the Scottish bar where we re-met the Scottish man and his leg-splinted wife who were distinctively merrier than two hours previously. We also didn't want to put all our eggs in one basket however, so we dodged the rain which was now falling in biblical proportions, and headed back to the Irish bar to toast our success and plot our escape route from Lukla, the little village on the hill where we seemed destined to be stranded for an exceptionally long time.

The next day with the weather still very much inclement and news channels across the world now reporting on the hundreds of climbers and tourists stranded high in the Himalayas, no planes were flying so we all bit the bullet and started trudging down the mud-filled valley through the rain in an effort to reach Surke, a small village which held the key to our escape. Finally we saw what we were looking for, a flat field with a helicopter on it. On reaching the field, we had to wait before a relatively old helicopter landed within meters of us. This was my first time in a helicopter, and after seeing all the previous helicopters struggle to take off and then fly through a very narrow gap between two exceptional strong looking trees before plunging down and over the side of a cliff edge, I doubted whether this was the best introduction to the sport. I was also paying £600 for this evacuation, and as a team, we had all agreed that after being stuffed in by far the oldest helicopter on the field, we should be being paid just for having the nerve to get on board. My confidence was slightly raised, however, when I saw the pilot who would be taking our lives in his hands. A suave looking man with a broad smile, dressed in jeans, riding boots, a leather flying jacket with stereotypical fur trim, and the obligatory pair of aviators, stepped out of the old beast and quickly ushered us into the chopper ready for take-off. Although he was by far the coolest looking pilot I had ever seen, I still had some understandable apprehension about the flight ahead, and so, as I sat next to Debbie but separated by a mountain of kit bags, we managed to hold on to each other for dear life as the aging machinery rattled and roared, and with a big gap in the door still showing, we somehow managed to slowly inch our way above the ground and down the steep slope between the trees and into the valley.

Fortunately the pilot did a grand job of not crashing, and we were subsequently flown to a field at the side of a military base in the middle of absolutely nowhere where we had the short wait of seven hours before being picked up again and flown to Kathmandu. It was whilst we were staying on the military base that we started to talk to the Nepalese pilot who quickly informed us that the helicopter we were flying in was older than he was. We stopped talking to the pilot before he could give us a rundown of the service history, and proceeded to wait on the base which easily rivalled the valleys surrounding Baruntse for its isolation.

We were eventually a day later than planned as we arrived at the hotel Manaslu. This proved a big shock to the system, as before we had left for the mountains, we had thought the hotel was average at best, and perhaps even a little dirty in places, but after arriving from the land of tents and tea houses, the Manaslu was like a palace to us, complete with showers and even a door with a lock for each room. We must have looked like cave men to the concierge dressed in a smart black suit and hat.

Unfortunately due to the weather delay from Lukla, our international flight was the next day so we were somewhat limited on time, which was no issue since no one particularly had much interest in spending more money after reluctantly handing over our credit cards to pay the helicopter bill which had amounted to $10,980 between 12 people.

I shared a room with Ian for the night where we had a quick kit explosion and the first shower after 35 days of climbing. With only ten minutes to go before needing to leave for the evening meal, I was left with no choice but to go for a quick five minute shower instead of the 60 minute bath I was hoping for. Nevertheless, everyone looked remarkably clean and we had all had a complete minute makeover on returning to the lobby.

A final meal at the famous Rum Doodle was enjoyed by all, which was then of course followed by the obligatory night out on the town; and then that was it, the end of the expedition quickly came to a close. All we were left with was our international flights to Delhi, a three-hour wait whilst Roy tried on the lipstick in duty free, and the final nine-hour flight to London Heathrow.

Chapter 27 – The Aftermath

Before the start of the expedition, I knew that there were many different ways the expedition could go, and many different factors that could influence the outcome of the expedition. Prior to meeting the rest of the team members, I knew that this would be the one area that really had to go well, but also had the potential to destroy the expedition and its objectives if we didn't perform well together. There were 12 incredibly lucky people who travelled to the Himalayas to climb Baruntse, and these 12 people just happened to be our team. No one expects everyone to get on well in a team, even if a team is made up of best friends, as when you spend 35 days living and breathing together, even the best teams fall apart. Our team was different though, it was destined not to work by the sheer fact that all 12 people were relative strangers, but even with this, somehow, we gelled together not just as a good team, but as great friends. Highly demanding environments and situations can break a team of friends, but in contrast, our expedition pulled 12 strangers together and we bonded over often arduous experiences.

Our goodbyes at Heathrow were understandably emotional, and I felt sad that, if I was to go on and climb Everest, it would be without the people that got me to the top of Baruntse and Mera Peak. But overriding this sadness and indeed happiness was the satisfaction that 12 people from all corners of the UK (and Ireland) had come together and become lifelong friends.

Walking through the double doors which was rapidly becoming a drill at Heathrow, I had made it back, this time with far greater success than Peak Lenin, and despite the fact that they were all numb, I still had ten fingers and ten toes.

It is a strange feeling meeting back up with family and friends at home after such a long time away in a country that has little resemblance to the UK. There was none of the hustle and bustle of Kathmandu for which I was glad, but in a small way, I missed the controlled chaos, the uncertainty, and the life of the people of Nepal. Kathmandu had been a far cry from Bishkek and Osh in Kyrgyzstan, and whilst some of the fundamentals were the same, in all truth, Nepal and Kyrgyzstan were really worlds apart, and it would be fair to say, Kathmandu has an addictive property that is very unique to that city.

I soon came back to earth with a bang though when I had to work out how I was going to cover the £600 helicopter bill which I clearly hadn't accounted for prior to the expedition. As soon as possible after arriving back in the UK, I also wanted to write and record a diary from Baruntse that would remind me of subtle features of the expedition such as Ian with his pants on his head, which I would have otherwise forgotten. Thankfully, I found writing this diary to record key events much easier to write than my dissertation, and infinitely more interesting considering no one fell down a crevasse in my dissertation.

Writing the diary occupied a few days which allowed me to slowly readjust to life at home. It is difficult to image how you will feel at the end of an expedition, and to some extent, despite being back in a country with infinitely better infrastructure, and a house with a solid roof and walls made from brick, it is hard not to miss the company of the 11 other people and Sherpas who I was surrounded by for such a long time. I soon finished writing my diary though, and I realised that I needed to quickly get back on track and find a sponsor for the Everest expedition. It almost felt like Everest didn't matter now that Baruntse had been a success, but I had to focus on the reason why I had attempted Baruntse and Mera Peak in the first place, it was all in order to gain experience and progress onto the dream mountain, Everest.

During my first phone call back home whilst I was still at Baruntse base camp, I had had some very unexpected but exciting news. A potential sponsor had tried to contact me whilst I was away on the mountain, and requested that I attend a meeting in London in an effort to make a deal. I was stunned since this was my very first success in finding sponsorship. I hadn't even had a meeting at this point, or even a remotely positive email reply, so to be summoned to the city for a meeting was exciting, if a little terrifying. I wanted to make sure I sealed the deal with this company, as I didn't see that any second opportunity would arise, and so revamped my whole presentation with further information and sponsor pictures from the very recent Baruntse expedition. I was set to see the CEO and so this induced even more completely rational fear than before.

It was still November when I went for a meeting with the head of communications and sponsorship in a nondescript logistics company which had revenue of €51.48 billion in 2010, has over 275,000 employees and holds a royal warrant from The Queen. The CEO was unable to attend, however I presented regardless to the member of staff who had enough authority to give my project approval. Despite the nerves, I managed to pull off a confident pitch, and put across as much information as I could. The plans were grand, ranging from an expedition to mark the Diamond Jubilee, to a marketing campaign for the company who usually sign sponsorship deals in the region of £50,000,000. What I was asking for was much less, and provided a value for money that even a professional international sports team would struggle to compete with.

I left the offices feeling that I had done all I could to seal the deal, and went away eager for a response once the CEO had browsed over the blueprints for an expedition which was perfect timing in every sense of the word. Planned for May 2012, it was just before the celebrations for The Queen's Diamond Jubilee, and crucially, it was nicely placed before the Olympics to avoid any clashes of audience, and was even scheduled to finish immediately prior to the start of the Olympic torch relay, a perfect time to capture the perfect audience.

I waited in eager anticipation for this response all the way through the remainder of November, and then all the way through December encompassing Christmas and New Year which isn't the greatest time to be worried about whether the answer will be favourable or a crushing blow to my plans. I had stopped my bombardment of companies, since I thought this a waste of time as I now had to concentrate on pushing this sponsorship agreement through and then focus on my preparations in Scotland and in the Alps where I would give myself the final tests before the ultimate exam. Unfortunately, even at the end of January 2012, I still had no answer as to the outcome of my pitch. In the middle of February, I became disillusioned with the prospect that this all might come off, and, fast running out of time for both winter training and to find a prospective sponsor, I reluctantly took Mum's advice and sent just a few more proposals out before taking a break in Scotland.

You can picture the scene, I was close to two months away from the biggest expedition of my life, yet I had no sponsor, and was rapidly running out of ideas. I had exhausted every little piece of information

I possessed; I had emailed, contacted and spoke to as many different companies as was humanly possible. I was now at a complete loss as to just what to do and what to make of the situation I was in. I knew that I should continue to train, just in case a sponsor came along and I suddenly found myself on board a plane bound for Kathmandu but without the lungs to make any form of respectable attempt. Finding the motivation for this type of training though is incredibly tough. Running to the point that everything hurts, and then maintaining that same intensity for 13 miles is incredibly demanding, but never more than when there feels like there is no purpose to the pain. Somehow I did manage to train, and what's more, I managed to better all my previous attempts during apnea training, adding more and more distance after the Baruntse expedition. I had been training each and every day, running, swimming and cycling countless miles.

But all this effort was for what purpose? I had done everything in my power to make the Everest 2012 dream a reality a success, but the one thing that let me down was the one thing that was out of my control, and the one thing that athletes, expeditioners and anyone who relies on funding and sponsorship fears. I had gone to extreme lengths to try and bolster my financial position. I had contacted the most powerful people that I could think of, and not just in Lincolnshire, England, or Europe, but the world. These individuals and organisations included Sir Richard Branson, the Sultan of Brunei, Mark Zuckerberg, Bill Gates, oil barons in the United Arab Emirates, atomic weapons manufacturer AWE who are notable for producing inter-continental ballistic nuclear missile weapons systems, the Barack Obama administration, Carlos Slim Helu, the richest person on the planet, Thorntons Chocolates who rejected my claim of part-ownership of the company, and even Everest the home improvement company who were unable to see what use double glazing would be on the mountain, clearly overlooking potential for the most orchidaceous, best insulated conservatory in all of Asia.

Chapter 28 – A Well Timed Break

I knew I couldn't maintain the physical intensity of training whilst at home, with what felt like the financial world hanging around my neck. As much as I forced myself out to run and to train, I wasn't enjoying it because I was so uncertain of my future, so I knew a break was the only alternative. After sending just a couple more proposals, I had decided I would go and visit a friend in Scotland where I would be able to take a break from all the sponsorship worries, but still maintain a good level of fitness and even improve my winter climbing ability which would no doubt come in handy whilst on Everest.

I quickly packed everything that I thought I would need, axes, harness, crampons, a variety of climbing gear and then a few other essentials into my big kit bag, then headed up the East Coast Mainline to Aberdeen.

Scottish winter climbing is world class, attracting athletes like Ueli Steck on the hardest routes such as 'The Secret'; and after experiencing the acquired tastes of Kyrgyzstan, India and Kazakhstan during 2011, I was more than looking forward to a return visit having not climbed in the country since the previous year.

We had planned to make use of Scotland's unique environment, which in the winter gives plenty of snow, especially towards the east, and combines this with some of the best climbing terrain in the world. Unfortunately, I didn't seem to be having the best of luck, and had inadvertently travelled to Scotland during the hottest winter on record which rendered almost all my possessions entirely useless.

In my kit bag, I had been very meticulous with my packing, and so had with me many different types of fleeces, many down filled garments, and generally the warmest pieces of clothing I had. Clearly I hadn't packed many pairs of shorts or anything with a remotely shorter sleeve, so when it came to climbing on the sea cliffs in bright, 24 degree Celsius sunshine, I felt slightly overdressed.

We very quickly scrapped the hope of finding any prospective winter climbing routes that were in condition, and had somehow come up with the solution which involved climbing on rock instead of snow. Neither of us had extensive knowledge of rock climbing which is surprising different from ice and winter mixed climbing despite sharing the same objective of somehow, gracefully or not, clambering to the top of a route. I was certainly the most inexperienced party having only ever previously rock climbed indoors at the not so well known Grantham Leisure Centre. Between us, we had no leading experience, and apart from the odd outing to the Himalayas and Glen Coe, had almost no idea how to place 'gear' into a crack which would act as the safety net in case of a fall.

After spending a good day locating potential climbing venues along the coast, we opted for a sheltered spot that was free of any other climbers, and had the great advantage of not being overlooked by anyone hoping to see world class climbers in action. The first thing I noticed about this type of climbing, apart from the lack of snow and rain in mid-February, was that it didn't take very much height to induce a certain level of vertigo, especially on certain sections that had many rock steps leading to the freezing North Sea below.

This type of climbing was something far different to what I was used to, far more committing with marginal protection placement opportunities few and far between in the weathered and eroded sea cliff rock. With winter climbing, there is always the comfort that despite the crevasses, potential for avalanche or the risk of hypothermia, there is soft white snow all around which somehow dulls the senses, no matter how steep or how many thousands of feet of air are below you. Being on rock makes every move absolutely critical; one false move here, even from five metres off the ground, and it can be game over. Indeed this is true of many winter routes, but there is something about the snow that helps keep your fear factor out of the red zone for just a little longer than whilst on rock.

Rock climbing is certainly beneficial when it comes to summer alpine, and winter expedition climbing. The more you are exposed to these 'on the edge' type situations, the more you become numb to some of the imagined danger, and it becomes possible to just focus on each individual move, rather than worrying about the potential for falling which becomes more and more obvious the higher you go.

There is something else about rock climbing which makes it an invaluable tool, even for lengthy expeditions. It is the problem-solving aspect, both in a metaphorical sense, and a more literal way. Being able to problem-solve on Everest is critical, especially when facing situations that are almost certainly out of your comfort zone. An unexpected queue at a bottleneck high on the mountain, or an unusually high avalanche risk are just two problems that will prompt you to problem-solve in a large scale. But there are also more fine and small scale problems to work out such as individual moves up the Hillary Step to an awkward pirouette, or attempting to fix a non-responsive oxygen bottle regulator as you climb up and into the death zone. All these variations on problem solving are solvable and are easily practised on a rock face where, although the specific problem is different, the thought process required to logically reach a solution is the same. And that in essence is all a rock wall is; it is a series of problems that need to be linked together, and then solved so that the overall 'problem' of climbing the face can be tackled.

So whilst I wasn't getting the most specific form of training on the snowless east coast, I was getting a very beneficial element of training that would simply add to my ability to climb on Everest. It also gave me space and time to think. I didn't have much time since the days were counting down extremely rapidly; however, whilst I had been stuck in a room for months on end sending desperate emails and trying to find the smallest of leads, I realised that sometimes, all that's needed is a break away from all the stress, just to see the bigger picture and put everything into perspective. Often, I found myself waking up to an endless list of tasks that had been building up constantly. I had to contact as many different companies as I possibly could, but the more companies I contacted, the more work I set myself in order to successfully send off the one proposal that might be my saviour. There comes a point though, where time away from the immediate task at hand is required, to take stock of everything, and work out a different game plan. I was constantly living by my own rule, that I would only work to plan A, if that didn't work, I would reassess plan A and try again, I simply didn't have a plan B as I had invested everything to make the expedition happen. Such a risky strategy in hindsight, but it is true that who dares wins, and additionally it would be true to say that no one who has ever achieved greatly in their life has ever done so without a healthy amount of daring; but it is managing the risk, that's the key.

And so my trip to Aberdeen had been a great way to let off steam, and add an element of cross training into my preparation programme, being ever hopeful. I also took a phone call from home whilst I was training. I had had an email from a company who wished to meet me again in London, although fresh from the defeat of the previous meeting in the city, I didn't hold out much hope, and in fact thought that this may be a little inconvenient considering the amount of work I had to catch up on after my break. This was interestingly also the first time I really truly doubted that I would be able to pull the dream off. I realised that I was drastically short on time, and I really didn't think that even if this latest development came through, I would be able to pull off everything in time. I thought at this point that even after everything I had worked for, perhaps it would be easier if I just didn't go, since this would make everything so much easier, especially reducing the level of stress that would undoubtedly build up if the expedition got the go ahead.

I forgot about this recent development and enjoyed the scenic journey back to Lincolnshire along the east coast, sad to leave a newfound home, but still recounting some of the best days of climbing I'm sure both of us had just had, in my mind. I was at this point blissfully ignorant about what developments could unfold as I hurtled through the British country side directly towards the epicentre of the earthquake that was about to hit; this was clearly the calm before the unannounced storm.

Chapter 29 – Can You Yell Hibu?

In 2008, a leap year that started on a Tuesday, many things happened that would affect the world for many years to come. 2008 was the year that Cyprus and Malta adopted the euro, Sir Edmund Hillary passed away, Fidel Castro resigned as the President of Cuba, Barack Obama became the first African-American president of the USA, there was an earthquake in Lincolnshire which registered 5.2 on the Richter scale, Jigme Khesar Namgyel Wangchuck was crowned King of Bhutan, Wayne and Coleen Rooney tied the knot, and pirates hijacked a 300,000 tonne super tanker off the coast of Somalia.

Unfortunately, 2008 was also the start of the world recession which as of 2013 is still an ongoing crisis having reached the infamous 'double dip'. Many students including me started university with the anticipation that the financial situation would resolve itself by the time we graduated. In hindsight, this way of thinking was slightly flawed as much of the world found that this was the greatest recession since the Great Depression of the 1930's. In 2008, I didn't take too much personal interest in business; however four years later, I was about to walk into a board room to pitch my idea to a business which like most businesses, would be cautious about spending in such a financial climate.

On the evening of the 6th March 2012, I travelled into London to find my accommodation for the evening. My budget was tight, so I headed for a hostel somewhere in the city close to an underground station. My feet were in pieces with my business/wedding shoes effortlessly slicing into my heels which meant quickly perfecting a discreet limp technique. I found my accommodation for the evening, there wasn't an English speaking person in sight, even the person sitting behind the desk at reception struggled with my RP British accent. Heading up many flights of stairs which were in need of a deep clean, I reached my dormitory for the night. Five bunk beds were crammed into the room, each with their own 'privacy' curtains which nearly stretched the full length of the bed. I dropped my bag with all the documents I would need for the following day, I phoned my mum and told her that the accommodation was great and I had been upgraded to a penthouse across the road, and then I clambered into the bottom bunk of my bed in which I could only dream about the proceedings for the following day.

All of a sudden, at 5:30am, and likely to the disgust of all the travellers I was sharing with, my alarm went off and I attempted to get dressed as best as possible without waking too many other people who had the potential to be carrying lethal weapons or at the very least, be extremely drunk. I resorted to putting on as few clothes as possible, and then made my way out into the hallway where I could get fully dressed uninterrupted.

I had recently been to a wedding which incidentally had the theme of James Bond, and so had a perfectly good dinner jacket type suit, not ideal for a presentation, but as long as I didn't need to wear the jacket with its satin trim and I could hide the pleated front of my dress shirt with a tie, I would get by. I did own another suit which I had worn for sixth form, but unfortunately I was still yet to fully grow into it.

So on the 7th March 2012, I travelled into London SW1 early and found the nearest coffee shop to the boardroom; I was sick with nerves. Whilst travelling back from Scotland, I hadn't expected my proposal to be taken seriously with so many previous rejections, and I had assumed that I would be seeing someone who would pass on my information to people who could actually make a decision, similar to my previous meeting. The evening prior to this new pitch however, I received an email which turned expectations upside down, and confirmed to me that I would be throwing myself to the lions.

Yell Group was the company, the inventors of the Yellow Pages, the famous directory synonymous with corporate contacts which seemed slightly ironic given the tack which I had taken in contacting corporations with my proposal. The email I received the day prior to my pitch gave me all the information I needed for locating the boardroom before 8am. The email also gave me the details of the members of staff I would be pitching to which subsequently accounted for 99% of my sickness.

The first member of staff on the email was the Group CEO; this came as a slight shock since I hadn't been expecting such an important figure at the pitch, however my shock grew worse as I read the 'also in attendance' section. There would be the Group Company Secretary and General Counsel, the Group CFO, and finally the Corporate Responsibility Manager. This sent chills through my body since I would be pitching to the most esteemed figures in the company. I sat in the coffee house sipping my hot chocolate feeling very out of place surrounded by business people all flocking in for their caffeine fix before a tough day in the city. I felt out of place and as an athlete, had little experience in this setting. I hoped that I wouldn't meet any of the company figures that I would be pitching to later in the morning, but I doubted that they would need to visit a coffee shop after flying in to the city on board their private jet, then onto the boardroom in a fully equipped Rolls Royce Phantom.

I sat in the coffee house until I became calm and was able to rationalise the situation I was about to enter. I knew that there was no need to panic. Although everything rested on convincing some of the most important people in business that I was the man for the job, I also knew that they were only human, and so would be able to understand my enthusiasm and vision for my project as long as I was able to get across the main points of my proposal.

I tried not to think of the worst case scenario which was only an immediate 'no' after all, and instead tried to remember all the points in giving the perfect presentation. This didn't help too much since the remaining 1% of my sickness was due to the fact that I had delivered some utterly abysmal presentations at university, and had failed on my last attempt at securing any form of financial investment. Again, I rationalised and I soon realised that many of my presentations at university had been disastrous since I didn't understand any of the content; this time, however, I knew everything regarding my pitch like the back of my hand. I would be talking from experience, and aside from learning all my numbers, everything else was purely my own concept which I had been living for the past two years; this time it would be impossible to forget my content, since I was the content.

I walked along the London street to the boardroom, the city now teeming with life as the working day started to get underway. I soon reached the location and stood in front of the building, excited, nervous, a bundle of energy with every emotion rolled into one. The building was grand, clearly out of the price range of most property enthusiasts. Large gilded doors and a long marble entrance leading to a modern, almost futuristic set of grand stairs. I rang the bell, and like a little school child, thought of running away before I could see who was behind these grand doors, but fortunately remained rooted to the spot as curiosity got the better of me.

Ushered in by the Group Company Secretary and General Counsel no less, I was taken to the boardroom where I had a moment to compose myself, get out all of my documents and my cherished proposal which by this point would have been infamous across the heart of the city. Surprisingly as I sat down, I felt very comfortable, despite the company I found myself in. My confidence was undoubtedly aided by the humanness of everyone sitting around the table, and rather than be cutthroat, they were clearly prepared to make the mood as relaxed as possible so I could get down to the job at hand and talk marketing and numbers. Starting the pitch with the basic details, I soon found a flow to what I was trying to explain. Every detail was covered from every angle, and it became clear that Yell could be the company that I would try to take to the top of the world. All of a sudden, a new element was brought to the table which just added to the possibilities and appropriateness of the expedition. Yell was in the process of rebranding, a very secretive process that could afford no media attention whilst brand ideas were still up in the air. Everest would be a perfect way to rebrand a company; every metaphor for Everest is reflected in business and in life, so this new angle, one which I clearly had not been expecting, was the last piece in the puzzle which would pull this deal through.

After countless hours pitching my idea, I left the boardroom and casually walked through the busy streets of London, and using my day pass on the Underground to full effect by embarking on my own tourist type day out. I wondered if any of these businessmen and women that I passed every few seconds were having a day like I was. Did anyone notice that I wasn't really the business type, and in fact just in disguise, attempting to earn a respectable yearly salary in a single day?

As I walked back towards my connecting train home, I tried to assess how the day had gone and what was the next likely outcome. I had been given no idea by any of the staff to whom I pitched whether or not they would come on board with my expedition or not, but whilst I didn't like the nervous wait, I didn't have any expectation of what the outcome would be so I was as calm as I could be given the circumstances. All I knew is that someone from Yell would contact me in a few days, and then that would be it. I knew for sure that if the answer was a no, then there wouldn't be an Everest dream for me in 2012, there simply wouldn't be the time.

On the train home, I coaxed myself into a quietly confident mood for no particular reason other than everything in the meeting had gone as perfect as I could have hoped. I thought that there was no point in thinking negatively, there would be plenty of time for that if the directors at Yell didn't feel that I was what they were looking for, so I tried to go over a moderately good scenario in my head to see what my next moves would be and what I would need to do to finally be ready in the unlikely event that the Everest project was on.

Chapter 30 – Incomprehensible Ecstasy

Later that evening as I rested at home after a long and exhausting day, my phone rang unexpectedly and I answered unaware of the drama that was about to unfold.

At 8am the same day, I had been ushered into the boardroom by the Group Company Secretary and General Counsel, and now I found myself on the phone to the same Group Company Secretary and General Counsel hours later. I wasn't expecting this call, so I was unsure what to make of it, especially given the very fast response time, and I assumed that it would be much quicker to give a 'no' rather than convince many people including the shareholders and give a 'yes'.

The conversation was roughly as follows. "Matthew, I will be very brief as I know you will want an answer after your pitch today. We have come to the decision that we will be partnering your expedition." Before I could utter anything in response, he continued, "And Mike (the CEO) thought it was one of the best presentations and pitches he had seen."

I was in utter shock. I couldn't think of any words to say except for a million thank-yous, and then remained in silence whilst the conversation continued on the other end of the line where I found out exactly what I would need to do to complete the deal.

I came off the phone feeling completely overwhelmed. I could physically feel the adrenalin coursing round my body. I had worked so hard for over two years just to pull the sponsorship deal, and suddenly all of that stored emotion came flooding in. I went through to Mum, and she instantly knew what had just happened, but neither she nor I could possibly imagine the stress that was about to be endured. I called my best friends and they were as shocked and surprised by what had just happened as I was. I was physically shaking with excitement for what felt like an age as I revelled in the euphoria that surrounded me. All this emotion was flowing from somewhere in my body, all stored from the very first day that I conceived the idea in the French Alps, to the disappointment on Peak Lenin, the unforgettable experiences on Baruntse and the special times in Scotland. Every little piece of training I had done was now for a purpose, and I would use all this energy to my advantage. I remembered a coincidental tip I had picked up whilst I was playing squash. Affirmation cards are pieces of paper that if read often enough, are said bring the change that is written upon them, or at least you will start to believe. I always carried around one card in my squash bag; it said "Remember 2012". 2012 was meant to be the year that squash finally made its debut in the Olympic Games, but alas it was rejected. I wondered for a moment whether all the training I had done for so many years was meant to lead up to this point; whether it was all meant to lead up to 2012, but not in the way I had intended it to. I had expected that I would be representing my country on the squash court, but instead found myself in the very late stages of preparations to tackle the highest mountain in the world.

And then it hit me, and it hit me hard to the point where I felt physically sick. For 30 minutes, I had been awash with emotion, but all of a sudden, as if I had all but run out of excitement, I felt a wave of panic sweep over me, and a whole new emotion enveloped me, something I had never felt before; I was under serious pressure to perform.

It dawned on me that in under a month, I would be flying to Kathmandu, then to Lukla, walking to the base of Mount Everest, the mountain I had dreamed of since a little impressionable boy, and attempting to walk in the footsteps of my own heroes. Every expedition I had previously undertaken and all competitions that I had ever played in were full of pressure, but that pressure was different, it was my own personal pressure, the pressure of my expectation upon myself to perform. No one else would be impacted if I performed badly, it would just be my own disappointment, and perhaps those close to me. But this time it was different, so totally different. Yell had come through to help me in my hour of need, but their offer of help was filled with external pressure that had been placed upon me to perform, not just for myself this time, but for someone else. I was being paid to summit Mount Everest, so I felt that there was no other option, I really needed to summit if I was to hold onto any credibility.

Of course this pressure from Yell was unintentional. A surprisingly human organisation for their size, they fully understood the pressure that I was already under, and so reassured me that as long as I came home safely, that would be good enough. But for me, that wasn't enough, the overriding goal is to always return home alive, but this time, there was an invisible and an inevitable pressure that meant I needed to perform when it really counted.

This new wave of panic swept over me and within seconds of feeling so happy that I could hardly speak, I was reduced to a panicking mess as I realised the task in hand. It wasn't simply the pressure of performing that hit me; it was the challenge of monumental proportions that was staring me in the face. I had been on enough mountains by this time to know that when it starts to hurt at altitude, it really hurts; every inch of your body in agony, just wishing for a release from the pain. This is what I had faced previously, but unlike in the run up to Baruntse, I felt drastically unprepared, unconfident, and very small. This was Everest after all, the mother of all mountains, the biggest one out there, and full of dangers that strike fear into the heart of even the most hardy mountaineer. I managed to calm myself down, and concluded that I would cross each bridge when I came to it. The first bridge was to get some form of sleep that night which I knew would be almost impossible. I was overcome with every possible feeling, but had been comforted by all the right people. I went to bed an emotional mess that night, but safe in the knowledge that I had secured my funding for an Everest expedition in one of the worst global financial recessions ever seen.

Chapter 31 – Progression and Preparations

After the rollercoaster of the 7th March, I started to get organised as quickly as I could since I knew time was very much of the essence. In order to make my schedule, I would have to do so much, and effectively fit it into the final three weeks that I had left in the UK. To do this would mean making endless lists that I could tick off before creating more lists. Because I had so much to do and could afford to miss nothing out, I had lists for absolutely everything, and somehow managed to fine tune the organised chaos that I was living.

Amongst my chores for the final three weeks, I had to go to Reading to finalise the expedition contract with Yell, I had to book flights to Kathmandu, and contact an expedition leader to actually confirm my place on an expedition, something that most people do over a year in advance; I also had some final training to finish, I had to contact as many different media sources as possible as well as conducting TV and radio interviews, and finally I had the most exciting job of all which was to go shopping for all things feathery.

My first job was to get down to Reading where I would be able to sign my contracts and meet with all the staff at the Yell headquarters where I would be given a briefing of what I was actually required to do. Up until this point, the only thing I knew was that the company wanted me to summit Everest, but I didn't know their rationale behind their sponsorship; was it for media attention, was it linked into building the new brand, or was it more intrinsic to the company, revolving around intra-employee motivation?

I soon found out that Yell were indeed launching a new brand, however the directors and people who make the overall decision had still not been able to come up with the new name of this initiative, although they knew very clearly the direction the company was taking. This was very exciting for me, with the prospect of not just being able to attempt the climb of Everest, but being part of the rebranding process of a FTSE constituent, although I wouldn't actually know which name I would be taking up Everest until I reached Everest base camp. Aside from the rebranding and the unnerving consequences if the expedition didn't quite go to plan, there was a concerted effort to motivate employees working within the company. I knew that this is one of the most undervalued assets of this type of expedition because the effect is not easily quantifiable. If the expedition was purely a marketing strategy, there are methods to calculate roughly what profits the expedition has made to the company, however this is often short term and often goes unnoticed by the employees.

The directors at Yell were very keen to use the expedition and the metaphors surrounding Everest to interact with employees across the world, by creating various initiatives and challenges that employees could be part of after seeing the exploits of the expedition. As the climber, this was particularly rewarding to know that something that I was doing could help motivate and drive productivity at the very core of the business.

This alone told me that the company had a very human side, but I was shocked by the amount of attention I was drawing as I moved from room to room in the headquarters. Members of staff were genuinely interested by the challenge, and getting behind the efforts which only helped to calm my nerves and dispel any fears that I may have just signed the contract binding me for life to a faceless corporate giant.

I now knew that the expedition would serve two purposes, it would be helping to launch a new brand, and it would also act as a motivation for employees. We then had to turn our attention to logistics. I had a very limited time to get everything up and running, and organising communications for base camp back to the UK proved decidedly tricky and expensive with sat phone calls costing up to £6 per minute. The key lay in liaising with the company I was going to be climbing with, and the contacts in Nepal. This tricky interaction between four parties was difficult and time consuming; however I knew that once I had everything together and was sitting on the plane to Kathmandu, everything would work itself out somehow.

For my expedition, I had chosen to work with the strongest and best possible team on the mountain. Henry Todd is a legend of the Himalayas, with the enviable nickname of 'The Todd Father'. Well known throughout the region, Henry operates the best expeditions on the mountain through his expertise in mountain logistics and weather, his use of the best team of Sherpas and guides on the mountain, and his interactions with Himalayan Guides, the best logistical team for the region. Some of Henry's past climbers include

Sir Ranulph Fiennes, Bear Grylls and Kenton Cool amongst many others. I met Henry in the picturesque, neither here nor there town of Grantham, Lincolnshire, where we discussed the expedition in great detail. Up until this point, with less than three weeks until the end of March, I was still not a member on an expedition, so it was with great relief that Henry accepted me as a climber in his team. I would be climbing with Dr. Rob Casserley and two other young climbers, which with our mean age of 21 years, made us the youngest team to attempt the mountain.

I had felt uncertain about which team to go with since the expedition on Baruntse had gone so well, I wondered whether I would ever be able to surpass that experience. The only consolation to this conundrum was that I was already good friends with some of the team members, and so thought that whilst the chance of meeting a whole new team of amazing people like I had done on Baruntse was slim, I also knew that by climbing with friends, it would give us a much higher chance of being successful as we could all pull together as a team from day one, rather than going through the long process of working out who was the alpha male, and who was and wasn't prepared to follow.

I knew that this was the best option for Everest, and I also knew that with the expertise of Henry and his close knit team, I would have the best possible chance of reaching the summit. As Henry had said, he would get me to the South Col, and then from there, it would be down to me; this seemed like a fair enough deal. I had already decided that I would climb from the south Nepalese side of Everest after having had the pleasure of trekking through this part of the world on the return from Baruntse. Many different factors can affect which side to choose, but as a general rule, the south side of Everest is the best bet.

So I had the sponsorship and therefore the weight of the world was no longer on my shoulders, and I also had the team, now what I needed was to make a once in a lifetime visit to the bank where I could make an unusually large transfer of funds to Nepal. This involved walking into the bank as usual, going to the same cashier as usual, and then asking to make a transfer, as usual. The lady on the desk asked where the money was going to, and was happy once she had located Nepal on the computer, although she clearly had no idea where this country was. She then asked how much I wanted to transfer at which point the red panic button was pressed and her supervisor came swiftly to the desk to check why a 'boy' of 21 was transferring enough money to put down a generous deposit on a city bachelor pad. The interrogation started immediately, with a whole series of questions relating to money laundering being fired at me, at which point I asked what money laundering was and whether it could be done with normal household appliances. Somehow I managed to blunder my way through the series of questions, and then watched the TV screen as exchange rates fluctuated showing the new daily rate. I became aware very quickly that the bank wasn't the best place to transfer money, and instead of a simple transaction where I had expected to pay no more than £500 to have my hypothetical money wired abroad, I ended up paying 3% on top of my expedition fees which when considering the amount, dramatically increased my expected expenditure. This was frustrating as I considered that I was paying money to pay money, but realised there was little point arguing, so left feeling very sick at the transaction I had just made. My parents always said that money used to burn a hole in my pocket, but having had the lump sum sitting in my bank for less than 24 hours, I waved goodbye, and added a whole new meaning to the phrase.

The transaction was complete, which to some extent confirmed that I would almost certainly be travelling to Everest, an overwhelming thought.

My next task was to prove ironic and perhaps a little satisfying as I had to work out a method of shipping the new brand flag of Yell to Nepal. Iswari, the Nepalese owner of Himalayan Guides who also happens to be the king of logistics to Nepal gave me the details I would need to ship the flag to Everest base camp. The irony is in the fact that the logistics company who would ultimately deliver the flag to Nepal was the same company who were potential sponsors of the expedition all those months ago; I wondered if they knew what was associated with the parcel that they would ultimately deliver.

I checked and double checked my lists. Slowly but surely everything was coming together; but I had saved the best for last. I needed to buy all the expedition kit that I would need that I didn't already have on the previous expeditions. On Baruntse, I had often looked like a tramp with ripped trekking trousers, and old base layers, but I couldn't afford anything else. Now, I had the chance to update some of my kit, as well as purchase the most 'Everest' piece of kit you can own. I wasn't sure where I was going to buy my down suit from, but I knew that this and all the other pieces of expedition gear could be found in the Lake District where I had previously bought my high altitude boots and various goose-down filled garments. I decided that my last bit of training could be done in the Lake District, and then killing two birds with one stone, I would also be able to kit out the expedition at the same time.

What I hadn't quite realised though, was that whilst down suits are commonplace in many mountaineering shops due to the commercial side of high altitude climbing, most of these suits, and in fact all the size small suits had been previously sold prior to the start of the Everest season. This presented a number of problems, mostly revolving around the fact that it would be nearly impossible to climb Everest without this suit. Frantically ringing round asking to beg, borrow or steal a suit didn't help matters, and I was left with the choice of either making one out of a BHS duvet, or having one specially made for me in the hope that it would be ready before I arrived in the Lake District. Fortunately I chose the second option, and I found myself days later waddling round a mountaineering shop in my shiny new, exceptionally hot suit. At this point, I also met up with another friend from the Baruntse expedition who clearly wanted a piece of the action in the bright yellow onesie.

I tried to hold myself back from spending excessively; however it is easy to lose track of purchases when each individual item costs in excess of £500. I recounted all my purchases later in the day and ticked off each one from my 'to get list'. Each item was fascinating. I had already used some weird and wonderful pieces of equipment on Baruntse, but now I was overloaded with new-fangled clothing systems and climbing gear. I recalled my collection of high altitude equipment; I now had a pair of boots, a down suit, a high altitude sleeping bag, and a pair of the warmest possible mitts to protect my extremities from the crippling effects of frostbite. Each one of these pieces of equipment was rated to below -50 degrees Celsius, with the Kevlar lined boots being rated to below -60 degrees Celsius. I knew from experience that the environment high in the mountains is extreme, however seeing the equipment needed to take me over 8,000m just gave an idea as to what I could really expect at the highest of altitudes.

We had shopped until I had literally dropped, so having purchased all the main pieces of equipment with just medicine and various personal items left to buy, we headed for Wasdale on the western side of the Lake District. Wasdale is famous for having the view of England's tallest mountain, deepest lake and smallest church. It is also reported as one of the many homes of mountaineering. Napes Needle is a classic rock climb situated in the Wasdale valley, and was one of the first recorded rock climbs ever attempted. I had, however, set my sights on a slightly different challenge which I thought would best prepare me for Everest. We had a limit of three days in the valley, so the challenge was on to make the most of the time. I already knew what I was going to attempt, and was positively confident about my plans. A full day walk whilst carrying 20kgs of water was one challenge whilst a run up to the top of Scafell Pike was another. The first challenge involved getting wet and then attempting to swim a long distance, specifically two miles of Wast Water. Parking up the evening before next to the lake, I was slightly daunted by the prospect of the swim. I had never swum in open water other than for a few minutes in the sea, and had never attempted to swim in a wetsuit before. The water looked black with a heavy breeze creating white horses in the centre of the lake. Despite the ominous appearance and my lack of experience, I was determined to attempt the swim. I could swim all day in a pool so I knew the distance was not a problem, and as long as I stayed close to the shore line, I would be as safe as possible, whilst being tracked from the lake side.

I woke up the next morning full of anticipation. The wind was not as strong which meant I wouldn't have to contend with waves too much. I got suited and booted, constantly looking out over the water as if waiting for something that would put me off the swim. I managed to get down to the shore line, and after waiting a few moments to compose myself, I stood up and walked calmly into the black abyss in front of me.

As soon as my head hit the water and the bubbles stopped obscuring my vision through my goggles, I very quickly knew that something wasn't quite right. I hadn't forgotten anything, I double checked. I put my head under water and immediately came up for air gasping. This wasn't going to plan, and I was getting increasingly frustrated with my inability to start the swim. After one last try, I realised that actually, I had developed an irrational fear of open water almost instantaneously. It wasn't the distance that scared me, or the fear that I would drown, but worse, it was fear of the unknown, the darkness which went on forever past my goggles. I was the only person in the lake which made everything ten times worse, as I suddenly felt very alone, and all too vulnerable. I sat in the shallows and put my head under the water, to try and calm my fear. I gazed again into the thick blackness, and as much as I knew there really was nothing to worry about, my imagination took hold and a whole manner of images appeared out of the blackness. I had travelled less than five metres, yet minutes before I was full of confidence in covering over two miles of the lake. I put this down to experience and quickly headed to the car, frustrated, deeply annoyed and aggravated by my pathetic attempt. I later learnt, however, that Margaret Hogg was murdered and her body was disposed of in the lake which gave me at least some reassurance that my fears weren't all for nothing. I also learnt that there may or may not be a 'gnome garden' deep in the lake which I would expect to be quite a frightening sight if, whilst swimming the length of the lake, you caught an inadvertent glimpse of many small heads looking up at you.

The following day, I managed to be more successful in carrying around 20kgs of water in a rucksack full of 2L water bottles from Tesco. This is a great way to build up strength whilst climbing up mountains which I was anxious to do after my epic day out on the fixed ropes on Baruntse, and this method also saves the knees through the ability to empty out all the water at the summit giving an easy descent back to the valley.

My final day involved running up Scafell Pike in under a quarter of the time that most people take to walk up the mountain. This would be one of my final training sessions prior to flying out to Everest and in some ways, getting to the top meant that I was ready to face my toughest challenge yet. This climb mirrored my first climb of the mountain all those years ago when I was a small boy, seeing the world for the first time and now, standing on top of the mountain once again, I was about to go and take on the tallest mountain in the world; a fitting end to my training in the Lake District, I thought.

Chapter 32 – Final Checks, One More Run

Despite having visited the Lake District many times in my life, I have never quite gotten over how quickly the countryside becomes flat as you venture out of the mountains. I wasn't so sad to wave goodbye to these mountains this time, as I knew that I would most likely be sick of mountains in a few weeks and wishing that I could find some 'Lincolnshire flats' in Nepal.

As my very final piece of training a week prior to flying to Kathmandu, I decided to run a half marathon which after my previous years of training came thankfully easy this time. Running gave me a chance to think about the expedition, about what I was letting myself in for, and the challenges that I would almost certainly have to face in a week's time. I wanted the expedition to go as smoothly as possible, I didn't want to miss home too much, and I didn't want to have anything to worry about. Thinking through all of these potential challenges with the luxury of spare time meant that I would have less to worry about on the mountain. I couldn't afford to miss home any more than I had to; I knew I just had to focus on the task at hand and make sure I stayed safe; if I managed this, I would then be home soon enough. I also tried to visualise what it might feel like to get to the top of the world. I didn't really have an idea other than summit pictures I had previously seen, so I let my imagination run wild again, and soon felt sick as my mind cunningly took me to what I imagined as the danger spot on Everest, the cornice traverse with a 10,000ft drop into Tibet and an 8,000ft drop into Nepal. I turned my concentration back to my running, and just let my feet carry me back home.

Prior to Baruntse, I had been working to perfect a regime to cope with the issue of weight loss at altitude by developing a diet before an expedition; specifically creating a diet that gives the most possible calories in the most enjoyable way. During any high altitude expedition, the body loses massive amounts of body fat and muscle tissue where it is broken down to provide energy when the body is struggling to survive in the rarefied atmosphere. To rectify this problem, I had come to the conclusion that cake and protein weight gainer was the best option. The local cheap food shop sells an extremely unhealthy gateau that solved the first problem and one of my sponsors provided me with a rapid weight gain formula that solved the second. The protein shake was easy to use; simply by doubling the recommended amount, weight can be gained relatively quickly; more complex to measure however was the 12 portion gateau. Prior to Baruntse, I had divided each cake into six portions which seemed to do the trick, but as my expedition to Everest was set to last for 70 days, I decided to up the dose and divide each cake into four servings. By doing this for long periods of time, enough weight can be gained to give some margin for sickness and the inability to eat whilst on the mountain. Clearly pre-expedition diets aren't an exact science; however simply arriving at the mountain heavier than normal is at least a step in the right direction and gives some confidence that when the altitude finally removes every trace of your appetite, you won't quite starve.

Somehow whilst at home, I never lost appetite for my cake, and could always rely on it when I struggled to hold down the gloopy protein shake. On top of food consumption, there was also the matter of staying hydrated. It would be all too easy to become dehydrated and become susceptible to illnesses and see a marked reduction in performance whilst travelling. I became careful in the last few days that I had in the UK to make sure I left no stone unturned, so that when I reached Nepal, I was ready to go. Unfortunately, with a busy schedule of interviews, especially one particular day where I spent several hours in a broadcast room in the famous city of Lincoln being connected all over the country to a whole host of radio stations, staying hydrated meant taking many trips to the toilet and trying to regulate my bladder as best I could whilst live on air. This proved quite difficult with no apparent schedule to the radio interviews, however it was the cake that was by far the most tedious and most messy to consume whilst chatting away to some radio presenter on the other side of the country and having the extremely weird feeling of hearing your own voice as you speak.

I then gave a TV interview before commencing a press photo shoot, one of which included standing in a rocky pit wearing my full Everest summit kit on a hot summer's day. Unfortunately I had only received my sponsor badges on the same day, so they were stuck on as best as possible with Sellotape. After spending several minutes after each shot picking the badges off the floor and repositioning them on the suit as best as possible, I came to the conclusion that they would have to be sewn on permanently if they were going to have any chance of making it to the summit with me. After scouring the internet for a guide to sewing onto a down suit became fruitless, I handed over the needle and thread to Mum who was bound to know the ideal sewing technique. Clearly she didn't quite appreciate what value the suit would have to me whilst on Everest as a mug of coffee was promptly knocked over it. Luckily this was rectifiable, but I still maintain that it was a plea for me not to go.

The next item on my list which was mostly ticked off already was the acquisition of some weird and wonderful medicine. Medicine for high altitude is exceptionally convoluted, with different doctors prescribing a completely different course of treatment for exactly the same ailment. This is mainly due the high altitude medicine being a relatively new area of study in comparison to many other areas of study in medicine. There are four main drugs on top of all the generic antibiotics and personal health tablets that should be taken to high altitude which could save a climber who may be on the edge of death. These concoctions are acetazolamide commonly called diamox, nifedipine, dexamethasone and aspirin. Aspirin is certainly the easiest drug to purchase and has beneficial effects for use when the body is undergoing acclimatisation. The next three drugs are slightly trickier, however if you happen to live in a flat county such as Lincolnshire, doctors are often most willing to hand over the tablets for the perilous voyage. Firstly, acetazolamide or diamox is a common drug administered to aid acclimatisation and for various ailments such as sleep apnea whilst sleeping at high altitude. Nifedipine is generally used for the treatment of HAPE (High Altitude Pulmonary Oedema) and dexamethasone is generally used for the treatment of HACE (High Altitude Pulmonary Oedema). Of course these drugs are stored sparingly at local pharmacists, usually for treatment of serious illnesses such as renal failure. Asking the doctor for these tablets, even if they are handed over easily, often involves a certain level of interrogation, and it is certainly a rewarding experience when you finally tell them the real use of these medicines; often this will make their day too.

There is one final drug which may or may not be used at altitude. It is famous perhaps for the wrong reasons, but sildenafil citrate's origins were actually in the dilation of blood vessels in the lungs which can help prevent HAPE at high altitude when used as prophylaxis medicine. Of course, nowadays, sildenafil citrate is commonly known as Viagra and has other uses which are certainly unwanted when sharing a cramped tent with two ladies, if you're lucky. Asking for Viagra is an incredibly long winded process and involves significantly more interrogation than the previous drugs. Once you have finally explained the innocent need of this medicine though, it becomes clear that a course of Viagra which lasts long enough for an entire expedition could potentially set you back £1,000 if purchased legitimately. I thought that perhaps the body and bank would both cope better without Viagra, and so, after an embarrassing conversation with a doctor I hoped never to meet, I decided to leave the order at the acetazolamide, nifedipine and dexamethasone.

Finally, after days of worrying and stressing, packing and unpacking multiple times in front of a TV camera just to get the perfect 'packing' shot, I was just about ready to go. I felt like there was more to do, but the only thing left was to quickly add some music one of my best friends sent me onto my iPod, which I ended up playing to death on the mountain, and then that was it, I had nothing more to do. I was briefed by Yell, I had all my equipment, I had my flights, my passport, and a bottle of whisky for Henry in Kathmandu. I called a few friends, and then made my way down to Heathrow Terminal 4 again for another expedition into the unknown. I waved goodbye to home. I hoped I would see it again.

Chapter 33 – The Jet Set to Everest

I had booked a room in a hotel for the evening which was as close as possible to the departure lounge of Terminal 4. In fact, the Yotel was inside the terminal and gave a surrealistic send off as I bundled into the small room with Mum, desperate for morning to arrive so we could evacuate our cramped sardine can-like quarters which went some way in preparing me for life in a tent which would almost certainly be less claustrophobic. I did have to make a final radio interview whilst at the Yotel and I ended up speaking live on air in a busy reception area with the constant PA announcement reminder that 'unattended baggage will be removed and may be destroyed'.

In the morning, I just managed to fit my two oversized duffle bags out of the small hotel room door, and onto the nearest trolley. I hoped that if I turned up early to the check-in, I would be able to charm the lady behind the desk into overlooking any excess baggage fees.

My plan clearly worked, and I managed to avoid any unwanted fees. This gave me a chance to get down to the difficult process of leaving Mum once again at Terminal 4 as I left, once again, for a country that felt like a million miles away, both in physical distance and in its difference in culture from the UK which I had readapted to since my previous expedition in Nepal. I love Kathmandu, its culture and character is like no other place on earth, but this didn't make leaving any easier. We kept the parting as brief as possible, as it would clearly be too emotional to drag out such a thing under the circumstances. One last hug to last me 70 days was enough for me to get through the first layers of Heathrow security and wave goodbye once again, both of us understandably much more emotional than last time, as perhaps just like Peak Lenin, neither of us had any idea of what I was letting myself in for.

Once in the departure lounge, I waited whilst I calmed down and then sat near the closest TV screen and tried not to fall asleep while I waited for my flight number to be shown. I met another man also travelling to Kathmandu, I told him I was trekking which was an easier way to avoid a lengthy conversation with a complete stranger and wasn't too far away from the truth. At this point, it is hard to describe the emotions I was feeling, especially when thinking about the climb ahead. It was almost like when you say a word so many times, by the twentieth time, the word you are now saying no longer resembles the original, and that's how I felt about Everest. I had been talking about it and thinking about it so much, all I now felt was that there was something looming ahead that was terrifying, but I could no longer describe exactly what was so scary.

I saw my departure gate flash up, and made my way in the general direction of my plane, clutching my high altitude boots in my hand which should have made the stranger slightly suspicious of my intentions to simply trek. On arrival at the gate, I had a chance to work out my plan for the flight. As with my previous trip to Nepal, I would be stopping overnight in Mumbai, however this time I would be alone, so I had to make sure that I made my connecting flight, or risk paying a hefty sum to reach Kathmandu, or an eternity in Mumbai Airport which wasn't on my bucket list. The first flight would be roughly nine hours followed by an eight-hour stopover in Mumbai Airport before the last two-hour leg to Kathmandu. That would be the plan at least, as long as I didn't get too comfy in the chaise longue I hoped to find.

After contemplating my strategy, I realised that my flight was running quite late and hadn't actually arrived at Heathrow yet, so I busied myself with continual sums and checklists which I hoped would all confirm that I was on the right track to get to Nepal, I hadn't forgotten anything along the way, and that I had enough money to correct any bad decisions along the way. Making sure all the kit is accounted for is absolutely crucial when travelling to foreign countries where you are about to undertake such a serious climb. It is often stated that as long as you remember your climbing boots, you could practically kit out an entire expedition once you get to Kathmandu, however in practice, this would add enormously to the levels of stress at a time where rest and relaxation are key before getting underway. In any case, it would be very uncomfortable to purchase the majority of the high altitude gear which is needed, since kit for Everest should withstand temperatures as low as minus 60 Celsius. Kathmandu is both incredibly hot and humid in the day, and so you would be incredibly lucky to avoid heat stroke which would be a further kick in the teeth even before the expedition has started.

Fortunately I didn't have any suspicions that I might have left something crucial behind, and so was left only with the slight sickening feeling as I continued on the path of realisation of what was actually happening. I couldn't dwell on my thoughts for long though, as all of a sudden, I found myself being ushered out of the departure gate and onto a plane which would take me across Europe and into Asia. My journey to the highest mountain in the world, Mount Everest, had begun, and although the real journey to the mountain had started years previously, I was now actually in the process of acting out my dream, no longer in my head, but this time for real.

The flight to Mumbai was smooth and the pilots did a fantastic job of flying the plane to a height just above that of the summit of Everest. I looked down at the clouds below me, and found it hard to believe that a mountain could protrude to such an altitude. At 30,000ft, if we had been flying directly over Everest's summit, we would have been only 295m away, almost touching distance; my attention was drawn to the hostile environment outside of the plane as the windows started to freeze over and occasional gusts of jet stream winds buffeted our Boeing 777.

Moving my attention back to inside the cabin, I realised that I had often laughed at comedians who made jokes about sitting in an aircraft next to noisy or annoying children. Being in a confined space next to a child for nine hours, especially with a window seat meaning there really was no escape, would probably be most travellers' worst nightmare, hence why first class was invented. I didn't have such a problem with this since I could just ignore everyone around me and get through my blockbuster trilogy. The child that I happened to be sitting with, however, clearly had an awful cold which was effectively distributed by a two way process, firstly through constant sneezing, and then through regular recirculation of the cabin air. I really didn't want to get ill when I arrived in Kathmandu as I had planned to leave the city as soon as possible, but with any form of illness, especially a respiratory one, going up to altitude, even to the relatively low village of Lukla is a definite no.

I tried to ignore my worries and except for covering my face every time the sneeze came, I just concentrated on the movies playing out in front of me, which unfortunately weren't doing much to help calm my worries. The first film I watched was *Contagion* which being self-explanatory wasn't a clever move and sparked fear into all the expedition members who also watched the film on their flight. The second film, *In Time*, was a step in the right direction; however, without spoiling the plot too much, the mum dies, and so this turned out to be an emotional film to watch having just left my mum crying at Heathrow only a few hours previously.

The rest of the flight was relatively plain sailing except for when the pilots asked for the flight attendants to all take their seats due to turbulence which clearly didn't give much confidence to the passengers who were of a nervous disposition, especially when it came to flying.

I arrived in Mumbai at around midnight, and overcome by the intense heat even at this hour, I started sweating profusely as I dragged my heavy high altitude boots into the airport. As soon as I made it into the airport lounge, I headed straight off to the comfy chaise longue chairs which were craftily hidden behind the escalators. I started to reminisce about my previous stopover in the airport since I was sitting directly opposite the very same chair that I had sat in with the team from Baruntse. I felt sad that I didn't have them there with me this time, but realised that although I was on my own for the night and it would be my job alone to make sure I didn't miss the connecting flight, this was all part of the journey.

As I tried to sleep, I cursed at the mosquitoes that seemed intent on biting me. I didn't remember encountering any mosquitoes the previous time, and so had no insect repellent or anti malaria prophylaxis so I became a little concerned about the recent theme of catching some sort of illness, and then tried to forget and sleep, resting my ear to my alarm clock.

Usually not a morning person, I somehow managed to catch my flight after eight hours of intermittent sleep and nightmares about the mosquito bites that were beginning to show up all over my hands. This proved a very fast flight, where within two hours, I was back down to earth and this time in Kathmandu, Nepal. Clearly everything on this day was running at the same time, so whilst it had taken two hours to travel around 1,000miles, I spent the next two hours moving no more than 100metres through the severely understaffed visa control section of Kathmandu Airport. 400 people all shuffled along inches at a time in the heat and high humidity, all taking in the new sights and smells of the place. There were no mosquitoes here and apart from the wave of jetlag that was coming over me, I was ready and excited to get into Kathmandu and wander round, this time as an experienced city goer.

Chapter 34 – The Java Coffee House

Henry was expecting me, however hadn't foreseen that I would be in such a queue, so left me in the capable hands of Rajan, one of Iswari's men and a familiar face once I had managed to push past the hordes of people offering to push my heavily laden trolley, for a small fee of course.

Quickly escorted to the comfort of an air conditioned minibus, I was whisked across the city to my hotel where I could finally collapse and wait for the arrival of Henry who I hadn't seen since our pleasant encounter in Grantham's very own Costa Coffee.

I met Henry some hours later after I had managed to get some semblance of control over my baggage and handed over a bottle of blended whisky. Being far from a whisky connoisseur though, I had forgotten that Henry had asked for a malt whisky instead and not knowing the difference, I couldn't understand or justify why two bottles which both contained whisky had a price difference of over £100, so stuck to the cheapest Johnnie Walker I could find since it was the only name I recognised.

I also met Paul for the first time with Henry. Paul was also climbing Everest and would eventually make up a second team of climbers under the umbrella of our expedition who would also attempt the summit. We spent the first few days in Kathmandu together with Henry getting to know how the expedition would work, how Henry worked, and how we were going to plan the walk-in to Everest.

Unlike when I climbed on Baruntse where the walk-in had been as a big group arriving at the mountain at the same time, this was a much more relaxed affair with no requirement to stay as a group or walk in alone. This was much more flexible since there was no rush. We had over two weeks until we were actually allowed to get to base camp, so the idea would be to acclimatise as gently as possible and make the most of the luxuries in the valley, after all, we would be spending around eight weeks in a tent, so there was no rush or urgency to start sleeping under canvas.

This mentality also extended to Kathmandu, and whilst Henry wanted us to leave the polluted city as soon as possible so that we could get into the cleaner air of the mountains, we still had some shopping to do and the weather wasn't exactly being kind to the planes attempting to land at Lukla, with most being forced to turn around and retreat to the safety of Kathmandu Airport.

Within two days of being in Kathmandu, I realised that Henry's office was in fact the Java Coffee House. Unless he was organising extensive logistics for Everest, he would be in there drinking coffee and the occasional banana smoothie which proved to be exceptionally popular, especially when both Paul and I found ourselves stranded in Kathmandu for days on end where we ended up with around 20 smoothies between us. During this time, I visited Shonas famous mountain equipment shop once again, and purchased a spare pare of summit mitts just in case I managed to drop my first pair which would undoubtedly cause a whole world of problems, especially if at high altitude. I also had to move hotels several times during this period, and after precariously balancing my kit bags on the top of a local taxi, headed across Kathmandu in search of the Vajra hotel, where I shared a room with Paul which happened to be the hotel library.

The next morning I started to feel quite sick, and realised that unless I had been attacked by any book worms in the middle of the night which I would certainly not rule out given the state of the library floor, I was actually starting to suffer the effects of the illness I most likely picked up from the child on the plane. As the day wore on, sitting in the coffee house and drinking as many smoothies as possible to pass the time, I began to feel worse and worse, and at one point, even started to worry that I was feeling the effects of the onset of malaria. Henry reassured me and I tried to convince myself that if I was going to be ill on any part of the trip, now was the time to catch something so that I could get over whatever it was before reaching the mountain.

The following day, despite feeling rough, both Paul and I had packed our bags and vacated the library for some other poor soul to sleep in. Today, we would be attempting to fly out from Kathmandu in a small Twin Otter aircraft and safely make the journey to Lukla, where we could spend a day resting, hopefully building up more strength in the fresh mountain air before commencing the slow process of the walk-in.

Henry's expeditions are simple to understand once you have been on one for a few weeks, however, after only the third day in Nepal, I was still confused as to how I would meet up with Mollie and Becky who would be part of our summit group and where the rest of the climbers were who would also be climbing on Everest in various waves.

From a number of days in the coffee house, I started to build up a relatively good picture of who would actually be climbing and who wouldn't. Firstly, there would be Rob who would arrive five days after we made it to base camp; he would be climbing with Becky, Mollie, both arriving in a few days, and me for the summit push on the mountain, if we made it that far. Then there was Valerie who would be climbing exclusively with one of the Sherpas in Henry's team. Rick and Ryan were two Americans who would be joining us at some stage to also climb Everest along with Paul. Richard would be arriving in Nepal in a few days' time, and would be climbing on Everest, but only as far as camp two to build up experience and hopefully come back and try the whole mountain in a year or so. Then there would be Roger who would be climbing with Kenton who was going for his tenth summit of Everest, this time filmed by Keith. Finally, Bonita and Bob would be attempting Lhotse, the mountain next to Everest, joined by the South Col, having both previously climbed Everest.

All this was very confusing as I tried to remember all of the names whilst we travelled to the domestic section of the airport through the early morning rush hour. I often wondered why there were so many vehicles on the roads in Kathmandu. Where were all these people going to? There were exceptionally high levels of unemployment and poverty in the city, and I couldn't believe that all these commuters, far more than in London for example, had anywhere to actually go, maybe they just drove around the city all day.

We walked into the domestic airport lounge and took our seats whilst the enigmatic and smartly dressed Iswari and his assistant went into various rooms to secure our flights for the day. We waited for five brutally long hours in the airport, all ready to go and start the walk-in to Everest when all of a sudden, the announcement came that all planes to Lukla had been cancelled. Both of us couldn't quite believe that we had spent all this time doing absolutely nothing except watching the hustle and bustle of excited and some increasingly frustrated people around the airport.

The only saving grace to our wait was that Rajan had given us two new Nepalese phones that we could use to call back to home whilst at base camp. Nepal clearly was a bit behind the times in terms of technology as we were both handed our new Nokia 1280 phones, both in bright pink and with the classic game 'Snake'. But clearly they were made for use in the mountains with 22.5 days' (540 hours) worth of standby battery power and a flashlight for finding the toilet tent late at night.

We were both despondent at having to leave the airport after waiting for such a long time, but secretly I was quite relieved as this meant that I could have more time to recover from my illness at a lower altitude before heading to the mountains, although I was torn as to whether low altitude and smog was better than the higher altitude but crystal clear air of Lukla.

As we had exhausted all our shopping lists and really had nothing left to do in Kathmandu, we headed straight for the coffee house where surprisingly we found Henry enjoying an early afternoon break in the city sun. We joined him for the rest of the day and were later joined by Mollie who had finally made it to Nepal after enduring the same horrors at Mumbai Airport. Mollie would be trekking in with Kenton and a group of 28 trekkers who would be visiting Everest base camp before returning home, after which point, Mollie would then continue up Everest with the rest of the climbers.

We had been promised some more luck the following day, and both anxious to leave, we decided to make another attempt at flying to Lukla. We arrived at 7:30am, and then after a two hour wait, we made it through the general airport lounge and into departures. The departure lounge was a relatively depressing concrete bunker type building which was quickly running out of spare seating. Here we met Mollie again and her group of 28 trekkers who were anxiously waiting for their flight. Kenton, the group's leader, had already managed to catch an early morning flight to Lukla; however didn't have any baggage, so in all, the trek to base camp was quickly turning out to be a 100mile long mess. We were confident that today would be the day though, so we waited patiently in the increasingly hot room until around 11am. Iswari said that planes to Lukla had been temporarily stopped due to weather, and Becky's international flight had just landed, so Paul and I walked over to the international arrivals where we met Henry who looked to be as calm and relaxed as ever. After another 30 minutes, visa control was obviously going slowly once again, and Iswari called to say that flights were back on, so we hurried back to domestics to avoid missing our flight. Things seemed to be moving a bit better now in the airport, and we were hopeful of catching a flight. After another four hours of waiting, we got the all clear from Iswari and stood by the door ready to board our plane which was waiting outside for us. Things seemed to be taking a long time for some reason, and we contemplated sitting back down, but anxious not to miss our plane which could be our only hope of getting away from the city, we remained standing patiently by the door.

Gradually the sky seemed to grow dark and ominous clouds started to appear on the horizon. We feared that this might mean that cancelation of any further flights would be imminent, and our fears were confirmed after a plane load of people walked through the door looking deeply shaken with sick expressions. We later found out that these poor people had been on their way to Lukla when bad weather had engulfed their plane, forcing the pilot to divert back to Kathmandu through what was extremely turbulent weather. We remained at the airport for another two hours hoping that the storm would pass, but by 5:30pm, torrential rain and a thunderstorm had surrounded the airport forcing the announcement that all planes would be cancelled for the remainder of the day. For over two days, we had waited in an airport for 15 hours and still, we found ourselves going back to our hotel room getting increasingly frustrated and agitated that our adventure could not just start.

Keen to look on the bright side, I was gradually getting over the illness, and another day in Kathmandu was not detrimental to our overall schedule, plus the evening meal gave a big portion of the group the chance to get to know each other with Paul, Richard, Mollie, Valerie, Henry and Becky all in attendance.

Chapter 35 – Third Time Lucky

At the evening dinner, we had decided that we would all try and go as a group the following day. Since Kenton had managed to catch one of the only flights that managed to get to Lukla by getting to the airport early, we decided that we would wake up at 4:30am and try again with the aim of all walking-in together. I had a much disrupted sleep due to the two Germans clearly catching up on a lifetime of experiences on the balcony right outside our window which was single glazed; not that that mattered too much though since it was also impossible to close.

As it always does, 4:30am came around 30 minutes before 5am and as always far too soon, but remarkably, still in a state of semi consciousness, I realised I was feeling much better than the previous day, so I was finally excited to be leaving Kathmandu and starting the long trek in to base camp. Breakfast would be had in Lukla if we managed to actually get there, and in any case, it's probably wise to take the Kathmandu Lukla flight on a relatively empty stomach to save embarrassment if turbulent weather is encountered. Strangely, everything on this day seemed to be going to plan and we guessed that this was probably due to having Henry with us. As Kathmandu airports go, we were fast through to departures and before we knew it, we were getting on a bus to take us to our little Twin Otter that sat waiting for us after the previous days of heavy storms; I hoped it wasn't damaged.

Henry had a chance to point out a dangerous and idiotic mountain guide to us, who also happened to be sharing our plane and in turn, everyone gave him a disgusted glance, but although no one actually knew if he had done anything wrong or what it was, we quickly learnt that it was always a good bet to listen to Henry.

As we all squeezed into the small aircraft, everyone said a little prayer and hoped that in an hour or so, we would be at Paradise Lodge and not simply in paradise. The aircraft shook violently to life as the pilots managed to start the engines and as soon as the fuel trucks had disconnected, we were on the move towards the runway.

On reaching the runway, the pilots saw that there were no other planes landing, that the engines were still turning, that the wings were still connected and nothing was on fire, so we lined up and with even more violence than start-up, we picked up speed, gradually at first, and then with the engines rattling on full power, we reached take off speeds and gracefully lifted off the ground, the pilots skilfully swapping their pre-flight checklists for the daily newspaper. Somehow, I had managed to get a seat right at the back of the plane right next to an extremely concave window which as I have never experienced before, gave stunning forward views along the side of the plane and in the general direction that we were flying. This was great as it meant for the first time as a passenger, I could watch the direction that the plane was actually flying rather than looking at all the tall, pointy looking outcrops of rock whizzing past the window. As we approached Lukla, it was great to see our steep approach angle, and then the sheer cliff faces at the end of the runway all zooming into focus. From my viewpoint, I could see how high or low we were in relation to the runway which gave me the privilege of being the third person to know whether we were going to hit the perimeter fence, overshoot into the brick wall/mountain at the end of the runway, or kiss the tarmac perfectly on the centre line. Fortunately for all involved, it was the latter.

Within half an hour after having passed the Lukla security which consists of an open gate, we walked into the Paradise Lodge which brought back many memories. The last time we had been in this lodge, Kenton Cool had politely come over to our table to talk to the smitten Debbie after being summoned by Andrew. This time, Kenton was once again in Paradise Lodge which made me laugh a little inside, but as we found out, Kenton couldn't actually go anywhere because he didn't have any of his 28 trekkers and some of his bags were still missing.

We stayed in the lodge to have a welcome breakfast, whilst watching the steady stream of planes flow into the airport in an effort to move the large backlog of people still stranded in Kathmandu but hoping to get into the mountains as soon as possible. It was good to know that we would be trekking in as a group, since it meant that unlike before when it would have just been Paul and me, there would be many people to talk to and much to talk about which is crucial when faced with a two-week walk-in. As we set off, Henry gave us some pointers about the trek to come, and also where we would be stopping for lunch. There was absolutely no rush, and as always when acclimatising, it is absolutely vital to move as slowly as possible, rest often and drink plenty. These are the three key rules to moving well at altitude, especially in the long run. Essentially, time spent allowing the body to ease into high altitudes at the beginning of an expedition is acclimatisation in the bank for when the expedition starts to have a more vertical profile and the altitude gains become serious. For now though, we were just happy to potter about at a leisurely pace, being over taken by all those trekkers who were clearly desperate to get to the next village, but would be regretting their speed with the pounding headache which would probably follow the next morning.

After a few hours, we stopped for lunch by the exceptionally long bridge which crosses a gorge in the remote village of Phakding along the Khumbu trail. Along the trail all the way up until the final settlement before Everest base camp, the food menus are always the same. Western foods mixed in with some local delicacies are common in every tea house, with the only difference being that the price gets more expensive the higher you go. As with many things in the valley, there is certainly no access for motorised vehicles, so everything ranging from food to clothing is carried by porters coming from Lukla or lower down in the valley. This way of life is often amazing to watch as very often, especially lower down the trail, porters are seen carrying anything from steel tables and chairs to whole carcasses of raw meat in the general direction of Everest.

Soon after leaving Phakding it started to rain which required the donning of waterproofs; however, Henry wasn't keen on walking in the rain which came as a nice surprise for all of us, so we stopped short of Josalie in the little village of Bengkar. Josalie was another few hours onwards, but as Henry explained, there was no point in getting wet since there was no rush after all. Even after the warnings that we would be taking things very slowly from the offset, all of us were anxious as to what type of mileage and altitude we would be gaining in the first few days, but the first day of enjoyable strolling put everyone at ease.

At Bengkar, everyone started to bond well in the tea house, and many laughs were exchanged which was a vital part of actually enjoying the expedition rather than going through personal hell on your own every day. As the evening drew on though, I began to realise that I was losing my voice and by the end of the evening, except for a low pitched grunting sound, I could barely speak at all. I hoped that a good night's sleep would cure this illness once and for all, especially being in the clean air which was noticeably better than Kathmandu since you couldn't actually see it.

I turned in for the night and for the first time in days, enjoyed a very long, uninterrupted and traffic-free sleep. It was bliss.

Chapter 36 – From Bengkar to Bengkar

Waking up from my slumber, I realised how lucky I was to be in such a place. Through the window, the sun was shining and all around the Khumbu valley, there was tranquillity. The daily commute for the porters and the trekkers hadn't begun yet, and it was strange to see the path go off into the distance without a soul to be seen.

I packed my bag ready for the day's walking and headed downstairs to meet the rest of the team for breakfast. Henry was obviously concerned after my previous illness and asked how I was so I opened my mouth to speak and despite the best of intentions, nothing happened. I hadn't needed to speak since the previous night so hadn't realised that by the morning, I had completely lost my voice and was only able to communicate through hand signs, generally directed at my throat and mouth.

I was clearly not fit to continue the walk and so was advised to stay put. At this point, I realised that I would probably be walking to base camp on my own, which I was slightly fearful of, since I only knew half of the route and didn't really have any experience at finding a reputable tea house and finding meals throughout the day which isn't as hard as you would think judging by the poverty and pollution in Kathmandu, but still requires some traveller expertise such as avoiding fresh vegetables which have often been washed with unsafe, non-drinkable water. I also didn't particularly want to do the whole walk on my own, so reluctantly went back to my room to sleep off whatever was still affecting me, as the rest of the group headed onwards to the famous market settlement of Namche Bazaar.

Being notoriously good at wasting time, I wasn't too bothered by the prospect of becoming bored since I guessed I could just sleep for most of the day and then most of the night. I was clearly still ill so perhaps my body needed the rest and maybe I could continue the next day and somehow catch the rest of the group up in two days' time or so.

During the 3rd day in Kathmandu, I had decided to self-prescribe a course of flucloxacillin thinking that because my previous attempts at administering antibiotics had all gone well and as long as I took the full course, I wouldn't come to any harm. I continued taking these throughout my first sick day at Bengkar, and decided that it might also be good practice to douse my throat with salt water which would help to fight off any afflictions of that area. I was surprised to see that going downstairs to the dining room to craftily take some salt from the tables, then going back upstairs to mix it with my water, was particularly time consuming and all of a sudden, it was dinner time, then bed time soon after.

I hoped I would wake up the next morning feeling at least a little better than I had previously, and after reading about Scott's terrible journey to the South Pole, swiftly fell asleep.

The next morning to no surprise, I practically fell out of bed and crawled to the dining room of the small tea house. I hadn't got any better overnight, and in fact, actually felt positively worse than I had the previous day or even in Kathmandu. I managed to call Paul so that a message could be relayed to Henry, and then tried to sleep as much of the day away as possible.

At lunch time, I realised that the day was really starting to drag on and I was losing any positivity that I had before flying out to Nepal. Despite all of the effort for the last three years, I was actually struggling to make it to base camp, and more than that, I worried that I may not actually make it there at all. As soon as that thought came into my head, my mind started going crazy with the thought of having to abandon the expedition at such an early stage, and how I would possibly explain this when I got back home. I pictured the face of the CEO who had put so much trust in me when I had to tell him the dreaded words and I cringed inside. I couldn't go back yet, I still had so much further to go, yet I hadn't even made it to Namche hill which is the first of three main hills you have to actually climb on the walk-in to Everest. I tried to take stock of my situation; I was in the middle of absolutely nowhere, there were no British people to be seen and no one spoke English, or any other language that I could remotely understand for that matter. I felt so alone at that point because I really was on my own. It wasn't like I had reached Everest and then had to bail off in a dramatic rescue attempt or anything remotely interesting. I was simply lying in my bed waiting for something to happen, either I would get better, or if the worst happened, I would have to go home.

Clearly I wasn't thinking straight, which in hindsight is understandable due to being confined to an oversized wooden coffin for hours at a time with no one to talk to or to give me a sense of reality.

I knew that I should at least try to get better, so took out my large supply of aspirin and put a tablet into my water bottle so it would dissolve into some sort of solution that I could gargle with and at least take away some of the discomfort of the suspected laryngitis. Aspirin is one of the mountaineer's wonder drugs since it lowers blood pressure and thins the blood which is perfect for high altitude travel where the altitude and cold temperatures tend to make blood quite gloopy which is much less effective at travelling around the body delivering oxygen. Regrettably I had brought non dissolvable aspirin tablets with me and therefore couldn't quite reach the desired solution even after many minutes of exhaustingly shaking my bottle until hundreds of pieces of tablets swam around in the mixture. I couldn't summon up any more energy for any more physical activity except to walk to the sink and gargle the many small pieces around my throat. I tried to forget the pain and retreated to the comfort of my bed. I had now been in the tea house for around two days constantly and my motivation was very quickly evaporating away. I could feel that I was gradually getting better and I guessed that perhaps tomorrow, once the pain had subsided, I could get on with the walk-in.

I hadn't spoken to anyone all day and so decided to call Mum to talk through my predicament and also test out the voice for the first time in a day and a half. Fortunately the voice just about held up and I came off the phone with a rejuvenated view, coming from someone who was able to look outside my small box of torture.

I tried to sleep for the rest of the day in order to recover as best as I could, waking only just in time for dinner. On going downstairs, I realised that the tea house was now full of French and Sri Lankan trekkers who had decided to rest here for the evening. At the best of times my French was ropey and my Sinhalese even worse, but with a crackling voice which seemed to fail consistently on every third word, communicating was proving futile. In the end, there were a few familiar words exchanged, and then the international language of hand signals took care of the rest, including the lesser known hand signal for ordering a deep fried, pastry covered Mars Bar which took a while to perfect.

Again, despite the long hours in bed, I managed to sleep once again, now having spent close to three days in almost solitary confinement. I simply couldn't wait to leave this place which although probably an attractive place to rest for most trekkers, was quickly becoming my worst nightmare.

Chapter 37 – Along the Lonely Road

The next morning I woke up full of energy. I was determined that today was the day that I would finally leave my confined quarters in search of the next tea house, even if it was only slightly closer to Everest; anything had to be better than staying here.

The owner of the Bengkar tea house seemed quite sad when I left, as despite not seeing each other very often, she knew that I hadn't left the house once, and was clearly resting for some reason. I hoped that she didn't think I wanted to take a long term rental agreement out since I was staying far longer in one place than many trekkers do, especially this far down the valley. After paying for my stay which amounted to almost 5,000 Nepalese Rupees (£35), I got my bag and headed for the door and the sweet smell of fresh morning air.

I hoped that I would reach Namche; however, it was at the top of an exceptionally long hill which probably wasn't the best way to keep recovering from whatever illness seemed to keep recurring. Taking the pace as slowly as I could, I plodded on up the hill which had some rock step sections to allow the porters to haul up their enormous loads in the steepest parts. I wrote a diary entry of the walk to Namche which said "Not sure I remember any of the walk from Baruntse, even after only six months". I tried to think why I couldn't remember any of the walk, even after such a small time scale, and first came to the conclusion that it must have been because this time, I was walking the other way. I was clearly trying to kid myself, and eventually came to the proper conclusion that most of the group were so severely intoxicated during the walk from Namche to Lukla on the Baruntse expedition, that many members were as close to being blind drunk as it was possible to be without actually falling down the sheer precipice at the side of the unfenced path.

Amused with myself, I carried on up the hill taking in all the sights and smells of the valley, technically for the first time.

At one point, I was stopped at an army checkpoint due to being an unaccompanied trekker. I contemplated just carrying on up the path, but then spotted the oversized assault rifle in the cabin. After a lengthy process where I had to call Henry on the mobile and use a passing Sherpa to translate the conversation to the army officers, I was cautiously allowed to carry on with my journey.

I had been warned by the officers that there was a police checkpoint ahead which I would also need to pass, although the army guards could not give me any papers to allow me to pass this next obstacle which could potentially leave me in quite a limbo. I took the gamble that the police checkpoint would probably be less fortified and equipped than the army checkpoint, substituting the assault rifle for a pocket knife, and so would most likely be able to pass with relative ease.

I saw the police checkpoint ahead, and also saw that there were many people passing at the same time which meant that the police would probably not spot a small figure travelling through the crowds. As I reached the post, I put my head down and carried on up the steep incline. Unfortunately, at the same time as I reached the post the crowds thinned dramatically and those that were left were of Nepalese origin and so I didn't blend in quite as well as I had hoped. I got passed the checkpoint though and after ten metres, I thought I made it; that was until heard a man screaming, so I turned around and saw a young police officer running up towards me. Luck seemed to be on my side, however, as when the officer reached me almost choking from the effort of his short sprint, I realised that the officer was in fact a young boy wearing very suspicious looking clothing. At the same time as he reached me, a Ukrainian family also reached my point on the path and were clearly intrigued by all the commotion I was causing. I had previously talked to the father further down the path and he quickly resumed our conversation which gave the police boy enough evidence to suggest that I was in fact a Ukrainian trekker who had left the family and was now being told off by the family elder for previously abandoning them. The police boy smiled and headed back to his cabin, happy that he had stopped a runaway child from escaping to a remote village or perhaps even Everest base camp.

As Henry had said, it is best not to tell anyone your business; along these trails, you never quite know who you are talking to, so for each person who questioned the motives of the young looking solo trekker, I was simply on my gap year exploring the Khumbu. As I was unable to lie, anyone who asked how long I was travelling in the Khumbu seemed surprised that I was planning a 70-day stay in the area. They probably thought I was mad; what possible attraction could be in the Khumbu valley that has almost no links with the outside world that could keep someone occupied for so long?

On reaching Namche, I was pleasantly surprised that the hotel recommended by Henry was in fact the same hotel that I had stayed in on the way out from Baruntse. I thought I had better stop comparing this expedition with a previous one as it was a completely separate entity entirely and I was clearly becoming soppy and sentimental. Having said that, my spirits were significantly lifted when I remembered some of the previous antics which occurred in the hotel and once I arrived, I called one of the team members from Baruntse who was sick into a dry bag after previously having crawled up the stairs in the same hotel during one particularly heavy but unforgettable night in the market village. I later heard rumours that this single night had kept the bar in the village open for the whole of the winter season without the need for any customers.

I enjoyed the moment of reflection before heading down to the dining room for a lunch of traditional Nepalese *momos* which are meat or vegetable filled pastry cases. Whilst eating, I met a pharmacist and his son who were also out trekking to Everest base camp and hoped to climb the nearby Kala Patthar. Pharmacology is clearly a fascinating subject, and during our short time together, I learnt many weird and wonderful facts including the uses of flucloxacillin, none of which matched my symptoms and it quickly became apparent that ciprofloxacin was the much better choice all round. I guessed that I needed more practice before becoming a pharmacist, and possibly a copy of the BNF, but all things considered, this had been the first inaccurate self-administration of medicine that I had made during all my expeditions and at this early stage in my career, mistakes were bound to happen, I just hoped that I would be more successful in administering acetazolamide, the powerful high altitude drug, if I ever needed it.

The next morning, I hoped to get away early to avoid any queues on the path ahead, as I knew that the next section would be one of the most popular sections of the whole walk, possibly the most remembered, and certainly one of the many highlights of any trek in the area given the right weather.

Ascending the steep hill out of Namche, I turned the first corner and there it was, standing many thousands of feet right in front of me. Sagarmatha, Chomolungma or as it is called by western climbers, Mount Everest, stood before me. Clouds rested gracefully around its summit with the famous snow plume catching the jet stream winds.

It was a truly poignant moment in the expedition and one which I will never forget. I had seen Everest before from the summit of Mera Peak and Baruntse, but this time was different, I was looking at a place which I had been dreaming of standing atop for so long on *the* expedition that would potentially take me there. I looked around and there were crowds of trekkers all standing and staring in the same direction, all amazed by the height, it was majestic, towering above all else, I'm sure everyone was thinking the same thing as me, how would you even begin to climb something that massive? And that's when it really hit me. Here I was standing thousands of feet below the tallest mountain in the world which was over 30 miles away, and all I could think of was, how the hell am I going to do that? The mountain top looks to be in another world, it was standing so tall that there may as well have been a warning sign saying 'don't even bother'. I had been to over 7,000m before, but here I was, looking up at something almost 2,000m taller, just wondering if perhaps this time, I had bitten off more than I could chew.

It is hard to describe the emotion whilst looking at Everest, knowing that it is the objective of the expedition. As I gazed up, it was as if I could feel the presence of the mountain, its ultimate power and control over the environment which surrounds it; quite simply, this was a mountain that commanded respect.

Chapter 38 – In the Shadow of Everest

Now fully in awe of the mountains and environment that surrounded me, I passed the crowds who had flocked to the area to see one of the seven natural wonders of the world. A day before, I had been confined to my bed with illness, yet at this moment, I felt the excitement building in me once again; the magic that Everest has was captivating and whilst I was scared to admit even to myself that I would be trying to climb it, the thought of physically being high on that mountain was all the inspiration that I needed to haul myself to base camp, no matter what stood in my way.

Perhaps before, out of Everest's gaze, I was losing sight of my reasons for trying to climb, but to see the mountain in reality is enough to put the world to rights for a moment at least.

Tengboche was the next village which I had to reach. Tengboche is famous for its monastery and religious significance in the area and holds a special place in mountaineering with all expeditions to the south side of Everest passing through the village. Unfortunately though, reaching Tengboche from Namche isn't quite as simple as it sounds, and after descending to the valley floor, the hill leading to Tengboche can be seen towering up in front of all who hope to reach its lofty heights. Clearly the local tea house owners were quick to see the potential for malnourished trekkers beginning the long path which zigzags its way up the hill much like an alpine road, full of hairpin bends which alleviate at least some of the torturous gradient. To cope with this problem, several tea houses have been built at the base of the hill which serve food throughout the day and have a prime position overlooking the route which can either be of use to trekkers who prefer to strategise their ascent of the mountains over a plate of chips, or can indeed be a hindrance as trekkers quickly become psyched-out, preferring to tackle the hill when they are fresh the next morning, therefore providing further income for the tea house owners.

Since it was only 11am when I reached the base of the hill, I decided that I would tackle it the same day and so began the long process of ascending to Tengboche through a series of very small but deceptively tough gradient gains. Along the way up the hill, I met a leader who had seen my group on the previous day and reported that they looked in good spirits as they trekked further into the Khumbu. This gave me some comfort knowing that the group were only a day or so ahead and equally it was nice to hear the names of familiar people being mentioned when for the past three days I had only heard vague conversations being conducted in Nepalese or French. In fact, I hadn't spoken to anyone since the group had left Bengkar and so it took me a few moments to refresh my ability to physically speak, hoping that some audible sound came out when I opened my mouth.

The leader also mentioned that Tengboche was full for the night which confirmed the statements made by a tea house owner at the base of the hill. This wasn't quite the news I wanted to hear after having taken one hour to get two thirds of the way up the hill hopeful of a good rest at the top. Clearly I would have to carry on further up the valley after reaching Tengboche, but with tiredness rapidly setting in due to the strength it had taken to get up the hill and the change in altitude, I was starting to doubt whether I would make the next village.

Tengboche couldn't come quickly enough, but when it eventually did, it marked the ascent of one of three of the most significant hills on the walk-in, the other two being to Namche which I had already tackled, and Dughla Hill which has the occasional and unfortunate name of 'Shit Hill', closer to Everest that was still yet to come. Looking round the settlement, I saw that nothing had changed since my last visit, and so knowing that Tengboche was a place where illness is often encountered due to the large amounts of trekkers who stay, I headed to the nearest path that would take me to the next village on the Khumbu trail. Luckily enough, Deboche was the next settlement which was only 15 minutes away, and I had been reliably informed that there would be at least some room in one of the tea houses that formed this isolated community.

On arriving, I found that the first lodge, the Rivendel which was one of the nicest looking lodges in the area owing to the fact that it did not appear to have an outside toilet, was sadly full. A little worried that it would soon be getting dark and I still had nowhere to stay, I headed to the next lodge which although almost full, had one room available for a solo trekker. Due to the fact that no one in the valley was unfortunate enough to have no friends to trek with, I made myself at home and tried to enjoy a few hours in bed before I could go down and get some food in what I hoped would be a relatively uncrowded dining room.

Since I had made it to the end of Deboche to find my accommodation, I realised after studying the map that the rest of the group were in Pangboche, another famous village along the Khumbu trail due to it being the historic home of many of the best Sherpas on Everest and indeed other mountains in the Himalaya. Pangboche was only 1.5 hours from where I was staying, but after speaking to Henry earlier in the day, he made it clear that I wasn't to rush the walk-in just in an effort to catch up with the group; there would be plenty of time for that at base camp. I would try to make Pangboche the next morning, hopefully before the rest of the group left, and there I would be able to have my first proper rest day on the walk-in at a high enough altitude to maintain my acclimatisation, but at a low enough altitude to be able to recover.

As I went down the almost vertical staircase which looked to be made from a solid tree trunk by mountaineers for mountaineers, the noise coming from the dining area was getting noticeably louder. Not being one who enjoys a room full of faces suddenly stop their conversations and turn to face you, I thought that I would try to enter discreetly and find a table with the friendliest looking people as quickly as possible. It didn't matter if they spoke English or not, but in a small way, I hoped that I chose a table with the least English speaking people present as possible so I didn't have to go through the confusing conversation to explain who I was, why I was here, and why no one was with me. Of course there are many solo trekkers who travel through the region, but the majority tend to have their own local guide since most have not been to the area before and are looking for the best sightseeing trip possible. I wasn't quite as enthusiastic about the sightseeing as there would be plenty of time for this after the expedition; for now I had bigger fish to fry.

As I walked into the room, the conversations quietened and without being too obvious, the faces started turning to the door, then back to the table to enquire about the identity of this stranger. I didn't make the discreet entrance I was hoping for, quickly walking to the safety of a free seat, but soon finding out the table it belonged to was reserved and that people were sitting according to their room number rather than the table where they were least likely to be interrogated. Slightly worried where I might be seated, I stood in the middle of the

173

room next to the stove, and waited for my instructions, whilst the conversations returned to their previous levels.

I sat myself at the end of a table with some friendly looking people, and was relieved when for the first 30 seconds, no one at the table spoke which indicated they might all be solo trekkers themselves and this might indeed be the loner table I was looking for. As soon as that thought entered my head though, American accents started springing up all around me, and soon, I was negotiating my way out of social suicide by explaining that I did indeed have friends, but they just happened to be ahead of me which certainly drew in the sympathy vote; after all, who would leave their friend in such a scary place with yaks and naks (female yaks) on the loose?

I started to fit into the group, and enjoyed their tales which they told as only Americans can. I soon found out that I was in the company of a Navy Seal, and whilst this was initially scary, I later learnt that he too was a solo trekker, although he did have a local guide which made me presume that he was in a sea or air based team, as pathfinding on land clearly wasn't his strongpoint. As the conversation drew on, we reached a point where it was time to ask the members around the table where they were from. As the answers came in, I smiled at their exoticness and patiently waited for the question to reach me. San Francisco, California, New York, Edmonton, Hong Kong and Lincolnshire; everyone seemed to be baffled as they tried to work out whether Hong Kong was indeed part of China, or a separate entity in its own right.

I listened along with the rest of the group to the tales of one couple who were descending after suffering altitude sickness at Everest base camp. They also added their disapproval of base camp itself, stating that they were disappointed that it was just a sea of tents, and that they could have seen the same sight at any campsite in America. I'm sure everybody was wondering at that point how any trip to base camp could have been misinterpreted so badly.

Politely excusing myself from the table of relative strangers, I slipped off to bed and finished the final tablet in my week-long course of flucloxacillin and, happy that I would finally be ascending free from any medication, drifted off into a deep sleep, content with the thought that I might be able to catch the group up before they left for the next village after their days rest in Pangboche.

I managed the next day's walk in an hour, moving through the cold morning air in Deboche, past the stone masons who were busy constructing even more tea houses to cope with the ever increasing demand from trekkers, and reached the familiarity of Pangboche. It's this village that is famous for many of the Sherpas who work on Everest and the surrounding mountains and it is this village too that is the home to both my Sirdar (head Sherpa) from Baruntse, Nuru Sherpa, and my Sirdar to be on Everest, Kame Nuru Sherpa. It is once you arrive at Pangboche that you know the expedition is really getting underway, and to help assist you in the mountains, Pangboche is where you can also receive a blessing from the highest ranked lama in the area, Lama Geshe; which I hoped to do during my rest day prior to continuing with the acclimatisation.

Reaching Sonam Lodge in the village, I managed to time my walk just right, catching the rest of the group as they prepared to head off with Henry further up the Khumbu trail and closer still to Everest which was now in constant view. We still had two thirds of the walk left to do, but we also had well over a week in which to get to base camp, so we still had time to walk at a leisurely pace with the absence of any rush. I would stay at Pangboche with Becky who was feeling ill, and we would later be joined by Bonita who was returning from her climb of Island Peak which was to act as acclimatisation and a prelude to her attempt on Lhotse, the mountain next to Everest.

Initially, the lodge and indeed the whole village was eerily quiet, with no sign of life except for a few teams of trekkers who slowly walked past the window. The tranquillity of the place was refreshing and was the perfect setting for a rest day. It soon started to snow, and the dusty paths and desert-like shrubs around us were slowly transformed into their alpine counterparts. Ama Dablam, the mountain which is said to be the Matterhorn of the Himalayas due to its impressive spiralling ridges and distinctive pyramidal shape, was in full view of the lodge, and provided the perfect image to gaze up at when the view of Everest became shrouded in cloud.

During the rest day, we saw Kenton again who was doing a good job of keeping all 28 of his trekkers in check, and then with his departure, it was time to spend the day eating, drinking and doing not much else. Popcorn, yak burgers, and Pringles were the foods of choice for the majority of the day which went at least some way in helping our bodies to recuperate from the previous few days of strain.

It is often hard to notice if any real change is happening to the body, and without medical equipment, acclimatisation often goes unnoticed. But due to the slow procedure of our acclimatisation, the stress of the altitude would increase very gradually throughout the day and whilst it would be enough to force adaptations to occur in the body, we hoped it would not be a case of too much too soon where at a certain altitude the body simply breaks down, so it had to be everything in moderation, that's the key.

Chapter 39 – The Blessing

As all good things come to an end, it was time for me to leave Pangboche and head further up into the mountains. Before I left, however, I decided that I wanted to visit Lama Geshe to receive a blessing to climb on Everest, something which is very important to the Sherpa community who take their faith very seriously. This is perhaps unsurprising given the nature of the terrain on which they work and the danger that often comes unannounced when you least expect it.

To receive a blessing from Lama Geshe, it is first important to make sure that you have everything required for the ceremony. This is mainly a traditional Khata scarf, and an offering, usually consisting of some rupees or dollars. The first hurdle to get through in receiving the blessing is the unexpected trek to locate Lama Geshe's house which is positioned as one of the highest in the village. The path steeply ascends past many Mani stones which are prayer stones with religious incantations and symbols carved into them that in keeping with local custom, should be passed clockwise, the direction that the earth and universe revolve according to Buddhism.

Once I had managed to locate the house which was hidden away and had beautiful views looking out to various 6,000m and 7,000m peaks, I walked inside the smoky building and said 'Namaste' as loudly as I dared to draw some attention to myself in the seemingly deserted house. Out of the mist, a woman ushered me through a maze of rooms and I was eventually sitting in Lama Geshe's room watching on as he performed a blessing for another group of climbers. I hadn't intended to do this part of the journey on my own, but since everyone from my group had already been to see Lama Geshe, I would have to very quickly learn what to do by watching the other group before I had my turn in the hot seat.

All too soon it was my turn to sit and face the lama, and the experience was somewhat ethereal. He chanted many words which I hoped somehow related to a safe passage on Everest, then I was given a handful of blessed rice grains which can be thrown on the mountain as a way of overcoming fear in the hardest and most dangerous places. Before I could leave, we bumped heads and I was given a *sungdi* (a blessed cord) and a cup of tea which had the suspicious taste of being infused with lashings of alcohol. Perhaps slightly linked to the tea, I left the house feeling much better about the expedition, myself and everything in general, and quickly found myself bounding down the path back to the lodge to collect my bag and head off higher up the valley.

It had been previously planned that to aid our acclimatisation and spend as short a time at base camp as possible, especially in the early days of the expedition, instead of heading straight to base camp from Pangboche, we would head up to Chukhung, the highest settlement in the valley that we were in, before dropping down and following the Khumbu valley once more to the base of Everest. Chukhung was still over a day's walk away, so I had to make a stop overnight in Dingboche before carrying on the next day. I was now becoming utterly confused as to the names of the villages that I was supposed to be staying in, and so I had to refer to the map every five minutes to make sure I hadn't overshot the actual destination; and with almost every name on the map ending in 'boche', I saw some great potential to stay in the wrong village which although not disastrous, could be quite confusing with the marked reduction in cognitive function at this altitude.

Finding Dingboche by lunch time, I stayed in a lodge that was recommended by Henry and to my surprise, found him to also be staying in the lodge overnight which gave some much needed company where I managed to learn a few interesting facts about the use of supplemental oxygen on Everest and what I could expect when reaching that point in the expedition. We also managed to fit in a few off topic discussions such as the science behind the aerofoil, a brief history of WWII, riveting on the Titanic, and the world championships of Hobnob, cream cracker and boiled egg eating. This proved an interesting and diverse range of topics all round which may partly have been due to the ever increasing hypoxic environment that was building up around us.

Before turning in for the evening, it seemed a good time to visit the HRA (Himalayan Rescue Association) clinic based in the village and as luck would have it, the doctor based at the clinic happened to be giving a talk on the dangers of high altitude and what effects, both in the long and short term, altitude could have on the body. Clearly everyone else in the room was trekking to base camp and then returning home as they gasped in synchrony as the doctor explained the further perils of venturing above base camp and what high altitude mountaineers might face high on Everest itself. Despite the fact that the lecture was highly educational, I couldn't help feeling a slight worry about a whole range of ailments which can come and go as soon as the body is unable to cope with the demands of the environment. The good news however was that many of the ailments, even the most serious such as fluid on the brain were treatable as long as a fast descent was made and the correct medicine was administered, but as pointed out, once high and exposed on the mountain, the chances of a successful rescue and an escape from these illnesses becomes more and more unlikely.

I thought about this subsequently on the walk to Chukhung the next day, and tried to convince myself that I was healthy, and if any of the symptoms did indeed rear their heads, I would be able to manage the situation, somehow.

Chukhung itself brought back more memories as being the first piece of civilisation after descending from Baruntse. Arriving once again before lunchtime, I was able to also see the beauty of the place, and the impressive mountains that surrounded it. For the first time since Namche, Everest was hidden from view by the impressive wall of Nuptse and Lhotse, the two main neighbouring peaks to Everest. There were also stunning views of Ama Dablam, Taweche Peak and Cholatse which all have stunning lines and ridges, all pointing to dramatic summits.

Going inside our chosen lodge, it was relaxing to be out of the wind, but still with the beautiful views of the mountains through the windows. The clouds were providing the perfect entertainment, circling around the summits and being buffeted by the jet stream winds which weren't due to abate for almost another month. Once all but the heaviest clouds had been ripped away into the blue sky, the entertainment looked to continue inside the lodge. There seemed to be a party of Chinese climbers all hoping to make the summit of Island Peak the following day and, saving their preparations till the very last minute, they were now being taught, and very slowly learning the skills needed to climb up the fixed ropes which were in place on the mountain. To most climbers, learning to 'jumar' is quite simple: the jumar, a metal device with a handle, clamps on the rope and then it is slid upwards with the mechanism inside preventing it from sliding back down the rope should you fall. Clearly explaining this in Chinese is a much lengthier process, and for a full four hours, the budding climbers learnt how this system worked and how it stopped them falling off the mountain all together. I wondered if any of the people being taught would actually remember all of this advice when they left the lodge in the freezing cold of darkness the next morning, to perhaps take their first steps on snow.

Whilst all this entertainment was happening throughout the dining area of the lodge, it seemed the best time to start ordering some food to replenish stores which had clearly been depleted during the walk up from Dingboche. Prawn crackers always go down well, as do deep fried Mars Bars which can be found in abundance at almost all tea houses in the area after many Nepalese owners happily adopted the fourth best thing to come out of Scotland since the screw propeller, general anaesthetic and *Braveheart*.

In all, we stayed sat in the dining room in Chukhung from 11:30am until 8:30pm. This proved to be one of the most difficult periods of the walk-in, since there was absolutely nothing to do. Even with the stunning nature all around us, we were bound by our instructions to do as little physical activity as possible outside of the actual walking to and from villages, and since we were at the end of the valley, there weren't exactly many places that we could travel except for back the way we had come. We needed to stay at this altitude overnight however, as this gave us extra time acclimatising before the dreaded stay at base camp which certainly was starting to lose its appeal given the boredom encountered in a relatively 'exciting' lodge when compared to a tent.

Henry had informed us before we left Dingboche that the rest of the group had trekked over the high pass at the end of the valley to aid acclimatising before arriving at Everest itself; however, as we had no guide to follow what was an extremely rough track by all accounts, we would need to head back down the valley and rejoin the usual path following the Khumbu valley. To make extra value of our time in Chukhung without getting lost on the high path, there was a peak above that we would be able to attempt before descending, known as Chukhung Ri. The mountain, although a relatively straightforward walk, is deceptively steep in places which provided a short and sharp reminder of the best pace to climb at, once in the company of ever thinning air.

From the top, the views were simply magnificent, and aside from providing the perfect opportunity for me to start learning how to operate my camera with gloves on due to the biting wind, it was also a good opportunity to try to call home and for the first time, relay some positive messages about how the expedition was unfolding. I had gotten over the difficulties faced at the start, and was now beginning to enjoy the environment in which I found myself. I reminded myself not to take this for granted either, as I would soon enough be in much less comfortable terrain, surrounded by real dangers of the big mountains such as avalanches, crevasses, seracs and the ever present danger of life threatening illness which would never be too far away.

Chapter 40 – End of the Road

The descent from Chukhung Ri was marked by no noticeable increase in oxygen, which was frustrating but understandable given our relatively short time at altitude. To drag the walk-in out for one more day, we would stop once again at Dingboche, the little village that was the stopping point prior to Chukhung. I was getting familiar with these types of villages now, and was much more at ease in the presence of locals who never failed to smile when the top row of a five-storey house of cards I had spent the previous two hours constructing collapsed, bringing with it the rest of the house. I had realised further down the valley that as we ascended, things would become increasingly expensive and this was proven on leaving Dingboche for the second time, where toilet paper, Mars Bars and all chocolate bars were all individually more expensive than one night of accommodation in a tea house.

The rest of the walk-in was marked by similar findings and events as the previous ten days, which included the long uphill march to Lobuche, the final stop before Everest base camp. We learnt that on this day, the rest of the group had reached base camp themselves, so in all reality, we weren't too far behind and could rest easy in the knowledge that we would be spending just a few less days in the confines of our tents.

This day was also the day that we slowly made our way up to the Dugla Pass. The climb away from Dugla is a long, tough slog, where the summit can be seen right from the very start of the climb. Once at the top, the scene is eerie and gives a chilling glimpse back into the history of Everest which has been marked by some tragic years such as the 1996 storm. Many memorials including that of Scott Fisher's make their mark on the horizon to help remember those lost on the mountains slopes. Of course Everest, just like many popular mountains in the world has a deadly side which needs to be respected, and these memorials certainly go some way towards refreshing the mind about just how fragile life can be in the places which the expedition intended to travel. Take for example the Khumbu Icefall; the famous flow of ice which is home to blocks of ice ranging from the size of a football, to the size of a multi-storey car park. All these structures are unstable, and moving through this environment is effectively a giant life-sized game of Russian roulette which can remove life before a sound is even uttered.

Moving onwards from the sadness in remembering fallen mountaineers, the next step was to take the path even higher up the valley towards Lobuche where we would meet Pierre from French - speaking Quebec. Pierre was a determined trekker who was unwavering in his desire to see the best of the valley and make the most of his time in the country by intending to wake up at 3am and drag his poor guide up Kala Patthar, to Everest base camp, and then back to Lobuche in a single day. His guide was clearly going through an adolescent phase and didn't like the prospect of starting a walk of such proportions without any mention of breakfast, but Pierre's admirable wish to see the valley in all its glory most likely won out the next morning.

The following day, I woke up, admittedly much later than Pierre, but with the same enthusiasm since this would be the day I finally reached Everest base camp. This would be the day that after all those years; I would finally be able to get to the business end of the valley where the beginnings of many dreams are made. Another cause for celebration was the hope that I would soon be reunited with my kit which was making its slow voyage from Kathmandu to base camp. During the 14-day walk-in, I had been in possession of only two base layers, one pair of trousers and definitely not enough pairs of socks, all of which I had worn to the absolute limit. This had proved not to be adequate and severely degraded my ability to sit close to anyone in any social setting, which was greatly exaggerated by the fact that I hadn't had a shower since the Yotel at Heathrow Airport. This would all change the next day though, as with the best of luck, I would have plenty of new clothes that probably still had the labels in and I would also be able to enjoy the luxury of a base camp shower which was a novel prospect having gotten used to the whole-body-double-wet-wipe routine during previous expeditions.

From Lobuche, the incline was gradual but relentless as we headed upwards, ever closer to base camp. Hours of trekking ensued where we had the pleasure of overtaking those less acclimatised than ourselves, and then watched in disbelief as porters carrying what looked to be all their worldly possessions in a basket moved past us at a jogging pace which either gave the impression that they couldn't wait to get to their destination, most likely base camp so that they could drop off their load, or that they were so well developed, the altitude at a meagre 5,000m really had no effect over their small bodies.

Just before lunch and after negotiating what felt like the thousandth rocky chicane, a metal tower started to come into view and I started to wonder whether we had walked so far that we had simply re-entered civilisation and come to a modern metropolis. As the tower came more and more into focus, I was reliably informed that it was the mobile phone mast at Gorak Shep. Gorak Shep which translates to "Dead Ravens" due to its complete lack of any vegetation or obvious signs of life is the farthest outpost of civilisation before reaching Everest base camp itself. The mobile phone mast which provides a very sluggish internet reception to the tiny settlement gives some indication of the importance of the location, since by using the signal from this mast, it is occasionally possible to make a mobile phone call from the summit of Everest without the use of a sat phone. Whether good or bad, every time I visited Gorak Shep during the expedition, whilst I was pleased that I was able to make a reasonable phone call back home, it never failed to astound me that this little place with its hi-tech satellite mast which could be used to access any site on the internet or make a phone call to any country in the world, didn't even have the infrastructure to build a flushing toilet.

Whilst stopping for lunch in Gorak Shep where the main outside toilet is literally overflowing with years of frozen human excrement, I began for the first time in the expedition to notice the effects that the altitude was having on my body. At 5,164m above sea level, Gorak Shep is relatively high so the effects of the altitude hit most trekkers and climbers that venture through the area; however, I couldn't quite put my finger on the exact symptoms. All I knew was that the air felt noticeably thinner, perhaps due to the decreasing temperature at this level, and simply getting up too quickly from a seat was enough to send your head spinning uncontrollably whilst reaching out to grasp at any form of support around you. As soon as we resumed the walk to base camp, I could feel the exertion which was slowly taking its toll on my body. Every effort to clamber up an awkwardly positioned rock was double what it had previously felt like, and my head felt fuzzy, as if it was rapidly trying to produce a report on what was happening inside my body but all the information kept getting lost in translation. Unable to tell me what was happening, it left me with a headache instead, a constant reminder from my body that I was either dehydrated and/or reaching a level of altitude that I wasn't quite acclimatised to yet.

The path from Gorak Shep to base camp isn't steep, and in fact it is mostly flat with relatively little altitude gain, but even flat sections of walking were becoming increasingly difficult. I gazed up towards the summit of Everest and wondered how I would feel if I ever made it that high, which given the current circumstances seemed very unlikely.

Just prior to stopping for lunch, we had been given a slightly out of focus view of what looked like a sprawling campsite. This view was unmistakably Everest base camp, however I didn't stop to pay any attention since it was still so far away which meant putting any fathomable scale to the place would have been extremely difficult. Once we were in between Gorak Shep and base camp though, the small blobs of orange and white started to resemble tents, and soon enough, the whole of base camp was visible as a rural sprawl across the glacier. Tents and prayer flags littered the horizon and the impressive scale of which just gave an immediate indication of the effort and logistics involved in pulling an Everest expedition off. As we descended from the final ridge and across the glacier for the first time, the entrance boulder came into view. This boulder is the limit for trekkers who aren't allowed to venture into the world of base camp for various reasons, and this boulder also marked a memorable point in my expedition. Covered in flags and surrounded by trekkers, the boulder gave an impressive view over much of base camp. As I walked towards it, I had been longing for this moment for the full 14-day walk-in, since to step over the threshold meant I was no longer a trekker, but a climber on a mission to scale the highest mountain in the world. Although it may seem like a relatively insignificant moment in the grand scheme of things, I felt incredibly proud that with the efforts of so many, I had at least been able to make it this far, which in my mind at least, was a very significant step.

Chapter 41 – Base Camp Life

Having crossed the threshold and now starting to move with an added spring in my step into base camp, the next mission on the agenda was to actually find the correct base camp. As I looked across the vast wilderness, there were tents everywhere, with dozens of teams all merging into one seemingly unorganised mess. I had no idea where Henry's tent was, so started to gently amble through the various different camps. First into view was the hi-tech camp of Russell Brice's Himex team with its mini bar and carpeted sun-dome tent which would eventually go on to tell a very strange story later in the 2012 Everest season. After this camp went past, so did many, many others all with the same yellow and orange tents which meant telling each camp apart proved almost impossible. There were no boundaries to each camp, only subtle differences in tents or camp layout showed where one camp might end and another might start, at least in theory anyway.

After asking a Sherpa from a random expedition, Henry was this way as he pointed to the end of base camp which still looked a remarkably long way away. Trudging up the icy scree path, we made our way towards the far end of base camp, passing the HRA rescue tent, and carrying on around car-sized boulders which were inconceivably resting upon small stilts of ice. Reaching near the end of base camp, we asked another Sherpa who pointed us in the opposite direction back the way we had come from. Clearly we were lost, and after a relatively exhausting day walking to base camp, the desire just to reach the correct camp and fall into a cosy sleeping bag was rapidly intensifying.

Finally after retracing our steps, in the distance perched on the highest hill of base camp was the mess tent in which sat the unmistakable figure of Paul with his baseball cap. The feeling of finally reaching this milestone in the expedition was incredible, mixed with a tinge of exhaustion, but we had finally made the long journey from Lukla to the correct tent at base camp. In the tent with a plate of food in front of me, I just sat content in the knowledge that I had reached such an amazing place. And base camp was amazing, the altitude had severed my appetite from me, so my full attention was directed outside the doors of the mess tent where Sherpas and porters busied about with a million tasks to be done in preparation for the first wave of climbers to move through the icefall. The scene was incredible, on one side the icefall tumbled precariously upwards towards the Western Cwm, and on the other, perched on the edge of the icefall was base camp with hundreds of occupants creating their own little home from home in this moonscape environment where clearly, humans weren't mean to thrive, or even survive, not in the long term at least.

After very slowly chewing through my meal, trying as hard as possible not to show my lack of appetite which is always a worrying time in the mountains since food means fuel, I thought it was about time to find a suitable tent to make my home and then start the long process of unpacking and sorting close to 40kgs of gear not including everything I had carried to base camp myself. I picked a good tent which had all the important amenities relatively close at hand; these were the mess tent, toilet tent, comms tent and shower tent. I hoped that I wouldn't have to re-pitch my tent halfway through the expedition since base camp is built upon a constantly moving and melting glacier, and often, tents can either sink or stand proud from the rest of the glacier after much of the ice around them has melted. I would have to take this as it came, so just concentrated on finding my bags and getting them into the tent.

It quickly became apparent though that I couldn't quite control the bag situation either, and many people on the expedition had some of their kit missing. A few people had all their base camp luxuries but no high altitude gear, and some people had the opposite. Luck clearly wasn't on my side as I subsequently found out that I had none of my bags, and all of a sudden, my dreams of a shower, fresh clothes and a comfy night's sleep seemed to evaporate. Clearly I would be roughing it for the night in a spare summit expedition -40 rated sleeping bag. It is interesting to note that -40 degrees is the same in Fahrenheit as it is in Celsius but at the time, that piece of trivia seemed irrelevant to me as all it really meant was unless base camp experienced a record low night time temperature for the season, I would be extremely hot and probably wouldn't sleep too well during the night.

After dinner, the struggle to sleep finally began and would last until the sun came up the next morning. I spent much of the night between being roasted alive and then unzipping the bag and within minutes reaching near hypothermic temperatures. This apparently never-ending cycle of rolling over, unzipping, re-zipping and then repeating lasted for a full 30 minutes when to my horror, I realised that I needed to pee. For the previous 14 days, if I needed the toilet during the night, all I had to do was get out of bed and find the head torch allowing me to navigate a frozen wooden building, but this night was slightly different. I was cocooned in a huge sleeping bag and a silk liner wearing very little, and outside, the temperature was a parky -10 degrees Celsius, perhaps colder with wind chill. My pee bottle was still lost somewhere in Nepal and a quick search of the few contents in my tent revealed nothing of use except my drinking bottle which I couldn't bring myself to use again if I had to pee in it. I contemplated trying to pee out of the open rear door, but concluded that that would most likely end in altogether unwanted consequences, so decided there was nothing else to do but start the long process of getting dressed, putting boots on and opening the tent door, all the while trying not to make too much of a sound waking the tent occupants next to me. Within a minute I was back inside the tent, freezing cold and starting the next process of undressing and getting back into my cocoon, trying to find the optimum position of the zip to achieve thermal equilibrium and avoiding sweaty legs and frostbitten arms.

Unfortunately, the situation didn't improve and I spent the whole night debating with my body about the perfect position in which to sleep, by which time the sun had come up and I found myself thoroughly exhausted. During the night, I had had to get out into the freezing night three times to pee and so to describe base camp at 2am as Baltic was certainly a well experienced understatement.

As morning came, so did the exacerbating heat of the sun which beat down over base camp and fried everyone who was left in their sleeping bags. Once the sun is beating down upon the thin tent fabric, the temperature inside rises rapidly until it becomes so unbearably hot, it actually seems tolerable to wake up from the slumber, get dressed and then stagger up to the mess tent becoming so out of breath that it takes two stops over the course of 10m, before looking back at the ridiculously low gradient path and wondering if you have aged significantly during the night.

This was to be the first full day resting at base camp where we could take stock of our surroundings and hopefully recover enough to contemplate heading up into the icefall the following day. Amazingly enough, both my kit bags arrived in base camp and I was given the news as soon as they arrived. I knew all the happiness that this would bring such as no more midnight rambles through base camp and the ability to sit in base camp feeling relatively clean, at least for a few days before the novelty of a shower wore off. I had hoped though that my bags would have been dropped off at the top of the cliff overlooking my tent so that at least I could just roll my kit down to my tent, but it seemed that the porter had had quite enough of carrying my equipment from Lukla for two weeks, so I had the task of somehow dragging my kit to my tent. At sea level, this voyage would have taken any mere mortal less than 30 seconds, however at base camp which stood at around 5,400m, I struggled to even lift one bag, let alone hold it for a sufficiently long time to haul it to my tent before coming back for the second instalment. The full process took me at least 15 minutes, at which point I called it a day on the exercise front and with my newly found sleeping bag, retired to the comfort of my tent and went straight to sleep.

Chapter 42 – Recurrence

Despite my previous illnesses further down the valley and in Kathmandu, I was happy with the way that I had recovered and made it to base camp. I remembered the time in Kathmandu where I had been worried about flying out and beginning the trek when I didn't really feel like getting out of bed, or when I was down in the valley, isolated and trapped in my own personal box. I had doubted that I would even make it to base camp, yet here I was sleeping under the highest mountain on earth, a fact that I tried not to remind myself of as this simply added to the list of why this mountain would be so hard, or maybe even impossible for me to climb.

As I woke up from my midday siesta, I felt something in my throat and knew instantly that something wasn't quite right. Something worse than a tickle in the throat that spelled out impending danger. I had felt this sensation many times previously and it almost always ended in a cold, a chest infection or some type of man-flu, but however it ended, it was never good. I tried to calm my fears about it since I was at altitude and the mind can play weird and wonderful tricks when it is starved of oxygen, so I forgot about it and carried on with the rest of my day. Lunch, another siesta, some dinner, and then back for the longest sleep of the day, this time armed with my pee bottle and a sensible sleeping bag for the evening.

Almost as soon as I got into bed, the coughing started, and it only got worse through the night. I couldn't believe my luck, I had been ill three times during the expedition and I hadn't even set foot on the actual mountain, this was madness. My mind flashed back to the flight from Heathrow to Mumbai where I watched *Contagion*; clearly that wasn't a good omen for the trip. I didn't know quite what to do, so I spent the night developing a hacking cough that very much resembled the start of a Khumbu cough where the dry air compounds the symptoms and the eventual cough can be so violent that ribs can be broken and parts of the respiratory tract can be brought up.

This wasn't the start to the expedition I was hoping for, and having spent hours packing for a trip through the icefall the previous day, I woke up the next morning feeling miserable and having to knock the first foray onto the mountain on the head whilst the rest of the team made their way upwards. This was deeply crushing for my morale, as for a second time, I had had to wait behind whilst the rest of the team did what they needed to, to make sure they acclimatised well enough. I cursed my bad luck and headed towards the mess tent for breakfast once the sun started to cook the contents of my tent. The small incline to the mess tent was torture and everyone on the expedition found it amazing how such a small slope first thing in the morning can be so difficult. I sat with Bonita who had made her way up to base camp the previous day and dreaded the arrival of the rest of the team, who didn't really know why I hadn't made the first climb of the expedition and would most likely think I was work shy with an aversion to early mornings. Still, there was nothing I could do except wallow in self-pity for the morning and then wait for the abuse later in the day which would no doubt outline all the fun that I had missed including an avalanche that had nearly taken out the whole team in one fell swoop.

Whilst climbing on big mountains, it is quite easy to let small situations get on top of you and let them destroy morale. I knew this was happening to me and after what felt like three separate illnesses, I was getting tired of battling against more than just the altitude. After all, fighting up a mountain against the altitude and environment is hard enough without having to fight to remain in control of your body. The key is always to rest and rationalise the situation as best as possible and once in a more positive frame of mind, even more serious situations such as a close encounter with an avalanche can be overcome. I knew that the altitude and the effort it had taken to get to base camp had most likely taken its toll and having not fully recovered from my previous illness, I was susceptible again to further bouts. In my tent, I wrote in my diary to rationalise the situation. Whilst I may have been too ill to venture onto the mountain yet, it was still very much early days and we had still not had the puja ceremony which meant we couldn't sleep on the mountain yet. I was also waiting for the arrival of Rob who would be somewhere on the Khumbu trail making his way up to base camp, and Henry encouraged me to await his arrival which was reassuring since he wasn't due into base camp for another four days. I figured that if I only rested during this period, then I had every chance of being fit to climb. This mental torment continued every time my mind wandered to thoughts of my family, friends and my sponsors who had made this whole expedition possible.

I wasn't the only one going through this emotional anguish however, since Keith who was the cameraman for Kenton's climb had also picked up a mystery illness and unbeknown to me, had had to travel back down the valley to benefit from increased levels of oxygen at lower altitudes in order to become fit enough to not only climb Everest, but also carry heavy film equipment and climb ahead of Kenton to get the best shots on the mountain; certainly an unenviable task.

So with two climbers out of action and the rest of the team coming within touching distance of an avalanche, the Everest expedition of 2012 was going as smoothly as ever. We hoped that the puja ceremony that followed the next day would bring us some good fortune and at least let us on to the mountain without anyone being killed before we even made it as far as camp one.

The puja is a very important ceremony for climbers and especially for Sherpas who climb in the Himalayas. It is used at the beginning of an expedition on many big peaks and none more so than Everest. I had learnt on Baruntse that apart from a good excuse to drink, eat and get messy, the puja was also an ideal opportunity to get cold and for fear of undoing the good work of the puja, I never felt easy about leaving to get some warm clothes on mid-ceremony. So wearing my big down jacket like almost all the other climbers, the Sherpas just in their thin fleeces, we sat and observed the unique ritual. The first few hours tend to be quite longwinded as the monk reads sacred chants from a holy book in a very rhythmical style whilst juniper is burnt and prayer flags are anchored to the puja altar. Then, as the ceremony starts to draw to an end, the expedition members and Sherpas get to play an active role in the puja by throwing sacred rice and painting the faces of the other climbers with flour. More sungdi cords are presented to the climbers by the monk at the end of the ceremony and even if one is of an atheist background, the ethereal nature of a puja generally leaves a positive feeling amongst the climbers who if nothing else, have had a break from thinking about the next torturous ascent through the ever changing icefall.

Once the puja has been performed, expeditions usually start gathering in pace and once the first foray onto the mountain has been made, the days usually start to tick down very quickly, although it is always important, on Everest at least, to realise that there is never any real rush and there is generally plenty of time to acclimatise before the first weather window presents itself. For me, however, the expedition was starting to slow down rather than speed up, and the day after the puja, I found myself completely alone at base camp for the first half of the day. Our camp was relatively deserted as half of the team had gone back through the icefall with Henry to sleep at camp one, whilst the other half would travel halfway up and then come back to base camp for lunch. I sat in the mess tent and looked out over the icefall which was an immense sight. I took pictures of this amazing feature just so I could be reminded what sight I was waking up to every day. Although I was feeling quite sorry for myself, it was always good to remember where I was, even if I couldn't be in the exact position I wanted, which was somewhere in the heat between base camp and camp one.

Despite the obvious danger of the icefall, there was a beauty to the almost stationary waterfall; imagine a food blender full of ice cubes, all blended up for a few seconds, then increased in size millions of times where people become tiny ants dotted throughout this giant's maze, this is the beautiful chaos of the icefall.

This time alone at base camp continued over the following day, where some of the group pushed up to camp two; Richard who was feeling the effects of the high altitude made his way back to base camp and Rick, Ryan and Becky were recovering from their exploration into the icefall the previous day. In many ways, I couldn't bear to spend another day cooped up in my tent and feeling like I had mostly recovered from whatever had been affecting me the previous few days, I took the risk of taking the short trip to the end of base camp where I could start my video diary of the expedition. My coughing had subsided and after continual gargling with salt water, I had managed to avoid the illness progressing into anything much worse than an unwanted cold. I knew from previous times at altitude that once the body has rested in a tent for several days, it is very hard to get going again and continue to exercise, so it was important for me to take a small walk, just get some blood pumping round my body and to feel a little more alive than I had previously.

The venture to the end of base camp seemed to coincide with almost all of the yak deliveries to base camp which was great to film on video but made negotiating the path to the end of the camp very difficult as in places, it is only as wide as two feet, often with a precarious rock hanging above you on one side, and a vertical drop or a crevasse on the other. I hadn't quite bargained for this game of bumper cars and so found a safe rock as fast as I dared and waited for the first herd to navigate the treacherous path before heading off once more to trekkers point. I sat just before the entrance to base camp, looking out at what I thought of as 'free land' where the trekkers could quite happily make their way home back to the comforts of infrastructure and civilisation within a few days, whereas I would have to stick out the suffering for a number of weeks yet. Whilst I never wished to swap places as I knew how privileged I was to be here, I envied their freedom and lack of pressure and wondered whether I would be better giving my position to someone else who could make better use of such an opportunity; mainly just by having at least one quick climb into the icefall.

I made another phone call home and received the reassurance that I needed. This part of the expedition was going so slowly and worse, it was going all wrong, but all I needed to do was await the arrival of Rob, and then everything would go smoothly from then on, it had to. I had been through the mental torture of this kind previously on Peak Lenin and I have now come to the conclusion that the little episode in Kyrgyzstan had been much worse, although it was of little consolation at the time.

The snow started to fall over base camp that evening and everything was quickly turned into a dimly lit winter wonderland with impressive vistas everywhere you turned. Avalanches also came down this night, just as they had been doing on all previous nights; although you can't see the cascade of snow through the darkness, you can certainly hear and feel the destructive power which acts as a reminder that up here, like it or not, nature is very much in control.

On the 21st April, I awoke to the pleasant feeling that all was well, both physically and mentally. I hadn't been getting the best sleeps which can be attributed to the altitude which has strange effects once a climber is asleep such as Cheyne-Stokes respiration, where breathing gradually increases until suddenly it stops altogether. This can often go on for 30 seconds before the respiration cycle is restarted. Some climbers are able to sleep through this abnormal pattern which is often quite shocking to hear for the first time as a tent partner, but if the period of apnea which is created when breathing stops is bad enough to wake a person, extremely poor sleeps can result which is both frightening and frustrating for the insomniac.

Fortunately I didn't have Cheyne-Stokes respiration, but just a tendency to roll over a particularly hard surface and wake up, or display symptoms of a tiny bladder with the need to wake up to pee as often as four times during the night which isn't ideal as the desperation not to drop the pee bottle is tested to the absolute limit every night.

I had now been stuck in base camp for a full six days resting and recovering and my persistence to lie in bed all day seemed to be paying off. After the first two days, I had quickly run out of exciting things to do and my diary on the next four days was just an explanation and methodology of how I had written my diary; a time-wasting strategy with an ambiguous use of the Droste effect. Despite spending this length of time doing nothing at base camp, I woke up knowing that today would be the day that Rob arrived to base camp. This was great news for me as it meant I could finally venture out into the icefall for the first time and get some climbing in the crampons; although I wouldn't be venturing out today, it would have to wait until the 22nd by which time Rob would know if all his gear was at base camp and after an evening rest in the mess tent to recover from a rapid walk-in from Lukla.

Up until this point, the expedition had been going slowly, not just in the pace used to cover ground, but in the activity level, which from my point of view had reached zero if you didn't include three visits to the mess tent each day, a dozen trips to the toilet tent but not enough trips to the shower tent. From my first venture out into icefall however, time started to move very rapidly as my thoughts grew more and more to the vertical world above me.

Chapter 43 – Another World

My first foray into the icefall was only a short introduction to life on Everest, but one which had some significant differences compared to other mountains that I had been on previously. One big difference was the scale of the Khumbu Icefall and the methods used to move through it, mainly the use of ladders to cross a number of bottomless crevasses. I had practised all other techniques to cross crevassed terrain, but the icefall on Everest is different. It is like no other terrain on earth, it is unique to Everest and its size, imposing danger and constant threat of avalanche from above makes it a foreboding place. Perhaps one of the most famous glaciers in Europe is the Mer de Glace which flows down from the Mont Blanc massif to Chamonix but in comparison to the glacier of the Khumbu, the Khumbu Icefall as it is known, the Mer de Glace is simply dwarfed in every way. At around 12kms long, the Khumbu icefall is 5kms longer than its European counterpart, and has its lowest point around 2,500m higher than the highest point of the Mer de Glace. That said, both glaciers are equally dangerous having both claimed many lives and despite subtle differences in where these dangers can come from, great care must always be taken when venturing out onto this unpredictable terrain.

For my first experience of the icefall, we would only climb as high as the first double ladder which would still take an hour to reach and would fully test my lungs which hadn't been used for a number of days.

The first difficulty was actually finding our way onto the icefall which I hoped Rob would be able to help with, but since base camp changes every year, we struggled to actually find the place where everyone gears up with crampons and climbing kit. There also seemed to be no obvious path to the icefall, so heading through a variety of expedition camps, we walked past numerous climbers fast asleep in their tents, basking in the afternoon sun. After scrambling and slipping on the icy glacier of base camp for a good 20 minutes, we found what we were looking for; footprints in the snow. They stuck out amongst the whiteness and showed the path which led through a maze of ice formations which rang out with the gentle sound of water running underneath the brittle surface. After gearing up, we headed straight into the maze which gracefully zigzagged through giant ice waves, which after each ascent of a crest, led you to the next level, slightly higher than the last. Much of the ice would be melted by the end of the expedition, but now, the season was still young and the ice even in the heat of mid-afternoon was still mostly solid. We climbed on higher and higher, and gradually as the climbing got steeper and more exposed, ropes started to appear to aid the crossing of moderately wide cracks which ranged from a few metres deep to black bottomless abysses.

As the gradient steepened, the lungs started to work harder and harder, and the heart started to pump, the pressure now audible in my ears. Rob seemed to be going well with much experience at altitude, but I began to remember the torture that is climbing at altitude. It is a pain that is agonising in the present, but once an expedition is over and time has healed the wounds gained both physically and mentally from the strains of altitude, the mountains have a strange allure that makes them seem appealing even though the last efforts in them had been mostly torturous. I was now beginning to remember this pain, and the difficulty which is imposed on the slightest of gradients. Now a snow slope steep enough to jumar up was ahead. A slope this steep at sea level by all accounts would have been ascended in a matter of seconds, but now this was a hill of herculean proportions that ripped the throat to pieces as the cold air is gulped down to settle the oxygen debt.

Interestingly, the bit I was looking forward to the most in this first jaunt up the mountain was the crossing of a ladder or two. I actually looked forward to standing over what looked to be a bottomless hole, and then gradually inching forward. If anything, the care that would be needed on the ladders would give me some breathing space to slow down my breathing from a rapid pant to a more controllable frequency. As we neared the top of a section, I saw the first of two sets of ladders. It was a simple single ladder which looked to be an ancient type which perhaps had a few days of life left, most probably purchased from the now defunct Woolworths. Crossing this ladder proved quite simple as only one step was needed, and then we were across to the other side and away from the danger of the crevasse below. As we inched higher, we met the final ladder of the day, and our scheduled turning back point. This looked to be a more stable design, and closely resembled two ladders that can be purchased from B&Q, which were simply tied together in the middle with string. Rope would probably be a better term for the binding material, but to be accurate, I doubt the diameter of the cord could really be classified as rope, with the only piece of confidence being the number of times the string had been wrapped round to prevent any mid-crossing disasters.

There were two ropes running either side of the ladder which provided some form of loose support, but the key was to lean forward, down into the gaping hole, and then move an inch at a time, maintaining at least one point of the crampons in contact with the slippery metal rungs. Once I had the technique practised, I began to feel comfortable crossing the ladders to the point where on reaching the middle of the double ladder, I could jump up and down a few times, just to illustrate to myself that I was relatively safe, and that as long as the ladder didn't break or somehow fall down the hole, I would be fine.

After both Rob and I were satisfied by my ability to cross ladders and that we had reached a high enough point in the day to keep pushing the acclimatisation process on, it was time to head down and out of this icy world and back to the artificial security of base camp. I knew that the next time I ventured into the icefall it would be to reach camp one, the next station after base camp that most other climbers on the expedition had already reached. I remained reserved about how fun that day would be, since it would mean dramatically increasing our exposure to altitude and then dealing with all the different ailments that come with that, such as headaches and a general disregard for the will to live, and on top of all that, the day would begin at the ungodly hour of around 4am to give us the best chance of getting out of the icefall before the sun rose and whilst the icefall was as stable as it could be.

For now though, I was content with a day's work well done, and apart from Rob's trainers filling with water under the security of a riverside snow bank, the day's climb went without incident. Tomorrow would also be spent in Gorak Shep, the first settlement reached on leaving base camp, where we could email back to home and update family and sponsors on how everything had been going; fortunately I had now been in the icefall so the dreaded email of 'I've been ill and spent over a week in a tent doing nothing' did not materialise, although this would have been far easier for Mum to cope with rather than the pictures of her son climbing below ominous hanging ice cliffs and over ravenous crevasses.

For the day of the 24th April, the plan was set. Bob, Becky, Rob and I would wake up early, we would then head up the icefall and stay at camp one for a single night, then move up to camp two where we would rest with a possible climb further up the Western Cwm to the base of the Lhotse Face, and then after another night at camp two, we would descend back to the relative comforts of base camp. This plan sounded simple and effective, all we would need to do would be to pack our kit, then get the best night's sleep possible before waking up early the next morning and begin the game of follow the leader for three days.

Everything was set; the kit was ready, and my clothes were lined up in my tent ready to be changed into at 4:15 when my alarm was set to go off. I knew I wouldn't get a great night's sleep, simply because of the anticipation of what lay ahead, and the pain that would be subsequently endured. I also found it hard to sleep when I knew I had to wake up early the next morning, perhaps for fear of missing the correct time, but I didn't have to worry, I had my alarm set for 4:15 which gave me 15 minutes spare to get dressed and make it to the mess tent, simple.

After a somewhat intermittent sleep, I vaguely remember waking up at 4:08am and looking at my watch with that sinking feeling that it was almost time to get up. I quickly did the maths though, and thought it would be more beneficial to have another seven minutes of sleep rather than getting ready right now, and besides, it was freezing so the less time spent waiting, the better. The next time I woke up was 4:40am when Rob marched over to my tent in the pitch darkness and simply said, "Matt, what the fuck are you doing?" To which my reply was of course, "Waiting for my alarm, why?" It then dawned on me when I quickly scrambled around feeling for my watch that I had overslept by a reasonable margin, and since my alarm was in fact set, the cold was affecting its ability to wake me up. I got out of my warm cocoon as quickly as I could bear and began to put on clothes in whichever part of my body felt most at risk from hypothermia. Once the majority of the clothes have been put on, it is time to unzip the inner door of the tent and struggle for a number of minutes to put on the high altitude double boots which have an intricate system of laces, Velcro and zips to transform the foot into a highly portable oven.

I made my exit from the tent as gracelessly as possible, and then headed for the cook tent as quickly as my lungs would let me where I would meet the others for a quick breakfast before heading up the mountain. Luckily Bob was also struggling with the early mornings, and so I hadn't been quite as late as I had thought but nevertheless, this wasn't a great start to climbing on Everest.

After a warming breakfast of hot milk and cereals, we headed outside into the cold as the first rays of light started to hit the valley making it much easier to find our way through the base camp maze and to the entrance of the icefall. We threw some rice onto the puja altar for good luck and safe passage, and then headed out, firstly across the stone-covered glacier, then to crampon point at the base of the glacier where we geared up and got ready to tackle the world of chaos that stretched up and out in front of us. It was a wonderful sight to behold, with head torch lights high up the icefall from teams who had left earlier, and the sliding and scraping of shingle from the boots of teams still working their way through base camp. It seemed the icefall was coming alive all of a sudden as many climbers and Sherpas flocked into its icy clutches. Just as it had before, the climbing started to steepen after half an hour, and with it, the speed dropped and the respiration rate increased. All the climbers I could see in the near vicinity were spewing streams of condensation from their mouths as they gulped down as much air as possible. Even though all these sections were so different from the last, they were all so new to me, and so the icefall just went past in a general blur as we climbed from one roped slope to the next.

The icefall is a constantly changing labyrinth, and cracks come and go as quickly or as slowly as nature dictates. All this change therefore requires the use of so called 'icefall doctors' who climb up to various points in the icefall and repair any damage to ladders and roped sections, or even change the route if it is required. It is hard enough to climb any of these slopes in the icefall with just a light rucksack on the back, but to see the icefall doctors carrying full sized ladders through the ice cascades and up into the highest parts of the icefall is simply a show of mind-blowing strength and physical capacity. This view of human effort is equally matched, however, by the destructive powers exhibited by the icefall. As we ascended, the sight of ladders which had been subjected to the enormous pressures found in the icefall and subsequently crushed was just another show of the strength and brutality of this environment. It is truly hard to comprehend such a place and the forces which go beyond the scale of human conception.

At 9am, we found a relatively safe area in the icefall where we could stop for a rest, a bite to eat and to radio base camp to let them know our rough whereabouts. Although I didn't know it at the time, for those who had been into the icefall multiple times, words were used to describe certain locations in the icefall where on mention, someone on the radio at base camp would have a relatively good idea of where you were, how high you were, and in the right spot, may even be able to see you through a pair of binoculars. Sections in the icefall such as the Popcorn Field and the Football Field are so named after the avalanche debris and the flat section respectively; only in this instance the pieces of popcorn ranged in size from a football to a large family car.

It wasn't until we got going again after our rest that I started to feel the pressure and strain of climbing at altitude. As the sun came up, the icefall acted as a suntrap and consequently the physical effort of moving upwards one step at a time became even tougher than before. It was becoming a mental battle just to keep moving but at the same time, not out pacing myself. It is very much a double-edged sword in the icefall, since the harder and higher you climb, the quicker you move past the dangerous sections; however you move up into thinner air and so maintaining a fast pace becomes near on impossible, whereas on the other side, it is much easier to move slower and more rhythmical but your chance of being hit by an impending avalanche or falling serac is clearly increased by virtue of the length of time spent exposed to these dangers.

Towards the top of the icefall, there is another relatively safe section where a short rest can be taken, just to recoup some strength that has been sapped by both the climbing and the heat. Just as on Baruntse where we moved from base camp to camp one, I was starting to fatigue quickly with the weight of my rucksack which made my breathing shallow and ineffective, almost as if I had developed asthma over the course of four hours. I knew however that we weren't too far away, and once we were over the final dangerous section, we would be able to make our own way at our own speed along the final steps to camp one.

The rest was short-lived, and a sickening feeling moved over me, and I am sure the rest of the group; we all knew what was coming even if we hadn't been this high before. As previously described, the icefall has names which denote roughly what section you are in and how much progress you have made such as the Popcorn Field; in 2012 however, another marking post had been laid down artificially. Earlier in the season as camps one and two were being established, a young Sherpa crossed one of the top double ladders unclipped, as many Sherpas do, and tragically fell to his death. As the rescue team went into the crevasse to recover his body, a trail of his blood was left on the far wall of the crevasse. Knowing about this accident days earlier and the markings that were on the ice, I had no doubt that I would be fine, after all blood is a common sight in films and TV shows, so the mind would surely be numb to it. The sight that we witnessed, however, was truly sickening. Far different from any CGI or visual effects, this was real life and death was sitting there in the snow before us. I couldn't have imagined that I would be so affected by the sight until I saw the crevasse and my mind played out the events that must have unfolded.

Crossing over that double ladder gave a lasting memory of what toll the mountain exacts from our efforts to climb it. As we crossed, Rob told us to keep looking up, don't look down for it was a sight that even eyes accustomed to death in the mountains would have found hard to take in. We all tried to forget what we had just seen and thought only of the poor Sherpa who had left his family behind.

The final hour to camp one was energy-sapping undulating terrain but by hook or crook, we would all make camp and have the luxury of collapsing into our tents. As the tents came into view, relief washed over me as I knew that I had at least made this step above base camp, but I knew that if I was asked to move any further than the tents in front of me, I would have been unable to go, so the reality of what we still had to achieve was rapidly sinking in as the Western Cwm and Lhotse Face, the site of camp three, stretched out for miles above us.

Sharing with Bob, we spent the rest of the day melting snow and ice for various meals that we would try to make, just to try and take the edge off the exhaustion that had now well and truly set in. We had made relatively good time to camp one, arriving at 11am, and this gave us the best possible opportunity to rest and recover.

We all knew that the key to this recovery was to eat and drink, but not to fall asleep which tends to make eating and drinking impossible. But poor Bob was so tired; I had to keep nudging him back to consciousness as he repeatedly drifted off to the place we all wanted to be. For the rest of the day, we basked in the tent, constantly melting and boiling the snow and ice to drink, and then eating some of the luxuries that we had brought up from base camp which revolved around chocolate and small cakes with as many calories in as possible. For our evening meal, we had all carried a range of boil-in-the-bag type meals which were essentially bags full of cold liquid gloop that needed to be placed in boiling water before they were ready to be eaten. The main problem with high altitude cookery is that water only boils at around 78 degrees Celsius at camp one, and that combined with the freezing air temperatures generally means anything you have cooked, regardless of how long it has been boiling for, will be cold once you start to eat it. This is just one of the many delights of high altitude mountaineering, and so with a stomach full of cold calories, we moved all our kit to the side and attempted to get some sleep.

Chapter 44 – The Long Cwm

It was starting to seem like every time I closed my eyes at a new higher altitude, I found it almost impossible to sleep. As I lay awake in camp one, I could hear that Bob was fast asleep, and I became frustrated that I was unable to do the same. The drug diamox is a useful tool in preventing sleep apnea, however I had not envisaged that I would need it so early in the expedition, so when I did finally take a dose, it was far too late to have any effect. I simply lay in my bag listening to my iPod and last remember checking the time at 4am, although what time I truly slept remains a mystery.

As the morning light hit the tent and gradually the warmth started to melt all the ice crystals that had built up on the fabric, I woke up to the apt song of Diana Ross's *Ain't No Mountain High Enough* playing in my ear. We had a few hours to spare in the morning where we could wait for the tent to completely dry out and warm up, and then begin the laborious process of melting more snow for breakfast and the water for the climb up to camp two. As the packing of all our kit was nearing completion, the Sherpas arrived at camp one after a rapid ascent through the icefall. They kindly offered to take our sleeping bags up to camp two, and after the previous day's exertions, no one could resist their help.

Out of the tent, we all looked up at the route that was to come which was mostly hidden by further pressure ice formations. We had been told though that once out of these formations and across the final ladder, we would be able to see camp two ahead even with a few hours of climbing left to do. This is often quite a demoralising situation since even after 15 minutes of torturous effort the camp still looks no closer than when you started. The route to camp two is a gentle gradient all the way, and in some places, it is arguably flat. The two difficulties with this stage of the climb, however, are the altitude which is beyond anything we had encountered previously on the expedition, and secondly the heat that is produced by the constant reflection of the sun from the ice and snow which is both energy sapping and a dangerous recipe for bad sunburn.

In comparison to the previous day, I was performing much better since this part of the climb is all about finding a good rhythm for both the feet and in terms of breathing. If you can manage this, then the distance from camp one to camp two can be covered relatively quickly in comparison to other parts of the climb, and this showed when we arrived at camp two before lunch. After lunch, we headed further up to the top of camp two which added another 100m of vertical height gain in the hope of a better night's sleep than the previous one. On the way down, a big avalanche came down of the West Shoulder of Everest just confirming the lack of stability in the area. After seeing this, we felt like we'd had enough playing for one day, so it was time for an excellent dinner prepared by the much loved Pasang Temba, and then back under the canvas in the hope of a good night's sleep.

Sadly sleep didn't materialise on this night either, and so with the wind battering the tent, I stayed awake listening to the power of nature and my iPod, hoping that some time in the near future, I would be able to enjoy just a few hours of revitalizing sleep. In the meantime though, there was still climbing to be done, so after a much appreciated lie-in and casual breakfast, Becky, Rob and I headed up to the base of the Lhotse Face to get some more acclimatisation metres under our belt and spot out the route for the next time when we would aim to reach camp three on the middle of the imposing face. Bob had decided that he would stay at camp two for a few days, and since he was attempting to climb Lhotse itself instead of Everest with Bonita, their acclimatisation plan would differ slightly from those of us who were attempting Everest. Becky, Rob and I felt relatively fresh on the climb up to the base of the face, and after 1.5 hours, we had made our maximum height for the day.

At the base of the face, we stared up at the vertical world above us which was simply astounding. Huge lines of rock with incredibly visible striated patterns stretching thousands of feet above us which at one time, thousands perhaps millions of years ago, would have been at the bottom of the ocean. We then focussed on the climbing route which went without deviation, straight up the face to camp three. Climbers high above us looked like ants as they motored on up to the camp which was being hacked out of the ice by the Sherpas. The face was incredibly steep, and it would take some miracle for us to get up there. Whilst not overhanging, it was simply the distance that meant this section of the climb looked by far the hardest we had yet come across. The route was also very icy and dry this year, with relatively little snow higher up the slope which was critical in bonding all the loose rocks and boulders together.

We would have to wait for another day to attempt this wall though, and soon enough, it was time to head back down to the faux comfort of camp two, where the seats in the mess tent were simply piles of rocks with a foam mat placed on top, if you were lucky. As we reached the camp just in time for lunch, we were also met by the familiar faces of Valerie, Bonita and Paul who had come up from base camp to camp two in a single push, having already had their stint at camp one a week or so ago. By all accounts from their reports, the icefall had almost completely changed after the avalanche from the West Shoulder, and the icefall doctors had been busy finding new routes and repairing the existing crevasse crossings.

Chapter 45 – Too Close

It seemed that I was finally given the opportunity to have a good sleep at camp two that night, and after ten hours of almost constant sleep, I felt refreshed and ready to get down to base camp where we could properly relax without the southwest face looming above us. We would leave some kit at the camp, such as our summit sleeping bag, a sleeping mat and some spare mitts which would wait for our return journey, providing the camp wasn't destroyed first which would scupper plans of having a remotely warm night on the South Col. Shortly after 6:30, and before any heat from the sun kicked in, we were away, slowly jogging down the Western Cwm without any crampons which would only impede our speed down to the first ladders.

We arrived at camp one in around 40 minutes, almost 2.5 hours quicker than the ascent had taken us, and so we sat on our bags outside our tents for 15 minutes which gave us plenty of time for a quick breather, and a chance to put some sun cream on and take some layers of clothing off before we roasted alive in the icefall. As we sat there, it was pure bliss. The face of Nuptse glistened, Lhotse loomed up behind us, and Everest towered over to our right, its bulk immense and beyond comprehension. In those few moments, everything was so peaceful, as if all around was floating through wispy clouds. There were climbers all about, moving up and down the Cwm, going about their business, getting from A to B. The Sherpas were also going about their business, transporting an endless list of essentials and logistical equipment from A to B and vice versa. The mountain had a magic to it, created by the illusion of the fluffy white snow all around us that meant everything was safe, and unlike horror stories of mountains exposed to relentless winds, this was a thoroughly nice place to be. It was tranquil; too tranquil.

As we picked ourselves up and off the snow, we attached our harnesses and crampons, and then set off into the top of the icefall where a whole manner of traps awaited us. We crossed the blood-stained crevasse with the same sickness as before filling the stomach once again. We then headed down, further into the icefall amongst the popcorn field, and soon after, turned a corner onto a steep roped traverse. And then it hit.

No one facing the other way would have seen the crack sheer off across the face of Nuptse, but everyone heard it soon enough, and immediately heads started turning. A wall of snow was hurtling towards the ground at phenomenal speeds, and from our viewpoint, the area of destruction was camp one. A whole section of the Nuptse wall had avalanched, triggered by a falling serac from above. As the crack raced across the face, the snow started to slide and then crashed like a thunderbolt into the ground and disappeared from view. The immense clouds of snow started to dissipate until everything from our viewpoint under the lip of the icefall looked relatively normal. Everyone around was silent, but with an overriding need to get to safety.

At first no one saw what loomed behind us since it was hidden from view by the top of the icefall, but less than a minute after the avalanche had occurred, an enormous snow-filled cloud bellowed its way towards us. Within seconds the sun was blotted out, and after a few more, everything went dark as the storm from the avalanche hurled its way into the icefall threatening to blow everyone from where they stood. Everyone around started searching for ropes, something to clip into as the rush of air intensified to full storm conditions with horizontal spindrift and a roar that only wind passing through a structure as unique as the icefall itself can create. Through the storm, we could hear Rob shouting 'Don't panic, don't panic'; certainly easier said than done when nature is hurling itself at you. After what felt like an excessively long time being battered by powerful winds, the storm slowly started to abate, and then like it had never even happened, the cloud started to dissipate and for a moment the sun shone and there was nothing but silence. Then, after everyone had finished checking to see that they were indeed still alive, the radios started going crazy. Every team was contacting their guides on the mountain to assess the damage from an avalanche that from camp two, blocked out the whole of the Western Cwm.

It didn't take very long for the three of us to realise that we had been sitting in the tranquillity that was camp one only 30 minutes before the whole wall slid. We were clearly very lucky that day, and yet we still did not know what damage had been done, and how badly camp one had been affected, although the general consensus was that with the amount of activity on the mountain, camp one may well be a mass grave with people buried as they slept under the morning sun. Being a doctor, Rob had to go back up the mountain to see if any help could be given to survivors who still had a chance of making it down the mountain alive. This meant that a traumatised Becky and I had to find our own way down through the icefall which just added to the stress and confusion of the situation, since just as the others had said, the icefall was now drastically different from how we remembered it. With all the activity going on, many climbers were now rushing down the icefall simply to get back to the safety of base camp, and this meant that we were able to latch onto the group of a Sherpa and a Korean climber who we could follow down the mountain. Everyone was clearly traumatised, no one spoke a word, and there was simply reflection. Reflection of our luck in escaping the initial avalanche, and the thought of many climbers still trapped up high on the mountain.

As we neared the bottom section of the icefall, our attention turned to the difficulties which lay in front of us, mainly the many rises which even though at a significantly lower altitude than what we had previously been at, were enough to deplete any energy that we did have left. This final hurdle provided the perfect distraction from what we had just witnessed, and it wasn't until we reached base camp that we were able to talk through the story of what happened with the guys who were waiting to climb up to camp two the following morning. We later learnt that Rob had managed to help a Sherpa who had been swept into a crevasse sustaining many injuries including a broken sternum and a lacerated tongue. Amazingly though, no one else was hurt in the avalanche and due to the falling snow being slightly higher than the site of camp one, we suspected this was the main reason that no one was killed or buried alive. This was good news for us all to hear, and after the sight of a helicopter rescue going up to camp one to rush the injured Sherpa to hospital, we felt we'd had quite enough excitement for one day, and so headed off into the dark to the now homely feel of our tents.

Now that we had been much higher than base camp, I had the best sleep of the whole expedition so far, and this pattern continued every night except for those where I knew we had to get up at some dark hour to venture up the mountain once more. Before I completely fell asleep though, I thought about the experiences I had witnessed in such a short space of time. In a matter of four days, I had seen the remains of death on Everest, and had come as close as I would dare to one of the most unavoidable dangers to life on the mountain. I was clearly living someone else's dream as no real world environment could conjure up so many possibilities and uncontrollable forces and yet still let men into the very heart of the storm. But with my altitude-induced brain cell depletion, I could reason with this philosophy no more, and so fell into a deep and soothing sleep.

Chapter 46 – Base Camp Routine

When discussing high altitude mountaineering, the question is often asked, 'what is the use of climbing halfway, only to descend?' This is where many years of human trial and error on Everest itself and many other mountains comes into play when determining the best way to safely scale the mountain. Clearly the more times you have to ascend and descend a mountain, the higher the risk becomes from threats such as avalanche and rock falls; but the modern method of acclimatization is crucial in gaining the best chance of summiting and importantly, the best chance of descending and reaching base camp alive and well.

On all the previous mountains I had climbed before, acclimatisation was a case of moving up to a camp, having a full day and two nights' rest, then carrying on higher up the mountain, making the exposure to altitude as gradual as possible without the need to descend thereby significantly elongating the expedition. With Everest though, due to its extreme height, it is necessary to first arrive at base camp in relatively good health, and then to ascend to camp one, then two before descending, and then on the next rotation, ascend to camp two, then three before descending all the way down the mountain. After this final rotation, climbers often move down the valley away from the mountain all together, and reach an altitude of around 4,000m which greatly aids the body's ability to recover from the previous stresses placed upon it from high altitude. Once a period of up to a week has been spent at this lower altitude, climbers will then head back to base camp and await a weather window where for a short period of time, the jet stream winds that buffet the summit are pushed north, giving a respite from unclimbable conditions, and an opportunity to reach the summit. This method of climbing and then re-climbing the mountain is essential to allow the body to undergo the process of acclimatisation, mainly involving adaptations to the way the body uptakes and delivers oxygen to vital organs and muscles such as increased red blood cell mass and an increase in pulmonary artery pressure to saturate the blood with as many oxygen molecules as possible.

All these adaptations which take place in the body go relatively unnoticed, however, when it is time to fully stretch the capacity of the body and attempt a summit push; these changes to the human physiology make a critical difference when attempting to survive in the so called 'death zone' above 8,000m.

Sadly, we weren't quite at this stage in the expedition, and having only been to camp two once, by all accounts we still had a fair amount of climbing and acclimatisation left to do. After our brush with the avalanche which had shaken up many people on the mountain who had been close enough to feel its lethal power, it was decided that we would take an extra day to rest at base camp, and then on the 1st of May, attempt our second rotation, pushing straight to camp two from base camp which admittedly filled me with a little dread after the physical effort it had taken to reach camp one in a single day.

During the rest days at base camp, we were blessed with two full days of rest which was addictive. Everyone else from our team was up high on the mountain, meaning everywhere was blissfully quiet in camp, and until the sun went down, we were able to bask in our tents for the duration of the day relishing in the cosiness of our small homes. Everything in my tent now had its own place, and whilst it was still a general mess due to the amount of kit we all needed for the mountain, I generally knew where everything was, even when I woke up at midnight quickly patting around the floor looking for my head torch and pee bottle which was as far away from me as possible but never more than a full arm's length.

To make the full use of the time at base camp, you have to be an exceptional time waster, something that I have been able to take full advantage of whilst on the mountains. Being specified as 'rest days', the time spent at base camp is for exactly that, resting. There is no need to go off for long walks or do any more damage to the body than what has already been done and what will be done on the next rotation up the mountain. So essentially, nothing happens.

There was some news that was starting to stir amongst the climbers however, having been passed down from base camp managers between teams. The discussions were very focused upon the state of the Lhotse Face which was in a bad condition for climbing being far too dry and icy, meaning that any loose rocks could easily break free from the face and potentially cause devastating injuries or loss of life to any of the climbers or Sherpas who were in the process of climbing the face. Many radio conversations were made between the base camps, and decisions were being made about what to do. There were also rumours starting regarding the safety of the icefall itself, and whether the large serac on the West Shoulder that hangs ominously over the icefall would break away causing devastation and certain death to anyone caught in the fall line.

The main cause of concern regarding the safety of the icefall was coming from Russell Brice's camp who were hoping to get a number of injured servicemen to the summit of Everest, however after the death of one of their Sherpas, they were seeming spooked by the hanging bulk of ice. This was only a minor concern of other teams since the Khumbu Icefall had been subjected to threats from above ever since a route was made through it, and so, it was the Lhotse Face which was causing most of the problems for teams who were trying to make a safe route from camp two to camp three, the objective of our next rotation on the mountain.

The eventual plan would be to create a new, much less direct route up the face which removed many of the dangers associated with falling rock and ice on the old route which had no areas of protection or any places to hide. This meant more rope would have to be carried up the face, and a team of Sherpas would have to fix the lines in place before anyone could reach camp three. This wouldn't be too much of an issue, however the next obstacle to be overcome was to fix the route from camp three to camp four which was proving extremely difficult given that the winds were far too strong for safe climbing, and in addition, the route above camp three was still looking extremely bare which meant any travel into the fall line of any number of rocky areas was far too hazardous for the Sherpas to even contemplate until new snow consolidated the exposed areas.

Situations like these were out of our hands as climbers, and so there was nothing we could do except wait for the 1st May to come around and then hope that when we reached camp two, some form of safe route would be in place to move higher up the mountain to camp three, the final acclimatisation rotation before the real thing. In any case, it was far too hot in our tents to worry about such issues, so instead of worrying about the possibility that in fact no one would be able to reach the summit, I just lay, soaking up the energy from the sun, mentally preparing for the struggle that awaited me.

Chapter 47 – The Final Rotation

At 4:15am the next day, I managed to wake up with my newfound alarm, and stay awake long enough to get dressed and make it out into the bitter cold of night in search of the cook tent. I hadn't slept as well as other nights, but I knew this was due to the thought of what lay ahead. Bhim the always smiling cook greeted us cheerfully whilst he warmed up some milk for us, avoiding the need to try to digest our cereals with frozen liquid chunks. We knew the drill by now and were soon standing by the puja altar throwing our rice for safe passage. This time there would only be three of us, Rob, Becky and me. We looked up into the icefall with trails of head torches dancing around as the early birds climbed their way into the Western Cwm. We headed off into the dark in the direction of the entrance to the icefall as slowly but surely, the dusky blue light took over from the darkness that had been standing guard for the night.

As we swerved around the first ice formations which as always seemed never ending, the sounds of our breath and our crampons on the ice were the only thing that gave away our intention to climb. As soon as we started to hit the elevated terrain, our pace slowed to the preferred climbing pace and our breathing grew deeper and deeper. By the time we reached the first ladder, we were in the groove where everything becomes automatic. Hands twisting to torque open the karabiner ready for the next rope change, and the opening of the jumar gate ready for the first steep section past the first double ladder.

We climbed onwards past the popcorn field and over the flat expanse of the football field. The breeze from the Cwm rapidly cooled the hands as they pulsated to maintain some warmth and some control over the ropes. As we passed the blood-stained crevasse, the same sickening emotions came flooding back with the thought of the unknown accident, and then soon enough after the testing rolling banks of ice, we were standing at our camp one. This was the first time that Becky or I had seen the destruction from the avalanche only a few days previously. Many tents, including our own were ruined and far beyond any form of repair. Bent poles were splayed from all corners of the flapping material which gently rippled in the breeze. The avalanche itself had not caused this destruction though, this was simply the rush of wind caused by the falling snow and ice; if the camp had been hit directly, there would be nothing left to see.

This was certainly not the place to linger, and having already taken our crampons off on a spot of relative safety at the top of the icefall, we were keen to keep pushing on to camp two. Even with the addition of only 1kg, I could feel the added weight of my rucksack pushing down on me, making every vital breath so much harder. I soon began lagging behind the other two, and could only make my own pace which had to be a continual methodical plod; only that would get me to camp two.

Sure enough, 45 minutes after Rob had made camp two, I struggled up the final rocks to the mess tent where I could only drop my bag and collapse onto the nearest stone seat. It had been a hard slog, but I knew that we would be resting the following day which meant I would be able to regain my strength for the climb to camp three. We met Mollie, Roger, Rick and Ryan at camp two, who began to tell us of their struggle up to camp three using the old route which was in the process of being replaced by the much less direct and therefore less dangerous route. It had been extremely cold and dangerously windy when they had made their climb and had needed almost full summit clothing to avoid getting frostbite or hypothermia when exposed high on the face. Their tale sounded ominous, and I was glad that we would be attempting a different route which would hopefully offer more shelter from the winds that they experienced. Sometimes it can be the wind that is one of the greatest dangers on the mountain. In extreme cases, the wind rapidly accelerates the cooling effect, also known as wind chill which at 60mph can lower a temperature of -26 degrees Celsius to -40 degrees Celsius. Becoming exposed to this level of cold, especially when unprepared can lead to clouding of judgement as everything is consumed by the relentless buffeting of the wind which isn't exactly the most welcoming form of weather.

The following day, we rested alone at camp two, looking up to the Sherpas who were busy high on the face protecting the new route, and also hacking out platforms so that more tents could be sited at camp three. It was amazing to watch such small workers moving like ants, and to think that tomorrow those small figures would be us if we had the go ahead to make the climb, and judging by the sight of the climbers and the radio conversations that were taking place, it sounded very promising that the new route was on the verge of being fixed.

Waking up on the 3rd May, we had an early breakfast and then made good progress to the base of the fixed ropes. The route was low in profile up until the base of the face, so except for a minor detour across a possible crevasse field in an effort to find the start of the new route up the face, everything was smoothly going to plan. We geared up near the base of the wall, watching how other climbers coped with the conditions on the first section. Like the old route, the first section was steep, almost vertical in places, but that was as technical as the route would get, the rest would just be a case of endurance and stamina to reach the camp. As we moved up to take our turn on the ropes, we stood directly under the face and realised just why the previous climbers had taken so long. This wasn't a wall designed to accommodate sloppy high altitude boots, this was a sheer ice wall which would have measured Scottish grade IV/V for its vertical nature and exposure.

The only way to climb this wall with no ice axe though was to heave up on the jumar and kick in as much as possible into the bullet hard ice. With each kick, another few inches could be gained until the other foot found a relatively undisturbed looking sheet of ice. When enough height had been gained, the jumar could be pulled up and then used as leverage to haul up just enough inches so that progress was gained. This first section was by far the most physically challenging piece of climbing; however from the top, the challenges became more psychological as turn after turn led to tough slopes that while shallower in gradient than the initial wall, were still steep enough to reduce the pace to a slow and demoralising plod. This carried on for several hours over terrain which blocked out the view ahead to the extent that camp three could not be seen until we were standing right beside it. Mentally this was incredibly tough, just climbing for an unknown goal, but when we did finally cross the lip of the final ice formation, the sight of camp three was enough to make the previous hours of climbing worthwhile.

As our tents hadn't quite been placed at camp three, we opened up another team's tent and after checking that no one was inside, we carefully sat in the entrance with the whole of the Western Cwm at our feet. We had to make no sudden movements for fear of snagging our crampons on the new tent fabric, and after finding the optimum position for all three of us in the doorway, we gained just enough shelter from the raging wind outside to allow us a chance to regain some strength for the march back down. Despite all the odds during the previous weeks of the expedition and even in the final stages of acquiring funding before I knew whether the expedition would be going ahead or not, we had made camp three on Everest which was the final stage of acclimatisation. From this point on, we would go down the mountain and along the valley as low as possible to await the weather window which hadn't yet reared its head. This was a significant milestone in the expedition, and we would only achieve a higher altitude on our way to the summit if everything came together. I also felt relieved since we were now higher than the summit of Baruntse, and I was certainly feeling more energetic now than before; clearly our acclimatisation plan was working which filled me with great confidence. For now though, it looked like we would need to head down the mountain as soon as possible since the wind was dropping and heavy clouds looked to be moving in.

We headed back down the same way that we had ascended. Although the older route would have been a much quicker and direct route to follow, it was still dangerous to use the route that was exposed to falling debris from above and which still hadn't received any snowfall to hold everything in place. The descent we were taking was still a relatively quick way down the mountain however, and soon enough, we were on familiar ground. Arm wrapping is one of the quicker techniques for descending where the rope is wrapped around the arm a few times and acts like a belay device, however it is also a tiring technique when there are many metres of fixed ropes still to descend. Once we reached the end of these ropes, we reached the top of the final ice wall which was far too steep to arm wrap unless you possessed the strength and high altitude ability of a Sherpa who made the face look almost tame by running down it head first. At this point, most of the Western Cwm had vanished into thick cloud which was steadily making its way to the base of the face. We hoped to find our way onto the proper track where crampon marks were visible as this meant avoiding any hidden crevasses or getting lost in the approaching fog. In the morning, we had had trouble finding the path to the new route simply because it was less than a day old, and so only a handful of people had used the new track which didn't leave enough crampon holes to allow the new route to stand out from the snowy landscape.

We hurried to the base of the steep ice wall after abseiling down the two fixed ropes which were fixed in place with a number of ice screws and intricate Abalakov threads, and then watched as the greyness in front of us turned into a full whiteout. There was nothing to see but the whiteness all around, an incredibly disorientating feeling which without a compass or some physical track to follow, can quickly lead from you being 'temporarily displaced' to completely lost. I had experienced whiteouts on a number of occasions including a particularly bad experience on Pillar in the UK Lake District where we had set out from the summit and descended completely the wrong way, and once out from the base of the whiteout and we had some features to navigate by, we quickly realised that we had also descended into the wrong valley which goes some way in showing how disorientating a whiteout can be even on smaller mountains.

On Everest however, aside from getting completely lost, there is also the very real possibility of unknowingly walking over a weak snow bridge and falling into a crevasse which without a rope, usually ends up being a fatal mistake. So far though, we had managed to find and follow the small path created by a dozen crampon-wearing climbers walking over the same route. We were clearly descending, and even if we couldn't see it, our altimeters confirmed the drop in altitude. As we followed the trail for some time, it gradually started to fizzle out into nothing, perhaps covered by light snowfall or simply shrouded by the bad light. We were now in potentially lethal terrain, all three of us travelling over a possible crevasse field. As we inched our way over seemingly untouched ground, we saw the distinctive signs of potential crevasses close by such as depressed areas of snow and lengthy cracks running parallel to the bergschrund at the base of the Lhotse Face. We clearly needed a rope, but since we had travelled as light as possible and weren't expecting to navigate over too much unprotected glaciated terrain, we were without and struggling to inch our way over to the old path which we could just see through the dense cloud.

By some miracle, we had missed all the crevasses on the Western Cwm and were very relieved to see the top of camp two poking out of the cloud still many metres below. It had been a lesson learnt, and although none of us fell into a crevasse that time, you can never be certain what is exactly below your feet and how deep the snow really is that you are standing on. Although we hoped that the same situation wouldn't arise again, we would certainly have to be prepared because with the number of uncharted crevasses in the Cwm and the route that we had taken, we had been lucky.

It had taken eight hours to ascend to camp three and then make our way gingerly back to camp two, sometime also called ABC or Advanced Base Camp due to the provisions and logistics established at the camp. As so much time had been spent on the descent, it was now 4pm and we still hadn't eaten since breakfast at 7am, so a late lunch of Rara Noodles was prepared by the cooks at camp two, and we sat and ate in silence, wondering how much differently the day could have ended, and also about the prospect of walking out from the mountain back to Pangboche to soak up the thick and refreshing mountain air which would give us all we needed to regain our strength for the final push, hopefully for the summit.

Chapter 48 – In the Search for Oxygen

Often one of the things that goes unnoticed by many expedition climbers is the ability of the cooks in high places. On Baruntse, the quality of the cooking by Surendra and his team was mind-blowing and the ability to produce a whole range of foods including full sized cakes in a pressure cooker was simply astounding. Everest camp two at 6,500m in the Western Cwm is potentially one of the most difficult places in the world where Sherpas have to prepare and serve edible food to hungry climbers, and their skill was again superb, surpassing many western trained chefs with their adaptability and creativity. It is often hard enough to cook at sea level, but when at high altitude where at certain levels you could comfortably place your hand in boiling water, a pressure cooker is the only method of cooking food sufficiently when the atmospheric pressure around you prevents any form of open air cooking at all. This limitation to a simple pressure cooker is again what sets these high altitude chefs apart.

On the evening before our descent to base camp, we were joined by Kenton and Keith, and together, the five of us were treated to some of the best homemade pizza we'd ever tasted, and for dessert, we were given a pastry-covered Mars Bar which was supposedly marginally healthier than a battered one. This surprise treat at the end of our meal more than made up for many days of cold tinned fruit which finished off most meals at base camp.

After our enormous meals, we woke up at the pleasantly late time of 8am and had a leisurely breakfast whilst enjoying the warmer temperatures than we normally saw when we woke up between 4am and 6am, before the sun had had any chance to take the sting out of the oppressive cold. Henry would rightly want us to have left camp two as soon as possible so that we could move through the icefall before the sun started to heat the ice, making it even more unstable than it inherently was. Not in any mood to rush though, Rob radioed Henry to notify him of our superb progress as low down as camp one whilst we were still enjoying the luxuries of camp two. We did finally manage to pull ourselves together though, and by 9:20 we had left the rocky shores of camp two and made quick time to camp one, but not stopping to wait for any potential avalanche to hit us, and instead carrying on straight through the icefall as fast as we were able to move. By the time we reached the final never-ending section at the base of the icefall, I was completely drained, and could only haul my aching body slowly over the unstable rocks of base camp before finally collapsing in my tent, just in time for lunch. We would spend the rest of the day resting and then discussing the elusive weather window which just happened to fall on my birthday in three days' time. The only problem with this though, apart from the fact that we had only just come down from our final acclimatisation climb, was that the route to the summit still hadn't been fixed due to high winds up on the exposed slopes of the mountain. This was something of a relief as I wasn't sure I could physically backup another climb up the mountain which would mean going back to camp two the same night if we were going to hit the summit right on the weather window.

Unfortunately for some who had already completed their final acclimatisation push on the mountain several days earlier, it looked like there would be around a ten-day wait before a summit push could be realistically made, as the deteriorating weather window in three days would likely put paid to any serious effort. What this did mean for a few of us, however, was that we had unknowingly made a great acclimatisation push just at the right time, and we now had the chance to move down the valley where we could rest for a few days before returning for the first proper weather window. This also gave some breathing space where we could completely switch off from the mountain, and then start to rethink about strategies and prepare the mind for what it would have to deal with much closer to the time.

After this dilemma which was now in the hands of Henry and the mountain gods, we all got some much needed rest and prepared to move down the mountain on the 8th May in four days' time. We also managed to have our latest nights on the mountain so far, and at the party hour of 10:30pm, we all piled out of the mess tent to quickly stare at the stars and then head to our own small tents once we realised how bitterly cold it was without the protection of the mess tent gas fire.

A full rest day followed which gave us all a chance to update everyone at home, and update our diaries which were far too heavy to be carried up onto the mountain. The day after we had spent the evening socialising, we were clearly getting into bad habits, finally stumbling into bed at 11:40pm.

On the 7th May, as it has been each year, it just happened to be my birthday, and on waking up, one of the strangest days unfolded. As it was technically a rest day, there was really nothing to do, so a fair proportion of the day was spent in our tents where I had the chance to once again call home and give them the good news that I had aged a year since they last saw me. Of course, spending your birthday at 5,400m above sea level in amongst a rock moonscape under the watchful eye of Everest isn't the way most 22-year-olds spend that special day, and I wondered if in fact anyone spent their 22nd birthday in such a place. As the day wore on, the evening arrived and soon enough everyone emerged from their tents after the days slumber where we enjoyed a dinner finished off with an amazing birthday cake adorned with many mini eggs around the side. It was amazing that Mum had been able to contact base camp to make such a request, and just as amazing that Bhim the head cook was able to fulfil it. A bottle of rum was also a welcome gift from the Sherpas which was enjoyed by everyone present in varying forms, from a straight swig to a rum-hot chocolate mix; definitely a heady concoction at the dizzying heights of base camp.

Our 11:40pm record was certainly broken that night, and in the early hours of the next morning, we headed back to our small tents once again, warmed with the thought of descending from the mountain tomorrow and a belly full of rum.

Spending my birthday in the mountains certainly wasn't something I had thought too much about, but to spend the day under the shadow of Everest, it felt right that I would share that day with the mountain which I would try to summit in a matter of days. It was now time though to head down the mountain in search of thicker air, specifically the air that resides in Pangboche which has the ideal combination of altitude and distance from base camp to allow a reasonable recovery. From Sonam Lodge where we would be staying, the tip of Mount Everest could also be seen, and after the first few days of trying to forget all about the stresses to come, this sight would provide the perfect motivation for the dreaded march back to base camp. Mollie, Becky and I had packed enough clothes and equipment for the six-hour walk down the valley, and at 10am we were ready to leave. All we had to do was to wait for Rob to give Becky some stitches for a deep laceration in the hand and then we could leave. As with everything at altitude though, things take ten times longer than they ordinarily would at sea level so after forgetting to tell the cook team that we were planning to leave before lunch, we obligingly sat for a quick lunch and then finally left for Pangboche just before 1pm.

During these last few days after coming down the mountain, there had been widespread rumours about the state of the Himex team led by Russel Brice who was still aiming to get a number of injured servicemen to the summit of Everest. We had heard previously that they were unhappy with the state of the icefall and that they were contemplating their next move, but as we left Everest base camp, we were shocked to hear that the final decision to walk away from the mountain had been made. Regardless of the motive for making the final decision, it seemed that there was no coming back to the mountain to carry on, and so many people lost their dream to climb Everest, for 2012 at least but as they say, the mountain will be there to climb for some time yet.

As we walked out of base camp, we could see the Himex camp at the lonely end of base camp, free of any commotion and eerily quiet. There was no one to be seen, perhaps unsurprisingly after the hammer blow that they had all received. At base camp itself, speculation was running wild and the media back home jumped onto the idea that as the Himex team had stated, the mountain was too difficult to climb this year. The speculation, however, ran in the opposite direction, suggesting that either the team had doubts about the feasibility and safety of getting injured servicemen to the summit, whether it was due to the relative inexperience of the Himex team on the south side of Everest compared to many other expedition outfitters, or maybe a combination of factors. Although this decision had very little effect on the decisions of other teams, it left many with the phone call back home to calm worried family and friends who had been led to believe that everyone still on the mountain would be climbing to their deaths; something that was clearly not the case.

We ambled down the valley back through the far reaching outposts of Gorak Shep and Lobuche whilst discussing the recent events. Seeing things from a different perspective, we felt sorry for all the climbers who were now facing the gut-wrenching decision of having to travel home empty handed. Hoping this wouldn't give any clues as to our own future on the mountain, we reached Pangboche in the fading twilight and were immediately relaxed by the homely feel of Sonam Lodge which gave a respite from the unfurling events at base camp. At the lodge, we met Bonita who gave a running commentary about the location of the rest of the climbers on our expedition who had descended a day earlier, but had opted for the more westernised Namche rather than the tranquillity of Pangboche.

As I got into my makeshift wooden bed that night after the delight of yet another pizza for dinner, I could almost taste the air which was so much thicker than that at base camp. This was of course my mind playing tricks on me, but there was something reassuring about the air at this level compared to the thin atmosphere high on the Lhotse Face which felt so sparse in comparison. Whatever the unlimited supply of oxygen was doing to me, I knew that coming down to this comparatively low altitude was going to give us the best chance of reaching the summit, and for the first time in weeks, I felt strong again.

Despite being blessed with the opportunity to wake up at whatever time we liked, the worn in routine of waking up early followed us down the mountain. It also seemed that the more we descended, the greater our appetites became. I was initially worried that I had caught another illness with a feeling of extreme hunger, but after seeing what everyone else had ordered for breakfast, it was clear that everyone was nursing an increased appetite. Almost instantly after receiving breakfast, we had ordered brunch and even placed our order for lunch with a specific time of 12:30 to ensure that we could make it through the day without starving. This period of intense hunger lasted for the whole period of time that we were at lower altitudes, and gave us an indication that our bodies were taking every opportunity they could to repair all the damage that had been inflicted by the rarefied atmosphere at around 7,400m at camp three; all we could do was to put fuel in the fire and rest our weary bodies for the final push.

The day after we arrived at Pangboche, we happened to meet Mike, a pilot from New Zealand who had been guiding some of his fellow aviators to Everest base camp. Whilst on the way back however, he decided to go for a quick run and after checking his GPS device, it appeared that he had run the highest ever marathon at an average altitude of well over 4,000m. Mike had also summited Everest previously with Henry's team and so we relived some of his experiences about what was still in store for us which was both reassuring and in some ways slightly terrifying since none of us would have contemplated running a marathon at such an altitude.

From my experience, running a marathon at sea level is definitely hard enough.

Rob and Paul also turned up on this day and with a dining room full of aviation staff all crying out for someone to play *Top Gun* on the TV, the atmosphere was just the distraction away from the mountains that we needed without having to trek down to Namche to pay another visit to the local bar which by all accounts was still living off the profit made by a certain Baruntse expedition the previous autumn.

Altogether we would have a total of three full days at Pangboche, which would turn out to be the perfect amount of time before we wanted to be back at base camp to finish off what we had ultimately come to Nepal to do. During the rest of our time in Pangboche, we competed in the 'Everest Olympics' where the main events were Ultimate Frisbee and a series of dead hang pull-ups, and I also had a chance to visit Nuru, my Sirdar from the Baruntse expedition. I was delighted to see him again and he too was happy to hear how the rest of the Baruntse team were doing. I also heard that Sonam and Dawa, the two Sherpas from Baruntse were working on Everest but on the north side from Tibet; I pondered the possibility of seeing them at the summit which would be a fitting reunion to see these two great Sherpas again at the top of the world. Nuru himself was preparing to leave for Gasherbrum I (one of a group of peaks known as the Gasherbrums in Pakistan) in a matter of days, and this went some way in revealing the lives of some of the Sherpas from Pangboche and indeed many other regions. Unlike western climbers who train for years on end to attempt a solitary peak, climbing big mountains back to back is the way of life for the Sherpas, and their strength and love for the mountains can only be admired.

Chapter 49 – A Matter of Numbers

As we left Pangboche on the 12th May, we walked up the now familiar Everest trail for the last time on this expedition. There would be no more Pangboche to Everest base camp as far as Everest 2012 was concerned once we had made this journey, and the next time we saw Pangboche again, we hoped it would be with memories of the summit of Everest at the front of our minds.

I started the long trek back to base camp with Mollie and Becky after we had previously discussed how long we wanted the walk back to take. Paul and Rob had come to the conclusion that they would like to do the walk in a single day to maximise their time at Pangboche, and whilst this was doable by all the expedition members, we decided against the single day approach, and instead opted to take two leisurely days getting back to base camp which would hopefully eliminate any pressure or further stress on top of what we were about to go through. Soon after leaving, we realised that this was a good plan, and after becoming temporarily misplaced along a nameless river valley and then hitting the steep hill below Thukla, we decided to call it a day and enjoy another humongous pizza and to rest our eyes before the final part of the walk to base camp was completed the next day. As we moved higher up the valley the following day, we started to see lone figures coming towards us wearing bright white t-shirts. Some of these figures were running, and others were merely ambling along with the flow, but they all had a definite purpose: to get as far away from Everest as quickly as possible. As these figures came nearer, we could see from the lack of various functioning limbs that these were indeed members of the Climbing With The Wounded team who were moving away from Everest. It was a sad sight to see, but made more bearable by the servicemen's greeting as they headed down the valley; although they were hurting, they were clearly gracious in defeat.

We made base camp on the 13th May, and according to the latest weather reports, we had six days before the summit push could be made. All the teams at base camp were aware of this weather system, and so it was destined to be a busy few days on the hill judging by the number of tents now amassed at base camp. Henry decided to show us the intricacies of the oxygen system in the afternoon which proved to be a comprehensive lesson in how to operate the apparatus once high on the mountain. Although the principles and methods of operation were relatively simple, it was important that everyone knew the ins and outs of their system before heading onto the mountain where there might be no Sherpa around to help with a problem. Later this day, we also realised the length of the discussions which had taken place to see who would be going up on the mountain in the first push. There was simply not enough equipment or Sherpa support to have the whole team go for the summit in one large push, so some tense moments followed when the eventual teams were decided amongst Henry and the Sherpa team.

I happened to be one of the lucky ones by virtue of the fact that Rob's team was going first. Eventually we found out that for the first summit push, the team would be Rob, Rick, Valerie, Mollie, Becky and me. After this decision had been made, there really was no turning back; we would be going for the summit.

During the final rest day at base camp, I enjoyed the luxury of a final shower, and then proceeded to get together everything that I would need for a summit push including my oxygen mask, my down suit, my large mitts and bulletproof high altitude boots which were ironically starting to fall apart after all the use they had seen throughout the Himalayas. In my bag, I tried to fit everything in, knowing full well that I would have to carry the whole lot up to camp three as a minimum, and gradually start dumping kit as I progressed up to camp four, where I would hopefully set out for the summit with an almost empty rucksack filled only with an oxygen bottle, some spare mitts and a few personal items. I also had to fit in my sponsor flag from Hibu, the eventual rebranding of Yell, which I would aim to fly from the summit if we were successful. I was initially worried about the prospect of taking the flag to the summit since it was delivered to base camp in a huge cardboard tube standing 3m tall, but fortunately, apart from one flag and a backup, 99% of the space was taken up by bubble wrap and air, clearly doing a great job of protecting a small piece of cloth.

Two last items went into my rucksack; firstly one of my Khata scarves from the growing collection in my tent, and lastly, three letters which I would take up with me, but I had no intention of reading them; instead they would stay in the back of my rucksack and it was simply enough to know that they were there, ready to be read if the worst happened.

As I was in the middle of packing, I was also properly introduced to my own personal Sherpa who would be with me most of the way from camp three to the South Col, and then by my side every step of the way from camp four to the summit and then back to base camp. Chhewang Dorjee was my Sherpa, and together, we would become brothers bonded by an unforgettable experience, either way.

This was a special evening for our team who would be leaving early the following morning, so special in fact that after dinner we were joined by Henry who accompanied us whilst we watched the film *True Grit*. The film's title alone had enough metaphors to satisfy the whole climbing team and the goal that we were about to set out to achieve. True grit was exactly what we would need to be able to brave whatever weather and conditions that we might experience high on the mountain, both to reach the summit, and also make it down alive without succumbing to summit fever. Often described in high octane tales where an expedition has gone so wrong, summit fever is a phenomenon which compels climbers to continue to the summit at all costs, including the ultimate price of both their own lives and also potentially climbers around them. This mentality is fundamentally wrong, being both dangerous and selfish. Instead of adopting the summit fever, we would approach the mountain as we saw the conditions in front of us, and if that meant abandoning the summit in order to keep our lives, then so be it. As the famous Everest climber Ed Viesturs had once said, "Getting to the summit is optional. Getting down is mandatory". We intended to stick by this fundamental rule.

The final thing I did that night was call home; I wanted to tell Mum I loved her and that I would be as safe as I could possibly be in such a place. I hadn't expected to make this phone call but it seemed the right thing to do at the time. Before, although I had realised a little bit of what a summit push on Everest meant, I was only just beginning to see the importance of what it all really meant and how big this really was.

Chapter 50 – The First Push

On the 15th of May 2012, I woke up to the freezing cold of 3:45am. The tent was covered in ice and any water containers were frozen solid as they always were at night. I quickly got dressed into my icefall gear, big down jacket and thick mitts to keep my hands as warm as possible in the polar-like air. I headed to the kitchen tent wearing my big boots which clunked up the same deceptive slope which even after all the climbing we had done, never seemed any easier. Once in the slightly warmer air of the covered kitchen tent, I met our climbing team plus Roger and Paul who had come to wave us off up the mountain, an incredibly kind gesture considering the allure of a warm sleeping bag and the realisation that they would have to wait around another week before they would be given an opportunity to climb the mountain.

The routine was always the same, get enough food inside to last for the duration of the climb up the ice fall, and enough fluids so that once the sun started to cook the Western Cwm, dehydration wouldn't be allowed to creep up. Once more, Bhim the ever smiling cook at base camp ushered us out of the rock-walled kitchen with its tarpaulin roof and over to the puja altar where for the third time before moving to the icefall we threw a handful of rice and prayed for safe passage. This time it didn't matter whether you were a theist or an atheist, this time, we truly needed all the luck and help we could get.

As a team, we carefully made our way over the moonscape that is base camp, and after Rick got over the horror of forgetting his helmet, we made our way to crampon point at the base of the icefall where we would begin the process of gearing up, a skill that was now well and truly automatic. Padawa was climbing with Valerie as her personal Sherpa from base camp upwards, just as he had done for the whole expedition. He also managed to spot Rick's helmet and brought it along on the off chance that someone might need it or that he could possibly barter a yak in exchange. After gearing up and putting on our big mitts to fight off the intense cold, we started up into the icefall which as usual gave sweet crunching sounds as our crampon points bit into the bullet hard surface. Pressure cracks sometimes shot across a sheet of ice, but these were the only noises we heard. As we slowly got warmed up and into the climb, no one spoke.

This climb of the icefall was just as it had been every other time we had dared venture into such a place, but this time, something was different, another element had been added to the equation. This time, it really did matter, the pressure of what lay on our shoulders was overwhelming and climbing up each ice pitch and across each ladder, we all knew that this time it was for real, we were intentionally climbing our way towards the death zone, slowly but surely.

I looked up to the left of us, and high above was the perching serac which looked ominous and ready to pounce on unsuspecting climbers at any moment. This serac sits upon Everest's West Shoulder which had been renamed Russell's Shoulder after the Himex team abandoned their expedition, citing this piece of unstable snow and ice as one of the major risk factors.

Through the icefall I was strong. Aided by the rest down in the valley surrounded by thicker air, I was now more than keeping up with the group and for the first time, found the icefall strangely enjoyable. It was still tough though, and I couldn't afford to become complacent, I had to make sure I paced myself in order that I would get to camp two in better shape than I had done previously, although I knew we would have a rest day at camp two which would both give us the final preparation for the summit push and give us all a rest from a tiring climb from base camp, this was still a climb which never seemed to get any easier. This may or may not have been wholly or partly due to the fact that camp two always remained at the same altitude, as did base camp, and that the distance between the two camps never changed, giving strong evidence as to why the same climb, conducted at the same pace, with the same altitude gain and up the same glacier never got any easier.

At the top of the icefall, we decided that we would keep moving and then take dubious shelter in our old camp one location which we deemed a little safer than the previous time and would give us just a few moments to recover from the icefall, change out of our warm clothes and apply sun cream before moving on. At this point at the top of the icefall, I was showing signs of fatigue, and once onto the rolling ice bank section, my speed dropped from a gentle plod to one step one breath. All too quickly I was showing the same signs as I had done every time I had previously been into the icefall, and I was certain that at each time, I was carrying too much weight on my shoulders rather than my hips which is the best place for carrying a rucksack load. I clearly was just the wrong size for the bag and even with slight changes in weight, my performance was directly affected, just like it had been all those months ago on Baruntse. As I stumbled my way into camp one, I was relieved to see that Mollie, Rob and Becky had taken shelter in a tent which clearly meant we were stopping for just a bit. I took my bag off hoping that my breathing would improve, but suddenly, I was finding it so difficult to breathe, I thought I might suffocate.

I had never been diagnosed as having asthma before, but here I was, sitting at camp one struggling to breathe and unknown to me, in desperate need of an asthma inhaler. Fortunately Becky had one and after two doses, I could feel my chest and airways begin to open as if by magic. I had never previously used an inhaler for asthma, and it seemed a strange time that I would develop the condition whilst at camp one on Everest, but I guessed there was really no great time to develop asthma.

Once I had recovered just enough to keep moving, we cracked on; this time I was leading the pace to make sure I didn't get left behind somewhere in the Cwm waiting for the magic answer to help me reach camp two without losing the ability to breathe. As I plodded on, I tried to get into my rhythm as best as possible whilst trying to keep the shoulder straps from compressing my shoulders and forcing me back into the shallow breathing pattern which had been my downfall at the top of the icefall. As we crossed over the final ladder on the Cwm, there was really no need to wait for anyone as camp two could now be seen all that distance away, and to prevent any major catastrophes should half of Everest, Lhotse or even Nuptse slide off again, we would continue the walk at our own pace. For Rob, this meant arriving in camp two in around an hour, a little more for the girls who didn't seem to be struggling under the weight of their bags, possibly the same for Rick, and then for me, well, who knew, it could be an hour, it could be five, no one was really certain.

The monotonous plodding continued for what seemed like hours, and eventually I lost sight of Mollie and Becky in front of me. I really was alone now in the Cwm, I couldn't see anyone ahead of me, and behind me any remaining climbers on their way to camp two seemed to still be in the icefall. It was a time of mind over matter. I knew that as long as my feet kept moving, I would eventually reach camp two, all I had to do was keep putting one foot in front of the other; such a simple task when thought about from the comfort of an armchair at sea level.

More time seemed to pass and with every passing minute, the icefall was getting hotter. Every step was becoming harder as energy and what felt like life itself was literally being sucked away from me. And then I heard it. A crack somewhere, up on a face, almost deafening and sickening in its audacity to happen. But where was it? I hadn't looked behind me for a while but a Sherpa was standing there, looking at me, motionless. He too had heard that horrible nauseating sound. I looked ahead and from my elevated position I could see the two girls, first sitting on their rucksacks, and then rapidly standing up in horror of what they heard.

Something in the distance drew my gaze. It was ahead, on the right hand wall of Nuptse, I stared at the wall as did the Sherpa standing next to me, and as we stood there, the rocks on Nuptse vanished into a cloud that was building and gaining momentum. An avalanche, once again from the north face of Nuptse, was building in intensity. It started as a small, invisible crack jutting horizontally across the face, and soon after, the face itself began to slide as snow hurled down the mountain with a thunderous roar. I could only stand and gasp, rooted to the spot, not believing what I was actually seeing. The avalanche was up the Cwm from me, but it looked enormous and horrifyingly, it was moving straight in the direction of Mollie and Becky who I could still see. They too were staring in disbelief, but then that changed to urgency which I could see even from my distant position. They both threw down their bags and ran for the shelter of a snow bank that might just protect them from any debris that was coming their way.

As I stood where I was, wondering what I was going to do if an avalanche wall reached me, I could think of nothing. There was nothing around me that would prove at all useful, and apart from a crevasse that was far too narrow for me to fit down and then be able to squeeze out of again, the ground all around me was featureless.

The avalanche wave started its gallop towards us down the Cwm, first in the direction of the girls, then in the direction of me and the mystery Sherpa. It seemed though that as soon as the avalanche hit the more level ground of the Cwm, it could not maintain its momentum, and no sooner than had it began than it was fizzling itself out into a spindrift cloud as a small reminder of the power of the mountains.

Once again, we had all been so lucky. Had the avalanche happened on the South West Face of Everest to our left, the situation could have been very different. But fortunately for all involved, neither this avalanche nor the next avalanche which occurred closer to the icefall reached us. Now more than anything, I wanted to be out of the danger zone and into the relative safety of camp two. I set off again, and although still not at a great pace, I was more than ready to finish the climb alive, and as I had begun to realise, nothing motivates you more than a wall of snow and ice hurtling towards you.

After all this excitement on the Cwm, I was happy to finally turn the corner into camp two. I was behind a big snow bank and effectively safe from most dangers of any incoming avalanches but I still had another 40 minutes before I could collapse into the mess tent. I knew I was absolutely crawling towards the camp; I was utterly exhausted and could find no let up from the agony regardless of what position I tried to climb in. After one step, perhaps two at most, my hands would fall to my knees to stop me keeling over as I took as many breaths as I could before I could count to 30. This perhaps wasn't the quickest way to reach camp two, but just like before, as long as I kept moving, I would get to the camp eventually.

Crawling up the final rocky slope, I was greeted by Pasang Temba who I was extremely happy to see since this meant I had made it, despite taking eight hours from base camp and around two hours after Rob had made camp two. I dumped my bag as soon as I possibly could, ripped off my crampons and then collapsed into the mess tent. I was in another world, not quite conscious enough to even contemplate the plate of food that Pasang Temba had cooked for me.

Despite all this pain, by the evening, I had almost completely recovered from the day's effort. Like everyone else, I had spent the afternoon snoozing in the heat of the tent in an effort to regain some of my strength so that I could contemplate getting back out into the cold and being in a fit state to eat dinner. Mentally the climb from base camp had been thoroughly draining, but even before leaving I had expected this to be the case, and as long as I had a full rest day at camp two, I would be fine to continue up to camp three. Everyone has a bad day on an expedition or a bad section of climbing, and for me, through the icefall from base camp to camp one or two was never good.

That night I slept straight through which was a great sign after many previous attempts to sleep at camp two had proved futile. The 16th of May was spent as a full rest day at camp two to everyone's delight which meant a lazy breakfast, a lazy lunch, and dinner at whatever time you entered the mess tent. In between these meals, time was spent dozing in our own tents with the comfort of our sleeping bags and sleeping mats. We had all perfected the art of resting and essentially counting the hours by, and this was the perfect thing to do before a big trip up a big mountain. You could not afford to allow any stress to sap vital energy; instead, lounging around in a sleeping bag that was so comfy it essentially hugged you seemed the best thing to do.

Again, another night was spent at camp two, and we knew that once we woke up the next morning and headed up to camp three, there would be no more rest days, from then on, our thoughts would be on the summit push.

Chapter 51 – The Lhotse Face

On the 17th May, we woke up early at camp two listening to the noise of radios sputtering a jumble of words. Everyone seemed to be talking and bustling around outside my tent, so something must have happened to make the people outside so chatty. When I managed to get dressed and put on my inner and outer boots once more, we were all briefed by Rob as to the situation high on the Lhotse Face. It seemed that a Sherpa who was at camp three had been caught by a falling serac and needed urgent medical attention. Being one of the only doctors in the near vicinity, Rob would have to climb up in front of us to help with the rescue and evacuation of the Sherpa, and then we would meet Rob at the base of the Lhotse Face once the evacuation had taken place.

It was quite a tense moment since we all knew that in a few hours, we would all be resting in our tents under the potentially lethal seracs of camp three. Even the Sherpas don't usually rest here, instead preferring to ascend early in the morning from camp two to camp three before the western climbers have woken up. It turned out that the falling serac had broken both of the Sherpa's legs and also one of his arms, and so climbing out of camp three for rescue certainly wasn't an option for him.

Due to this unexpected commotion on the face, we all left camp two later than planned with Padawa Sherpa leading the way to the base of the face. Since we were leaving much later than usual, the sun was fully hitting the upper sections of the Western Cwm and was making any form of climbing extremely difficult. Sweat mixed with sun cream constantly dripped in my eyes and the heat was exacerbating, compounded by the reflection of UV rays at us from all sides. We had put sun cream everywhere that had visible skin exposed. Even the insides of the nostrils had to be protected from the UV rays being reflected back up at us from the snow around our feet. On days like this, even the most unusual sun burns can occur such as sunburn on the roof of the mouth. Breathing cold air constantly through the nose is painful, and so opening the mouth to breathe can't always be helped, but this greatly increases the risk of burnt skin in the mouth which by all accounts makes eating and drinking extremely unpleasant.

As we climbed higher up the Cwm, we saw the unmistakable orange brace which was wrapped around the Sherpa being brought down the mountain by a team of guides and Sherpas. As he went by, we could see that he was wrapped in a sleeping bag and supported by the orange brace which would save him from further damage as he was dragged down the steep rough track.

We met Rob at the base of the ice wall, and in a group we all started to climb from the base of the wall in the direction of camp three. It had changed drastically since the previous time we had climbed it, and instead of sheer bullet-hard ice, the wall was now full of dents and boot holes from the amount of traffic the route had seen. The climb was much easier than before, but the volume of people now climbing to camp three slowed down everyone's progress. As we climbed higher, big chunks of ice came down from above as higher climbers hacked into the ice to propel themselves upwards. Then, as I reached the top and was given an opportunity to rest, a helicopter approached camp two down in the Western Cwm, and within moments, it was back into the air, skimming the Cwm and then it vanished in a cloud of snow over the lip of the icefall.

The climbing was much easier this time as we were all acclimatised, and the novelty of the queue of climbers above us slowed our progress meaning that we could effectively rest where we wanted, and as long as we kept up with the climber ahead of us, then the pace was more than manageable. As people started to slow down in front of us, we managed to overtake a few climbers and make our way directly to camp three. The route seemed much shorter than the previous time, and I hoped this was due to the fact that we were well acclimatised and on track for the summit, not just because someone had changed the position of camp three by a few hundred metres.

Rick was caught between a few climbers lower down than I was, and so I carried on, past the row of tents that we had used as shelter on the previous trip to camp three, and then along a flat section following Mollie and Becky who seemed to know where they were going. Camp three was deceptively large, mainly due to it being spread out taking full advantage of all the flattish areas of snow which were few and far between. As I carried on, the route narrowed revealing the true gradient of the slope, and then just ahead, I could see the distinctive figure of Chhewang Dorjee who was helping the rest of the Sherpas create our camp. They had come up to the camp earlier and on the same day, had hacked our ledge out from the side of the face and then erected our tents ready for us to get in once we arrived. This was just another show of the strength of the Sherpas who were a fundamental part in everything we did; without the Sherpas, we wouldn't have even left base camp.

As I reached the tent, I was helped by Chhewang who made sure I didn't fall off the side of the face whilst I took my crampons off and crawled into my tent. I tried to level everything out as best as I could inside and then got out my sleeping bag and mat whilst there was still some room to manoeuvre before Rick arrived. As soon as my mat was out, I just lay in the tent, feeling the effects of the altitude which was a signal to start slowing everything down. First position the mat, then rest, then get out the sleeping bag, then more rest. Rest was the key now since this would stop the heart rate from rising too much and would alleviate any bad reactions to being at high altitude. We were now effectively sleeping on the summit of Baruntse, and yet there was still another camp to go before we could even have a chance of getting to the summit of Everest. Each time we ascended to a new height, the task which lay before us was put into a new proportion which just went to show how high Everest really was. In numbers, 8,848m is quite simple, but it isn't really quantifiable in human terms. How can you imagine the height of Everest, even after looking at it from base camp or indeed another mountain? It is only when you start to get high on Everest itself that you begin to appreciate just what a challenge you have undertaken and how incomprehensible the forces must have been when Everest was created around 60 million years ago.

Once I had just about sorted the tent out, Rob came in looking for all our oxygen cylinders. I thought this was particularly strange since I couldn't see any in the tent, and being bright orange, they are quite hard to miss. But it turned out all the cylinders had been placed in the snow at the back of our tent, and it was now time to check them to see whether or not they worked. The good news was that after checking each one, they all had some oxygen in, but the bad news was that only a couple fitted the oxygen regulators that we had. This was clearly a problem as we would all be climbing on oxygen the following day, and so not being able to access any of the oxygen in the tank wouldn't prove to be very useful. It seemed that due to differing screw lengths, the good regulators which were made in Switzerland where everything is based around absolute precision didn't quite fit on the oxygen bottles, so an older type of regulator would be brought up to fix the problem whilst using the smaller oxygen cylinders to get us to the South Col. Once on the summit push though, we would be using large cylinders which meant we could have the precision of Swiss engineering when it really counted. With that, we piled the bottles back up trying to remember which ones fit and which ones didn't, and then closed up the door leaving the conundrum for the morning.

Once Rick had been able to negotiate his way past the queue of climbers and get his breath back outside the tent, we were ready to start organising the tent for a potentially long night at camp three. The reason for this uncertainty wasn't due to not knowing the length of time we would be physically spending at camp three, we would be leaving early the next morning regardless, but it would be the mental stress of spending time at camp three on oxygen that could make the night feel like an eternity. We had never slept on oxygen before, just like most people who attempt Everest for the first time. Although we knew how the oxygen system worked inside out, we didn't have any idea of what it would do to our bodies, or more specifically what it would feel like. Would it feel like we were on cloud 9, or would there be no identifiable change which would leave us confused as to what effect it would have on the summit climb? We really didn't have any idea.

When both Rick and I were sorted, it would soon be time to begin the lengthy process of eating and rehydrating before the long night commenced, but first, just as the rest of the group had done, it was time to test the oxygen supply. Because we would be on oxygen primarily when we were sleeping, we would only need one small cylinder between us which would be opened at a flow rate of 0.5L/min (litres per minute) which would be split between us, so each minute, we would be breathing 0.25L of pure oxygen mixed with the atmospheric oxygen around us.

Unlike diving cylinders which contain atmospheric air, the oxygen cylinders for climbing at high altitude contain pure oxygen operating in an open-circuit oxygen enrichment manner. The aim of the oxygen system is to allow the climber to breathe normal atmospheric air but with an added trickle of pure oxygen which is just enough to prevent dangerous levels of hypoxia and importantly, keeps the extremities warmer, preventing frostbite and allowing a better night's sleep at altitude. For Everest, a standard 4L bottle of oxygen is used, and when filled, around 1200L of compressed oxygen is squeezed in at 300Bar. For sleeping, between 0.5 and 1L/min flow rate is used, and so the cylinder will last for between 20 to 40 hours. When on the mountain, flow rates vary from 2L/min to 4L/min, and so one bottle will generally last for between five and ten hours. All these calculations were very easy at sea level, but once up on the mountain, it would be all too easy to get the numbers wrong, so everyone knew beforehand what sort of flow rate we should be on at each stage from camp three upwards.

Because we were new to this oxygen game, Rick and I first tried the oxygen at 1L/min but at this level, we couldn't really tell any difference, so being eager for something magical to happen, we turned the regulator to 6L/min and for a short period enjoyed the light-headedness that comes with such a high flow rate. We soon realised however that at this rate, the whole bottle would run out in just over three hours yet it was supposed to last us for the entire night, so quickly turned it back down to a more sensible level before turning the system off altogether to allow us to get on with our eating, drinking, rest and recovery.

Because our bags had seemed heavy on the previous few days due to all the food we had to haul up, we immediately decided to eat as much of the heavy food as possible, meaning that tomorrow, we would only have to carry up light energy bars and some cuppa soup sachets. The first thing to be devoured was a whole pack of Cherry Bakewells, and shortly after, a whole tube of Pringles vanished.

It is important to note at this stage just what a fantastic food source Pringles really are. Not only are they extremely light to carry and packed with essential goodness, the most important point to make about Pringles is the fact that they are completely caked in MSG. They are literally swimming in MSG, so much so that it wouldn't be physically possible to squeeze any more of this substance into a tube of Pringles if they tried. Monosodium glutamate is a type of salt which has many properties including that of enhancing certain food flavours, and importantly, inducing hunger. This property is a great asset for high altitude mountaineers since often one of the first things to suffer whilst camping at altitude is the appetite. With Pringles though, if you physically can't get anything else down, they are more than up to the job of revitalising your hunger and depositing some much needed energy along the way.

Whilst stuffing our faces, Rick and I then had the very tedious job of melting snow and ice for drinking water. This ongoing chore only stops once you go to sleep, so whilst awake, one person is always in charge of producing enough drinking water for both and ensuring that the tent doesn't burn down in the process, something I haven't always been reliable at.

This was the first time I had shared with Rick, and it was good to be able to talk over our thoughts for the climb ahead of us. I think we were both nervous about what was to come, since almost everything was unknown. We had both watched films and seen pictures of people climbing the southeast ridge of Everest, the same route we would be taking, but up until now, we couldn't place any of these images on the mountain. With anything taken through a camera, the scale is removed and it becomes hard to tell how steep or how exposed something really is. Whilst clothes may be seen to be flapping in the wind and some spindrift is being blown past the camera, it is difficult to imagine exactly what it would be like to be standing in those conditions, how cold and how extreme it really feels when not seen from the safety of the living room. We both talked about the rumours of large groups ascending the mountain and hoped that because we were in the first weather window, we would be ahead of the crowds. Rick had had to quit his job to fulfil his lifelong ambition of climbing Everest, and I had fought desperately hard to raise the necessary funds, but many people who were on Everest were there because they had a spare £40,000 lying around in some offshore bank account. They simply fancied the challenge of Everest, but perhaps didn't have the experience of others on the mountain who were as prepared as it was possible to be for such a challenge. Some others who were on the mountain had chosen their expedition organisers poorly, favouring the cheapness of a local company who lacked the more strict requirements of western based companies. We hoped that we wouldn't meet any of these groups on the mountain, as quite simply, they were dangerous.

As we chatted, the constant rise of steam from the melting snow and ice started to pour into the tent which was our signal that yet another pan full of water had started to boil and was ready for consumption. After it had been dispensed between us, I had a chance to check a cut on my finger which had been caused by a falling stone whilst we were walking along a river bed back to base camp. It had been quite a deep laceration but I had soon forgotten about it until my hand started to throb whilst trying to delicately pour water at camp three. I took the plaster off and to my horror the whole area around the cut looked rancid and didn't smell particularly great. There was still some grit under the flap of skin and it looked like the area was clearly infected. Being at altitude with a great reduction in oxygen, things like cuts simply don't heal and if left to their own devices, the area around any cut will eventually start to break down and go bad. Luckily Rick had some iodine tincture in his first aid kit which I carefully applied around the wound, and then covered in the hope that at least the finger wouldn't get any worse. As soon as I was able to descend to altitudes lower than base camp, the cut would begin to heal, but whilst nearing the death zone, the best I could do was to prevent any further infection.

I placed another lump of compressed snow in the pan and turned the gas up to full power. I put another in to fill the gaps and then noticed bits of colour on what was supposed to be white snow. I showed it to Rick and we were convinced that we were now about to melt yellow snow, not even contemplating that it might be the iodine from my finger which would add even more purification to the water. But in the haze of altitude, our brains were on half capacity, and so the snow was thrown down the Lhotse Face and the lengthy process of getting more water began again.

Everything goes slowly on the Lhotse Face. People climb slowly, people think slowly, making 1L of drinking water takes over an hour, and getting out to go to the toilet takes far too long. I was contemplating to myself whether I would need to go to the toilet, and whilst at any other time coming to an answer would be simple, on the Lhotse Face, to come to a decision is to overcome countless problems on incredibly low cognitive function. This was all part of personal administration, i.e. the ability to look after yourself without relying on anyone else unless absolutely necessary and I had decided that after seeing the trauma of Rick's toilet attempt, I would wait until we got to the flat ground of the South Col before exposing myself to the elements.

At 7,400m, water boils at just over 70 degrees Celsius, and so after heating our boil-in-the-bag meals for a full 15 minutes, as soon as the packets left the warmth of the water and were exposed to temperatures as low as -30 degrees Celsius, we were left with a less than an unappetising bag of stew and sausage. This was better than nothing though, and we knew that every bit of food that we could get down would be so much better for us than eating nothing at all. I found it strange that I was still so hungry since my appetite at high altitude usually vanishes, however this time, even before the Pringles were devoured, I found that I could eat whatever happened to be in front of me or within reasonable reach.

After dinner, we boiled one more pan full of water that we could use as a hot water bottle, and then hunkered down for the night. Snow was falling around the tent and the freezing condensation from the boiling water had jammed the outer zips up, so we shut the tent as best as possible, and then got into the best position for sleeping. The Sherpas had done a fantastic job at levelling out the camp and so we didn't have too many fears about the tent sliding down the mountain side, but there was always the fear in the back of our minds after the falling serac had injured the Sherpa so badly the same morning. This was made worse by the fact that we could see the debris of his tent right in front of ours, tent poles bent and broken, and torn fabric fluttering in the wind. We would have to forget this if we were going to stand any chance of sleeping, so the inner door was closed, the oxygen system was turned back on, and we then lay back hoping for the best possible night's sleep whilst the flutter of our oxygen mask valves opened and closed, sending a trickle of oxygen past our noses.

Sleeping that night didn't come naturally. We both had periods of wearing our masks, then periods without them in order to avoid the steady trickle of condensation from running down our necks. This was one of the hardest bits to get used to, and could only be dealt with by having an absorbent cloth or tissue handy to mop up pools of water as it formed around the seal of the mask. It would always be difficult to sleep with something on the face like a fighter pilot's mask for the first time, but the longer we persevered, the better off we would be when we got higher up the mountain. Eventually, at whatever hour, we both drifted off in a daze of hypoxia and nerves about what was to come. Neither of us knew for sure, but all we really did know is that it would almost certainly be the hardest thing we had ever done.

Chapter 52 – Get In Line

The sound of our alarms and movement outside of the tent marked the start. We had no idea at the time since the decision would only be made at camp four, but as it would unfold, once we awoke to the sound of our alarms at camp three, the summit push had begun. We would not sleep again for another 40 hours.

After we had put on another pan of water in the morning to fill our water bottles up, there was no time for a deeply sustaining breakfast; so instead, my breakfast consisted of not much more than a chocolate biscuit. After this small canapé, it was time to ditch everything that we wouldn't need higher on the mountain. This was mostly a bag of clothes that wouldn't be of much use higher up, but also anything heavy from our rucksacks that we could do without. People had already begun up the Lhotse Face, and now time was against us, we had to get ready fast. I put my down suit on with the intention of using it for its purpose for the first time. It felt amazing to wear such a garment of clothing, and for the first time, I felt like a proper Everest climber. My boots went on, then my gloves and protective layers, and then finally, my crampons went on. Dressed up to the nines, I was ready to greet Chhewang who was standing outside the tent ready to hand me my supply of oxygen and a regulator to fit the cylinder.

He helped me haul the bag onto my back, and then I stood there for a few moments, breathing a supply of oxygen with the intention of climbing for the first time. This was a morning of firsts, but none more so that the horror of seeing Rob going to the toilet. Completely out in the open, hundreds of climbers climbing right below him, a relatively severe drop at his feet, I couldn't quite believe what I was seeing, but this was the life of high altitude climbing, and like they say, if you've got to go, you've got to go. Earlier the same morning, both Mollie and Becky also had to go to the toilet in full view of gathering climbers who were on their way to the South Col. Fortunately none of these unsuspecting climbers lost their balance and fell off the face, but many of them could still be seen fleeing to the safety of the South Col some hours later.

As it was, I happened to be the first person from our group who was ready to start up the face. I had expected Rob to ask us to all stay together, but as soon as I was ready, Chhewang and I were off. It felt strange to be climbing with full summit gear including supplementary oxygen, and I couldn't tell if it was giving me any benefits at first, but then once my breathing had calmed down and I had persevered, I came to the conclusion that it must have been doing something, or at least it wasn't further impeding my ability to breathe, so I left the mask on to do whatever job it was doing.

Chhewang and I soon reached the fixed ropes just above camp three, and it became clear very quickly that we were at the back of one of the biggest queues I had ever seen. I hadn't seen this many people waiting in line for the Boxing Day sales, let alone on a mountain; for the second time that day, I couldn't quite believe what my eyes were seeing. Ahead of us was a line of people which stretched up high onto the face and had no visible start. The scene was incredible, hundreds of people stretched out in single file, all on one set of fixed lines. At the beginning, the pace was steady, even with so many people climbing the face at once. I was able to keep up with the climber ahead of me, and then have a rest when the pace stopped. Despite our progress though, it was simply not quick enough to reach camp four on the South Col, and so at every available opportunity, Chhewang and I would clip onto the adjacent descending rope and overtake as many people as possible before getting back into line and going with the flow. There was simply nothing that we could do except to go at the pace dictated by the climbers ahead of us. Every time that there was a chance to move around climbers ahead, we took it and gradually made up some ground, but it wasn't enough and I couldn't maintain the speed needed to overtake climbers who were still moving upwards.

When the pace slowed, it gave me a chance to see what the route was like ahead. The long line ahead of us suddenly branched to the left across the face, and then crossed the Yellow Band and eventually the Geneva Spur before going around a ridge and out of sight. It still looked like we had so far to go and yet I couldn't tell if we were making any decent progress or not. After 30 minutes of climbing, we passed the top tier of tents at camp three, and only then did I get the impression that we might not physically be able to make the South Col in time. We would keep going though and aim to pass as many climbers as possible before making any rash decisions.

This process carried on for many hours. For hour after hour, we climbed higher up the face, everyone following in line. Reaching higher up on the fixed line and near the branch left, I looked down the line behind me back the way I had just come from. The rest of the team were all close by now, and just as I couldn't see the start of the line at the top of the face, I could now no longer see the end of the line at the base of the face as people still kept pouring out of camp three with the South Col in their sights. Chhewang now left me on the face since I was in good company, and along with all our other Sherpas, he headed off to help prepare camp four for us. There was nothing more our Sherpas could do for us here, our pace was simply dictated to by the climbers in front of us.

The face itself was incredibly steep for its length. With each step, the body was hauled up to its new elevation, similar to a giant stepping machine. There would be perhaps two or three steps before the line would grind to a halt and the process of controlled breathing would start to control the panting induced by a few steps in quick succession. The aim was always to keep as much of the sole of the shoe in contact with the snow as possible and to avoid front pointing which is the act of balancing on the front two points of the crampons, an exhausting task for the calves.

Hours had passed since I had joined the long line up the Lhotse Face, but despite the slow monotonous pace, I knew we were getting somewhere since just ahead of me was the turn to the left that I had seen all those hours earlier. As I gradually reached the snow anchor that was securing the fixed lines to the face, I got ready to unclip my jumar and karabiner and make the transition to traverse over to the Yellow Band. Fortunately I managed to clip in properly and not fall down the sheer face, but looking at my oxygen line, I could see that things weren't working quite as well as they had done a few hours earlier. On the line which connects the regulator to the oxygen mask, there is a small gauge which flickers up and down according to the flow rate and lets you know that at least some oxygen is being passed into mask. My gauge wasn't really moving though; as much as I stared at it willing it to move again, nothing seemed to happen and I could feel myself desperately slowing down, perhaps psychologically due to the knowledge that my oxygen may have run out, or simply because something had gone wrong with the regulator and the flow had stopped, there may even have been a leak. I couldn't work it out for myself, and instead waited at the side of the rope allowing other climbers to pass me whilst I looked out for a team member. Becky came up to me and checked my regulator and saw that the flow rate was right down, clearly the reason that I was now struggling to breath, let alone walk. Becky went ahead and Rob came to check that everything was now okay, and then I carried on. Along the traverse in the direction of the Yellow Band which was a line of yellow-tinged rock protruding above the snow.

The gap between me and the climbers ahead had grown whilst I stopped to get my oxygen supply working again, but soon enough, as a compact group once again, our team quickly caught up with the climbers ahead and the slow pace that we had all been subjected to before just got slower and slower. There was nothing we could do now, nowhere safe to overtake without risking falling down the steep face. Other climbers were clearly slowing up and running out of their oxygen supply since they had started on a high flow rate and had not changed down when they saw the queue ahead of them. The queue in the morning was so slow that the pace would have been quite manageable without any additional oxygen, but many climbers kept their flow on high all through the day and eventually, were starting to show the signs of fatigue associated with a reduction in supplementary oxygen. This was worrying since we could no longer see above the Yellow Band, but knew that climbers who were in the same situation ahead could be slowing everybody down and were therefore preventing the line of climbers who were able to continue from moving anywhere but downwards, and even that would be difficult.

Rob was clearly getting anxious about the length of time that we were spending on this climb, and told us that we would be approaching camp four by this time if there were no queues, but now we were only half way, perhaps less. Seeing climbers ahead struggling on the rocks of the Yellow Band, Rob was becoming increasingly frustrated with the lack of climbing ability or will to move by many people who were ahead of us. It was clearly creating a dangerous situation, and the longer we were out on the face, the longer we would be exposed to threats such as avalanche and incoming storms. The threat was so great that at certain points, if an avalanche had hit the fixed ropes, 200 climbers would have been sent hurtling down the steep face, all tied on to fixed ropes and linked to each other. There would be no stopping, and with the number of climbers attached to each section of line, the pieces of protection holding the ropes to the mountain would have been ripped out in an instant. All this was worrying, and soon enough the colourful language started to come out as Rob tried to hurry up the 150 climbers in front of us. Phrases such as "Oi, Yellow Banders, it's not a f*****g picnic, MOVE!" were hurled up to climbers who slowly inched up the exposed rocks. This was laughable at first, but as a group we soon realised that many climbers ahead were seemingly oblivious to anyone below them, and so shouting at them seemed the only reasonable way of making any progress.

Hour after hour went by and with it bad weather came and went. Spindrift showers flew past us in the high winds and chilled us to the core as the small particles of snow found their way into every entrance or gap in our down suits. The wind simply added to the feeling of exposure on the mountain and every time a gust hurled its way down the mountain, everyone crouched down to avoid being hit head on by the blast of polar wind.

Despite this weather and the cold around us, I was still relatively warm and working hard despite the slow progress which stopped the biting cold damaging my progress or ability to keep up with the pace. Eventually it was our turn to climb on the rocks of the Yellow Band which was the first piece of true mixed climbing that we had come across, and had it not been for the altitude or the line of other climbers ahead, it would have been very reminiscent of the mixed training I had done in Scotland, mostly in very similar weather conditions. Unlike any other climbing I had done on mixed ground, this was different in that all confidence was placed in the fixed lines to hold your position. With 50 other people all hauling up the same line, the confidence was initially quite sceptical, but I soon realised that leaning back out from the slope was the only way to cross the rock sections. Because we didn't have ice axes due to their redundancy on Everest, it wasn't possible to climb as close to the rock as possible hoping that the crampons would catch on a small ledge. Instead, by leaning out, the rock was used as leverage as we hauled up the fixed lines with our jumars, much like aid climbers do when ascending multi-pitch big walls.

Fortunately, this technique of climbing the mixed sections was much easier than the finesse technique required to climb more Scottish and Alpine type routes, and so I managed to keep up with the climbers ahead and even pass a few more on the adjacent lines. Once past this bottleneck though, we were back into the plod behind the queue again and exposed to more foul weather which was blowing in from above. Loose snow and ice was continually being brought down by climbers ahead in the line, and this was then swirled around by the vortex like wind which seemed to circle the whole line of climbers below.

Now that the Yellow Band had been climbed, the next obstacle was the Geneva Spur. This ridge of black rock protruding out of the surrounding snow was named by the Swiss expedition on the mountain in 1952, the year before Sir Edmund Hillary and Sherpa Tenzing Norgay made the first ascent of the mountain. The route was now obvious as climbers as small as ants crawled over the spur. I envied the climbers who were nearing the top of this feature since Rob had said that camp four was literally 100 metres around the corner from the top of the Geneva Spur, but from our current position, there was still over an hour since we would see this view.

The continual climbing required on this day simply drained energy unnecessarily, but still, we had to keep pushing onwards towards camp four; we were now so far away from camp three that there really wasn't any other alternative. I was now starting to tire; I could no longer feel the positive effects from my oxygen system, although it was still flowing so I assumed that it must have been doing something. The Geneva Spur itself still looked so far away as we once again traversed over to the left and towards the base of the black rocks. More of Rob's shouting hurried the people in front of us as some allowed us to pass. The day felt like it had already gone on for an eternity, but even by looking down into the Western Cwm to see our progress, I couldn't see an end to the pain any time soon. As we reached the base of the Spur, Mollie and Becky were leading our small group with Rob, Rick Valerie and me behind, following at the same pace that we had become so accustomed to over many hours. In fact now the pace felt like it had been lifted, but I knew that in reality, it had almost certainly slowed down, while the physical exhaustion which had by now well and truly set in made the climbing feel anything but slow. There seemed to be more of a queue ahead and at first I couldn't quite tell what was going on. First Mollie and Becky went past the blockage, and then it came to my turn. Rob went ahead so he could assess what the route was like up the Spur and hurry people on if needed, and then it was my turn again. The blockage was a climber who was drunkenly fumbling about on the ropes. His oxygen had clearly run out and he had no obvious support. There were no team mates around him, and no Sherpas to give him extra oxygen. He was now a danger to himself and everyone else around him.

It was this type of climber who had been slowing down the progress of many faster climbers below, but there is nothing you can do to help a climber in this condition unless you happen to have a spare oxygen cylinder to hand, no one in our group did, and more, we were struggling to get ourselves to camp four without helping anyone else. Of course if this climber had needed rescue, then we wouldn't have thought twice to give him as much assistance as we could, but as it was, he was in his own world, fumbling with the simplest of tasks such as unscrewing a karabiner. Clearly he was struggling under the confusion of hypoxia, and had very little control over what he was doing, if any at all. As I asked him if I could pass, he seemed oblivious to my presence and carried on grasping at the gate of the karabiner to try to pull it off the rope without opening it first, it really was shocking to watch. I turned around and saw a Sherpa behind me who looked to be with the climber, and so as quickly and as safely I could, I climbed round the climber and got to the next anchor point as quickly as possible so that I wasn't on the same rope as someone who could quite easily fall off the face and potentially pull everyone else attached to the same rope with him.

It is quite angering to see that a climbing team has let one of their climbers fall into this state, but the climber in question had made a bad choice in choosing an expedition outfit who didn't have the proper logistics in place and had limited supplies of oxygen, something that is clearly critical in ascending above camp three for the majority of people. I hoped that we wouldn't meet any more climbers like this where I feared for my own life or that of someone physically so close to me. Climbing the mountain was a hard enough prospect in its own right without having to worry about factors like this which are often controllable and frustratingly so easy to avoid.

After passing the climber who would also make camp four eventually that day, it was time to follow Rob up and over the black rock with patches of snow. As the metal points slid over the bare rock, they screeched like fingernails on a blackboard. This would have been more off-putting for me had it not been for the volume of my constant breathing which became an all-consuming thing. I knew the sound my crampons were making, but all I could hear was a Darth Vader-esque noise of breathing which blocked out all other sounds. Soon enough, the constant screeching of my crampons also faded into the background, and became just another product of hauling myself over black slabs and shingle in an effort to keep up with the climbers ahead. The Geneva Spur itself is a very mixed affair, with both snow patches and bare rock running in bands up to the summit of the ridge. Following the climbers ahead, the elevation started off relatively gentle at its base, but towards the ridge line, the gradient on the spur rears up once more becoming as steep as the Lhotse Face itself, requiring significant effort to climb. This would be a tough section of the route in normal conditions, but with the length of time that it had taken us to get to this point, the final few steps onto the snowy ground at the top of the ridge were simply exhausting.

I would take one step, and then rest for as long as possible, waiting for Rick who was just behind me to catch up before taking another step. I physically couldn't go any faster, other than to haul myself up one step at a time, and then find a position where I could have some respite from the overwhelming lack of oxygen. As I crossed over the ridge line, I still couldn't see camp four but the route ahead of me was relatively flat, which was such a blessing after the constant elevated terrain for so many hours previously. I could see Mollie who was just ahead of me sitting on a rock by the side of the fixed ropes. She had run out of oxygen and was waiting for Padawa Sherpa who was just behind us and had a spare bottle of oxygen in his rucksack. I now had to get to camp four as soon as I could, since I knew that my oxygen would be running low, and if I ran out here there were now no spare bottles, and the going would get so much tougher than it already was.

Chapter 53 – The South Col

We were now traversing the back side of the Geneva Spur, and there was no snow to be seen. Black rock was everywhere, with each slab being cambered down into the valley below. There were no true flat areas, and the instability of crampons on this rock slowed the pace down even further to a crawl. There was now no one ahead of me to follow since Mollie had had to stop, so I had to drag myself along at the best possible pace I could. Loose rock was everywhere and presented the perfect opportunity to slip down one of the sheer precipices below. And then, as soon as I rounded a corner, and as if by magic, the South Col appeared from nowhere and on it was a small village of tents. This was mind-blowing; I couldn't quite imagine that such a place, so remote and so unwelcoming, could really exist. Piles and piles of oxygen cylinders were lined up in neat rows and there was a hustle and bustle of Sherpas and climbers, all of them wearing down suits looking like spacemen who had come to explore the place; it really was somewhere from another world.

I carried along on the traverse and eventually reached our row of tents. I looked around in utter amazement at the place. It was surreal, tents all around on this piece of flat expanse, perhaps the only true flat ground for miles and certainly flatter than base camp. As I looked above me, Everest stood towering high above my left shoulder, the route quite obvious with climbers visible near the summit. Then to my right, Lhotse soared up into the sky, both mountains an impressive bulk of rock even beyond the high saddle that I was currently standing on. Heading over to our group of tents, I could still only manage a slow plod but that was enough to eventually carry me to an open door of an empty tent belonging to our small expedition. I met Chhewang Dorjee who came to help me, and as always, he couldn't do enough, always attentive and so caring.

I crawled into the tent and opened up my sleeping mat and sleeping bag. I tried to blow up the mat as best I could so that some of the rugged terrain below the tent would be absorbed without further hurting my aching body. Now in my sleeping bag, I thought about what had just unfolded during the day. It had taken eight hours to reach the South Col, but on any normal day on Everest, it should have taken only five. Both Rick and Mollie got in the tent with me and we talked, trying to rationalise what just happened. Although we hadn't spoken for the whole climb, we were all feeling just the same about the amount of climbers on the route and the length of time it had taken us. It was now 4pm and we still didn't know really what was happening. Rob radioed down to base camp to talk the situation through with Henry, and then moments later, he came to our tent to deliver the hammer blow news that we didn't particularly want to hear. Although we didn't want a rest day at the Col due to the stress that this elevation places on the body, we also knew it was 4pm and we had very little time to rest or recover.

As Rob came over to the tent, he simply said, 'We are leaving tonight at 8pm to get in front of other groups'. And that was it. We had spent eight hours out on the Lhotse Face become more and more exhausted as each hour went by, and now, sitting in our tents on the South Col, the summit camp on Everest, the second highest campsite in the world sitting at 7,900m, only second to Camp VI at 8,230m on the north side of Everest, we were only four hours away from potentially the hardest and longest climb of our lives. This was never going to be easy, we all knew that, but we had never expected such a situation to arise as it now had. Equally, we all knew why the decision had been made as it had. We were prepared to spend a night at the South Col but only if there were too many climbers setting out that night for the summit, especially if there were too many 'dangerous teams' preparing for a summit bid. We also knew that a night at the South Col could be potentially detrimental to our ability to make a summit bid the following day since the body cannot recover at this altitude. At camp four, climbers are effectively in the death zone, an altitude where humans are not capable of surviving for long periods of time, and regardless of how much oxygen, food or water you had to keep you alive, if you stay at this altitude long enough, you will eventually die.

In the tent, we quickly made a plan of what we would do to best use our available time. First we would try and rest, eat and boil some snow and ice to rehydrate, and then one by one, we would get ready into dry socks and get kitted up inside the tent to be ready to go by 8pm.

Shortly after getting into the tent, I knew that I would need to go to the toilet on the South Col if we were leaving the same night. At around 5pm, I slowly got my inner boots on, trying to keep my oxygen mask near my face. As I heaved myself out of the tent, I had to leave the oxygen inside so Rick and Mollie could use it, almost immediately

I felt a loss of strength and proceeded to knock over a full pan of nearly boiling water into the tent entrance which had taken almost a full hour to prepare. I tried to salvage as much as possible, but starting the process again from scratch was the only option. I stumbled drunkenly to a sheltered point of camp four where the wind wasn't blowing too strongly, and then I commenced the fiddly process of unzipping the crotch zip at the base of my down suit.

Up until this point, the expedition had been a series of well-defined pushes. There were multiple acclimatisation pushes, and then once on the final summit attempt, there was the first push to camp two, the push up the Lhotse Face to camp three, and then the long drawn out push to camp four. But here, squatting in full view of every tent on the Col, I was enduring the hardest push of all. There were so many difficulties to overcome just to go to the toilet, it was truly ridiculous. There really was no room for stage fright, but the potential for frostbite in all the wrong places was a serious prospect. Not only was my bum in view of countless climbers and Sherpas, it was also exposed to an utterly Baltic -40 degree Celsius wind which was immediately chilling. Once I had got over these initial problems and the difficulty of undressing multiple layers inside the suit whilst making sure that the suit itself was open wide enough at the base, there was the actual push itself. In all my years of living, I have never experienced the true exhaustion of going to the toilet on the South Col. It was a remarkably difficult experience as I gasped at the empty air for the tiniest amount of oxygen. My thighs were burning just to maintain the squat position for long enough, but multiple times I had to straighten up out of fear that I might suddenly collapse under the strain. But after ten minutes of standing out in the freezing cold, I no longer cared about this pain or the Sherpa who constantly walked past me to collect snow; I just wanted to be back in the comfort of the tent, preparing for the goliath push that was still to come.

The sense of relief and achievement was immense as I tiptoed back to the tent. I was only in my inner boots and my feet were already feeling the cold, as were my hands which had all but lost their feeling altogether. This time as I got into the tent, I managed not to knock over the pan which was still full of snow and ice, and as smoothly as possible, I collapsed back onto my sleeping mat, happy that the ordeal was over.

We carried on, the three of us eating and drinking as much as possible in our own little world. We encouraged each other to eat and drink when the other had forgotten or looked too tired to continue. We were also monitoring our oxygen consumption, and were each receiving 0.5L/min of oxygen which was 1.5L/min split three ways thanks to the splitter. I kept the cylinder between my legs to keep it as warm as possible which ensured that we would get the best use from the available oxygen and not run out prematurely. At this point, there really was nothing more we could discuss, and so we just sat there in the tent which was continually buffeted by the savage winds. We were simply waiting for 6pm to arrive so that at least we had something to do, something to get prepared for. This was the hardest time, since all we were really doing was killing time, and just as before an exam or interview, every situation, both good and bad was flowing through our minds. My imagination was going wild, and eventually, I tried to forget about the climb altogether.

So much sooner than we hoped, 6pm came round. It had felt like an eternity, even the two hours that we had spent in the tent, but still, it was a nauseating feeling and too soon; I almost hoped that time would stand still for a while, and that 6pm wouldn't come creeping up on us. As we looked at our watches, it was time. Everything was laid out in front of us, our inner boots, our mitts, our oxygen systems, our spare mitts, dry socks and our heat pads, everything was there, ready to be sorted.

The first and most intricate job was the activation and application of the heat pads. They can be a real life saver since they provide a small amount of heat to areas that would ordinarily have limited blood supply and therefore are vulnerable to frostbite. The two main areas are the hands and feet, but simply opening the air activated packs and putting them in our mitts and boots wasn't enough. First they had to be activated, but this process relies on oxygen for the exothermic reaction to take place. There was only one place where we would find this much oxygen at this altitude, and so into our oxygen masks went the pads. Within seconds, I could feel them warming up and producing some heat of their own which confirmed that they had been activated. But now, instead of just throwing them in the boots and mitts, they would have to be positioned carefully for full effect. The foot pads were easier, being stuck under the ball of the foot, but the hand pads required more care. These were taped to our wrists, right over the veins which supply blood to the hands to ensure that the pads had maximum effect. Of course the tape had to be just right, just tight enough to maintain the position, but loose enough so blood flow wasn't restricted which would greatly increase the risk of frostbite.

The socks that I had been wearing from camp three to camp four were completely wet, saturated through with sweat and so they were quickly changed to avoid the very real danger of trench foot. Lastly, my gloves were sorted, my bottles were filled and placed inside my down suit, and then my bag was sorted with all the spare bits like spare mitts, goggles and glasses, none of which I would need until the sun came up unless the wind was blowing in our faces which could cause all sorts of problems to uncovered eyes. We checked and then double checked absolutely everything. Nothing could be left at camp four that we might need for the summit push. Nothing could be left to chance, and so everything was checked for a third time.

We were completely ready to go except for our crampons which would be put on outside the tent. There was still over 30 minutes to go though, and so it was time to completely switch off. Switch off from what we were about to do, what we had already done, and instead, think about home, about family and friends and of lying on warm sandy beaches, the surf washing over our feet. I reached for my iPod, something that I would be leaving in the tent for my descent. I started listening to my music and even though I was moments away from embarking on something quite extraordinary, my mind started to wonder. I remembered how I used to listen to my iPod before a squash match, something to help me relax under pressure and forget about the pain which I was about to try and endure. Squash never did make the Olympics in 2012, but here I was, once again listening to my music, but this time I was in my own Olympics. The music I was listening to brought many emotions to my mind, I thought about the dream of every athlete, to play in front of a crowd, and here I was again, but this time, it wasn't logistically possible for my crowd to watch me, they were my family and friends sitting at home, wondering how I was doing, where I was on the mountain, whilst I was sitting in the tent, thinking of them in return. I closed my eyes, taking in the power of what I was listening to, motivating, encouraging and pushing. In that moment, I didn't know if I could really do it, but I knew, just as they knew back home, that I would fight for that summit.

I heard footsteps, and then as quick as a flash, the zip came down. We looked at each other, and we knew, it was time to go.

Chapter 54 – Reformation of the Line

As I arched to get out of the tent, the darkness took me by surprise. We had been using our head torches in the tent, but for some reason, I hadn't expected such darkness around the front of the tent. I slid outside and looked up towards Lhotse; I couldn't see the top since the black rock just faded into the darkness of the sky around it. Chhewang helped me with my bag out of the tent and then my crampons, and then for the first time, I looked around at the tents on camp four right behind us. I couldn't quite believe if what I saw was real or whether I was hallucinating with extreme hypoxia. There were lights everywhere, head torches as far as I could see over the whole camp. The clanking of gear, the swishing of the fabric from many down suits all rubbing together as climbers and Sherpas made the final checks before heading off into the night. It was a truly fascinating sight to behold, the fact that humans could bring such life to a place which is ordinarily beyond the limits for living. We all huddled together around Rob and the Sherpas, and we worked out our oxygen flow rates, and roughly what was going to happen. The plan was to leave now whilst other teams were still busying around with their kit, that way we would be out of the reach of any 'danger teams' who were hoping to get by on the most minimal and risky of strategies.

I took out two sticks of chewing gum and gave one to Chhewang. I found that the ultra dry high altitude air saps any moisture and this eventually hinders breathing as the inside workings of the upper respiratory tract start to solidify and begin to obstruct any flow of air. We made one more check, and then that was it; we started off into the darkness. The feelings at this moment were overwhelming and I struggled to concentrate on what I was doing instead of thinking about the monumental moment. Rob went first, Becky followed with her Sherpa, and then I followed with Chhewang on my side. The rest of the team were close behind, and although I couldn't see any faces since everyone was so well covered up, I knew Valerie was right behind with her bright heat torch shining like a search beam up the mountain.

As we crossed the rocky section of camp four, we started to hit bits of snow and ice which eventually turned into one long ramp of compacted windblown snow up to the Balcony, the halfway point to the summit. It seemed crazy that from camp four, the summit is around the same height as Scafell Pike in the UK Lake District, just under 1,000m, but from every angle that I had seen Everest from it looked immense and just as tall as it had from base camp. Fortunately I could no longer see the route which was now shrouded in darkness and mystery.

The first section of the snow ramp was bullet-hard ice which was exceptionally slippery even with the security of crampons. There were a few slower climbers ahead of us, and so we unclipped and climbed round them unprotected. Whilst passing one of the climbers, one of my crampons pulled out of the ice and I felt myself slipping without anything to hang onto. My crampon juddered over the snow and then caught on an imperfection in the ice. I was now gasping and fighting to control my breathing after this slip and sudden acceleration to rejoin Rob ahead, but it looked like we now had a long gap to the climbers ahead who were most likely slow and had left early to ensure they made the summit before their turnaround time the following day.

The ice at the base of the slope soon gave way to snow, and from this moment on, I was working on auto pilot. Despite wearing my wrist watch, it was covered over by so many layers of clothing that quite quickly I lost all concept of time. I just followed, step after step, kicking into the snow, pulling up the jumar and then heaving my body weight upwards. The climbing was technically the same as it had been on the Lhotse Face, but this time, the circumstances were so different. Although there were climbers all around, I felt so alone. Each climber was in their own zone and I was just the same. The only noise was the kicking of my crampons into the snow and my own heavy breathing. I was lost in my own world of pain and vulnerability. I knew Chhewang was beside me though; he wouldn't leave my side unless he absolutely had to. He started to change my karabiners at each anchor but I didn't want him to, he was only doing so out of kindness and his need to help, but I wanted him to make sure he looked after himself instead of helping me by doing something I could already do. I wasn't a lazy western climber who insisted everything be done by the Sherpas, but equally I knew that Everest isn't really possible without their help. Chhewang soon understood that I didn't need him to keep unclipping and clipping me back in, but when he stopped, it agitated me that he was no longer helping me. The theory of what you don't know, you don't miss was taken to the extreme in my severely hypoxic mind.

After what felt like perhaps an hour, Rob stopped our group and we all turned our oxygen up to 3L/min in order to keep up a fast pace and get to the balcony, or at least catch up with the climbers ahead as soon as we could. As we stopped, I looked behind me and inside my mask, my mouth was open aghast. In front, there were perhaps ten head torches headed for the summit, but behind, there was a mile long string of head torches lined up all the way from my position, right the way back to camp four on the South Col. I struggled to perceive or comprehend just what I was seeing, and just how many climber were behind us. The line and the lights that shone from the head of each climber and Sherpa was beautiful. This was an artificial wave in such a place that is totally governed by the extremes of nature.

I was caught off guard by my breathing which had grown erratic whilst I was staring down at the line of climbers below me. I tried to refocus on my breathing and then when the group set off once again, keep a better rhythm. I couldn't put a number to the amount of people I saw below me but I knew that regardless of the fact I had never been in this situation before, there were a lot of people below me, perhaps too many. Since I didn't know what the route ahead of me was like, except for the images I had seen and from past climbers' accounts, I couldn't imagine whether or not the route that we were climbing could cope with all these climbers. I knew that there were bottlenecks in places such as along the cornice traverse and below the Hillary Step, but these challenges were still hours away, and perhaps by then, the line would have thinned out.

Again we continued upwards, the route constantly getting steeper and steeper with a mix of loose snow and more compacted windblown slabs. The slabs that we were climbing on weren't thick enough to trigger an avalanche, but when disturbed, they did have a tendency to hurl themselves downhill. For the first few hours, the route seemed relatively straight, and except for the occasional chicane, all the climbers were in one straight long line. As we got higher, bigger pieces of snow started breaking off and falling along the sides of the fixed lines, occasionally catching the legs of climbers who protruded slightly from the line. A few times, I was caught off guard and had to fight to hold my balance as chunks of compacted snow hit my legs.

This was all the motivation that I needed so stay as close to Becky's Sherpa in front of me, but of course there is only so close you can get to a climber who is wearing sharp crampons on their feet.

Once again the climbing became repetitive and routine. I wore a balaclava under my mask, and on top, I had my hood from my down suit fastened into place. All this equipment and clothing was smothering, and simply added to the feeling of being in our own world. The only comfort was the occasional flicker of a head torch behind, or the reflection of some clothing which caught the dim light from my head torch in front. Here, although we were climbing as a small unified unit amongst a sea of climbers, no one could really help you. If we were to reach the summit, we would have to rely on our own bodies not to break down when we needed them most, and our mental resilience and fortitude not to give in when for all we knew, we could be so close.

In reality though, we were not close. Time had all but stopped, and aside from the sound of breathing, the darkness was an overriding entity from which everything else occurred. Looking over to distant mountains, the thought of remoteness and vulnerability came over me, but this was due to the darkness. Again, I looked up to see the route, but it was shrouded from view. The darkness played tricks on the mind, and perhaps in the clarity of day light, a whole new perspective could be placed on the route ahead and the terrain we had previously covered. There were some benefits to the lack of vision, the main one being the exposure around us. We could have been walking with a safety net at the side of us, or on the contrary, we could have been walking with 10,000ft of vertical exposure at the side of each of our feet, but in the unknown of darkness, the exposure is almost completely removed from the equation, and only the vividness of the mind can elaborate on the fear of the unknown.

Whilst everything was so black around me, flashes of bright light in my periphery started to stand out from the darkness. At first, I thought I might have been hallucinating, but over what felt like a reasonable period of time, the flashes repeated again. Trying to catch them in the act, I stopped and turned to look out towards the border of Nepal and Tibet and immediately recognised an electrical storm in the valleys far below. It was a magnificent show of lights, and something refreshing that for a few moments at least, took me away from my little bubble, and allowed me to focus on something otherworldly. The bright flashes seemed to emanate out from a single point and then a patchwork of clouds was illuminated for a few split seconds before the darkness returned.

Due to the numbers of climbers on the route, there were bound to be some discrepancies in the speeds of groups. Fortunately we were one of the quick groups, having become well acclimatised and adequately prepared for whatever slog we were faced with to the summit. As a few more sections of rope went by, two climbers overtook and then slotted in between Becky's Sherpa and me. This was fine by me, as I didn't want to hold any fast climbers up behind me, but it soon became clear that these weren't particularly quick climbers, they were more sprint orientated as demonstrated by their pace. Initially, everything went smoothly, and the pace was kept constant which was important in avoiding a ripple effect down to the last climbers in the line, but soon enough, the climber in front of me started behaving rather erratically. All I wanted to do was to maintain a constant pace which up until this point had been working well, but clearly the climber ahead had other ideas. As he caught up with the climber in front, he would then rest for 30 seconds, allowing the climber in front to move ahead, and then he would sprint as fast as possible to try to keep up. For whatever reason, perhaps the increasing level of hypoxia, I found this incredibly annoying, and started to worry that I could no longer keep up with this slow-fast pace being set. The pace was so hard to follow, and was clearly having effects lower down the line where gaps and bunches of climbers were starting to form. Chhewang clearly saw what I was seeing, and we tried to go ahead but to no avail. Almost as soon as we had unclipped from the fixed lines, numerous bands of mixed climbing started to appear. This was no place to be unclipped from the fixed lines, especially as we couldn't see what was either side or ahead of us, so we both clipped back in to remain safe.

This erratic pace in front seemed to last forever with my lack of a concept of time, but no sooner had it started than we were back up with the group ahead which for no apparent reason had slowed right down. It was important for us to keep moving at a relatively constant pace; otherwise we would have to keep adjusting our oxygen flow rates to ensure we didn't run out before we had to. The line kept climbing for a moment or two, and then I spotted to my horror what looked like a guide teaching a client how to climb the mixed section on the fixed ropes. This was certainly neither the time nor place to be giving climbing instruction, and just showed the extent of the naivety of some of the climbers who set foot on the mountain. We had clearly caught up with climbers who had left much earlier due to their inability to climb efficiently at altitude, and were now presenting a difficult challenge for every climber behind them. They would have to be passed, but on this more technical ground, a slip could not be afforded whilst unclipped from the fixed lines.

Fate, however, was kind to us, as when we reached these climbers, an old rope from a previous season on Everest emerged from beneath the snow. It was taut and relatively worn, but good enough to use to pass the instructor and his client. I felt like a character going through a scene in *Alice in Wonderland*, I simply could not believe what I was seeing was real. I imagined that the next thing I would see would be climbers sitting down on foldable chairs enjoying the view, perhaps with a warm drink in one frostbitten hand. I noted though that my hands and feet were positively warm, and clearly the heat pads were doing their job well. Whilst at home, I could never truly imagine how I would feel whilst climbing these silent slopes, but I never for a moment envisaged that I would be closer to overheating than to getting hypothermia and frostbite. As soon as that thought entered my mind, a cold blast of super-chilled air blew past me, full of spindrift which coated every exposed piece of skin on my face. It really was bitter outside of my down suit, but in my own little world on the inside, I was doing well.

As we climbed ever higher, I could feel the oxygen working away. I always kept a check on the gauge in the oxygen line to make sure it was still working as well as it could in these freezing conditions. Taking the mask off my face to blow my nose, I drew in a breath of nothing. I knew it was air, but it felt empty and useless. Instead of the dense air at base camp or even camp two, this atmosphere that we were now breathing wasn't designed to support life, there was simply nothing to it. I put my mask back on and gasped a few times to regain my breath as the pace once again returned to its usual self. I seemed to have lost the climbers who had overtaken, and now rejoined the safety of Becky's Sherpa, remembering to keep my distance.

Of course my real comfort was Chhewang. For hours at a time, I didn't hear him speak, but I knew he was there right behind me and that was enough. We looked at each other occasionally, just to let the other know we were still good to climb, but we conveyed everything we needed to in a glance and a single word at most, for we knew that the job at hand was to keep climbing. As long as we didn't stop or slow down too much, we would end up somewhere up on this mountain. I still had no idea whether we would make the summit, but I trusted Chhewang, and I trusted the pace that Rob was now setting. That was all I could do.

Chapter 55 – Leading Into the Night

So far, the climbing had been in relative silence with only our breathing to keep us company. The darkness had played tricks and had deceived and altered our perception of the climbing that we were doing. We had no concept of time. The climbing itself was becoming increasingly tough. The gradual slopes nearer camp four had given way to steeper and more mixed terrain. Each band of rock that we crossed was another huge expenditure of energy as a high step followed to clear the rock band itself, which was then followed by an explosive heave to push the body up and over the section. In places the snow was deep which made the going tougher as the legs now had to push themselves and the snow forward to make any progress. As soon as the boot top went under the snow, I could feel the cold seeping through over four layers of protection and insulation; it was bitterly cold.

In the darkness, when I looked out to the side, I could see the edge of the mountain as a faint outline, but that was all. We had been climbing for hours, but yet the sun or its light was nowhere to be seen, we were still very much climbing through the night.

Up ahead, I could see a few gatherings of head torches. Perhaps these were climbers ahead of us who were having a rest. I didn't know for sure, but I knew that I too would love a rest, and for someone to give me some idea of where we were. There really is only so much climbing into the unknown that you can take before all motivation escapes you and finding out how much progress has been made and what is still to come becomes of paramount importance. As we climbed upwards, we gradually moved closer to the gathering, and I could see that Rob too who was in front of our group started to slow and then stop altogether in the lee of a huge rock which was a great result. As the rest of our group came up to join us, we realised that we were now in fact at The Balcony.

At 8,400m, The Balcony is essentially the halfway point on summit day in terms of altitude, but perhaps not in terms of time. It is at The Balcony that climbers usually change their oxygen tanks, leaving one half full tank at the balcony itself ready for the descent, and then change to a new tank which should last until the summit. Almost as soon as I reached the balcony, I started to hear the loud hissing noise of many cylinders and regulators being changed which was a cue for Chhewang and me to do the same. Being a Sherpa, Chhewang was climbing on an incredibly low flow rate and so didn't need to change his cylinder, but I would certainly have to. I knelt down onto the compacted snow and let Chhewang change the cylinder for me. It was much quicker this way, and was certainly a job for a composed Sherpa rather than a tired climber who would most likely cross thread the regulator and then look in horror as precious oxygen started to dissipate into the air.

Fortunately Chhewang knew exactly what he was doing, and within seconds, I was back on my feet and we were both ready to go. The teams in front of us had also still stopped at The Balcony, and so Rob told us roughly where we were and found out how everyone was doing. Everyone seemed to be present, except for Mollie which was worrying. She had been climbing right behind us at the start, but may have fallen behind or even turned round to camp four, we just didn't know. She was however with her Sherpa, and so there was nothing to worry about; either she would be following behind, or sitting in the safety of her tent on the South Col.

Everybody went up to 4L/min of oxygen flow rate on the new bottles which meant that we could maintain a good pace all the way to the summit if we ever got that far, and the extra flow would also keep us warm. Becky, however, was starting to feel the cold in her feet and was despondent after Rob said she should turn round if she lost any feeling in her toes, but after a failed attempt on Everest the previous year, it seemed that it would take more than just a risk of frostbite in the toes to turn her around. On Everest, there is a fine line between a calculated risk and a foolish one, but only time would tell whether she, or in fact anyone who was climbing on Everest that night was taking a justifiable risk or not.

Before we set off once again into the darkness, I thought it might be a good opportunity to have a quick drink from one of the warm bottles that I had stored inside my down suit. I tried to open the zip at the top of the suit, but it seemed that as much as I pulled, nothing would happen. I looked down over the top of my oxygen mask and saw the reason for the blockage. A huge ball of ice had grown around the zip of my down suit and was preventing movement of any sort from the zip. I knew the cause of this ice build-up though; through constant breathing into the oxygen masks, water vapour quickly condenses and drips out of the mask. On hitting the first bit of the suit that it comes into contact with, normally the top of the zip, this droplet freezes almost instantly, and gradually over a few hours, a large ball of ice builds up. I had expected this, and had tried to use an old base layer to trap the droplets before they reached the zip, but this only added to the tangle of the ice and zip. The ball itself was currently the size of a small tennis ball, but since it was stuck firmly in place, I just had to leave it where it was, and hope that if I reached the summit, I would be able to somehow knock it off so that I could get to my camera which was sitting in the depths of my suit in the hottest place I could find.

After ten minutes at The Balcony, it was time to leave before too many other teams came up and were prevented from changing their own oxygen systems due to the number of climbers waiting about. Mollie hadn't appeared, and so Rob gave the signal for us all to start climbing once again. As it was, I just happened to be standing oh so inconveniently on the route up to the summit, and so when Rob ushered me along, I found that I was now in front of our group. There were still a couple of climbers in front of me, but they were moving slowly, and it quickly became apparent that the ridge we were now climbing on was much more knife edge than the climbing before The Balcony. Chhewang motioned me to go past, and reluctantly, I unclipped from the fixed lines and tentatively went clear, being careful not to knock the other climbers off the side of the ridge, or fall off the other side myself.

Almost as soon as I had gone round and then clipped into the fixed ropes, I looked in front of me and there was only blackness. I seemed to be at the front of the line, leading some 200 climbers, and there was no one in front to follow. It was an amazing feeling, finally being able to make my own way up to the summit of Everest without trying to keep up with anyone else. As I looked around behind me, there were lights everywhere, but in front of me there was nothing. With Chhewang Dorjee, I led the way for around six hours of tough climbing. Even though I couldn't see the route and could barely see the snow in front of me, I could tell that we were going over what felt like repetitive ground. A series of rock steps kept emerging from the left, and each time, the route quickly steepened and went off into deeper snow, before passing the rock step and following the ridge once more.

Once we were back at base camp, Rob had said that I had been climbing fast after the balcony and was worried that we might actually summit in the dark, but I had no concept of this. I didn't know whether we were behind schedule, in front of schedule or even what the schedule was. In fact I didn't even know if we had a schedule, but all I could do was keep climbing. Each time I slowed down the pace, Chhewang was right there to encourage me to keep moving forwards. Rob too was right behind me, and so I didn't really know whether I was actually going too slowly. I wished that Chhewang or Rob would overtake me so I had some idea of what pace we should be doing, but no one did, and so I told myself that the pace was fine and I should just keep going.

Occasionally, the rocks in front and even the whole mountain ahead lit up for a few seconds as Valerie's head torch pointed upwards. Unfortunately it didn't reveal that we were almost at the summit but it did give an outline ahead that I couldn't quite work out. As I kept climbing up the steep, curved pitches, I could see a pyramidal looking section ahead. It almost looked like a perfect mountain top, but even in my hypoxic state I knew this wasn't possible. Despite not knowing much of the route above camp four beyond what I could see from the camp, I knew that there was a place called the South Summit, and then the route went down across a knife edge ridge known as the Cornice Traverse. From there, there was the Hillary Step and the final summit snowfield to negotiate, but from my perspective, I couldn't see any of that. The outline looked so much like a summit of a mountain, but surely that couldn't be possible. I wondered if we had climbed the wrong mountain by mistake, much like the climbers in the tale of *The Ascent of Rum Doodle*. Perhaps all these climbers below me were just following blindly, not knowing that actually, I had no idea where I was going.

Still, I followed the fixed ropes which had been keeping me on the right track along the top of the ridge, and helped me safely navigate tough mixed sections of rock which were much harder in a dim light with no clues of foot holds where I could safely lever up with my crampons. The pace was high, and after every couple of steps, my hands fell to my knees as I stood hunched over, gasping for breath. Chhewang was now doing the same, and each time I stopped, we both took our time to breathe. Up here in the thin atmosphere, everything is acted out on a level playing field. Sherpas are now just as susceptible to the stress of high altitude as western climbers, and regardless of athletic background or not, in this environment with only 34% of the oxygen at sea level, only the mentally strong willed and lucky will do well.

The closer we got to the pyramidal peak, the more I became confused about where we were. I hadn't seen anything like this in books or pictures, but perhaps that was because everyone sees this object in the dark and so a picture would only show the veil of darkness instead of an accurate topographic map which is what I needed. Soon though, Rob came up behind me and said that we were near the South Summit. I then realised that the projection ahead of us wasn't the summit of Everest, or indeed the summit of any other mountain, but the entrance point to the most technical climbing on Everest. On the last few pitches to the South Summit, the complete blackness of night was replaced by the grey blue grainy light of dawn which subtly illuminated more and more of the route ahead.

Chapter 56 – Technical Difficulties

Sunrise is always an amazing time on summit day, and on Everest, it was no different. We had been climbing now for around eight hours, all of which was in complete darkness which considerably alters your perspective on the outside world. Now, all of the unknown parts of the route were becoming visible and this simply added to the magic high on this mountain. Chhewang and I were still at the front, plodding away at our own pace whilst behind, the dark-suited figures of climbers and Sherpas stretched for miles down the Southeast ridge of Everest.

As I looked out to the distant mountains of the Himalayas, the familiar sight of the alpine glow appeared over the horizon and cast its dark blue light over all the mountains which were able to escape above the clouds.

On the approach to the South Summit which was now very much imminent, the world around started to get lighter very quickly as if someone was physically turning up the dimmer switch before our very eyes. To our left, we could start to see the shadow of Everest, a huge pyramid which stretched out perfectly as far as the eye could see to the opposite horizon. From the depths of night, the Himalayas were finally coming to life once again.

Strangely, I was still feeling okay which was far more than I expected considering the amount of ground we had covered and the altitude that we had reached. Now at 8,750m, we stood atop the South Summit of Everest. It felt absolutely amazing to get to this point, and I knew that once I got here, although there was still almost two hours of climbing left to go, I would almost certainly reach the summit of Everest, a place that for the first time as I looked over from the South Summit, I could see as clear as day. Standing on this secondary summit, we had just a moment to appreciate the views which were stunning, and also see the rest of the route that we still had to climb. We could essentially see the whole of the last technical section leading up to the summit which still looked so far away considering the ground that lay before it.

From here, Chhewang went ahead and descended the back side of the South Summit, and started along the Cornice Traverse. Of all the sections on Everest that I had seen, it had been the Cornice

Traverse that most scared me. This was a knife edge ridge of wind-blasted snow, stuck delicately to rocks which were few and far between. The traverse itself was essentially a cornice, and to step too high on the snowline meant almost certain death as the weak-corniced layer of snow would fall away beneath you. The figures themselves make for sobering reading. On the left side of the traverse to the summit, there is an 8,000ft drop down the Southwest Face, and on the right, down through the thin cornice, there is a 10,000ft drop down the Kangshung Face which is a quick trip onto the plains of Tibet. On top of this, the traverse is only wide enough for one foot at a time, and in places not even that, so it is truly a balancing act with the only good news being that it would be almost impossible to get lost here, as even in a whiteout, apart from forwards and backwards, there is nothing else, only air.

Following the Cornice Traverse, there were a number of tricky rock sections, that although they didn't possess the notoriety of the Hillary Step, were still difficult in their own right. Time after time, these rock sections forced the route out onto the exposed edges of the Southwest Face and were painfully slow to navigate with extreme care being needed to avoid an uncontrollable descent. The main cause of concern was the nature of the climbing which was now mostly mixed with very little snow on the wind torn edges. Climbing for hours over rock with crampons was very tiring due to its committing nature and the very real danger of the crampons skipping over the polished rock. These sections seemed to go on and on, endlessly going around a corner to find another section of rock to negotiate. Mostly this rock was off camber which meant any slide was only going to go one way, and unfortunately, it wasn't in the direction of the summit.

We had successfully negotiated these rock sections when it came time to face the Hillary Step. This 12m wall of rock named after Sir Edmund Hillary who first found a route up it was the last problem to overcome before the much easier snowfields leading up to the summit. From the base, the bulk looked much larger than I had imagined it to be, but equally it didn't look as frightening or exposed since there was a large bank of snow behind which would hopefully arrest any fall before the worst happened. I could probably count on this snow protecting me, but mentally, that was all the protection there was between me and a big drop into Tibet, so in my mind, it would save me from whatever, regardless of how thin it actually may be.

There were no climbers in front of our group, only Chhewang was in front of me, and this made the climbing so much easier. Although my pace was slowing, I didn't have to try to keep up with anyone, I just had to keep focused on the climbing in front of me which just happened to be the big slab of the Hillary Step.

Just like on the Lhotse Face, the move was committing, and full trust had to be placed in the anchors at the top which were holding a jumble of new and old tatty ropes from many previous years of climbing. Some ropes were completely threadbare, whilst only the odd one or two looked like they would support a human. I clipped my jumar into the best looking rope, and then with my spare karabiner, I clipped into as many ropes as would fit, and then if one or ten of them snapped, there would still be a fair few more keeping me on the mountain. This main part of the step required a huge effort to pull up and then remain composed enough to lean back and allow the ropes to take my weight. It took several of these exhausting moves before I reached the top of the main slab and an object that looked so small but so awkward that it alone could prevent the summit being reached. It was a small rock which forced the route over a vertical drop which was completely committing. The rock also had a gap from the top slab of the Hillary Step which meant that you could not simply step over it. I was completely baffled by this problem, trying to see if I was missing something obvious, but hypoxia was stopping most of my cognitive function and so I just stared at it blankly as if the answer would just pop into my head.

Strangely the answer did just that, but I soon realised that it was Rob telling me from behind that the best way to get over the rock was to straddle it and then whilst sitting on top of it, perform a sort of high altitude pirouette. This was easier said than done since halfway through this uncomfortable move, I found myself looking straight down the Southwest Face, but with one leg over, I was just about able to reach the floor and haul the other leg round to join it. There were now only a few smaller rock sections to overcome, and then we would be on the final snowfield.

I couldn't quite believe what was happening and where we were, as I looked back and saw just how high we were and what sort of ground we had covered. We were now higher than any other mountain in the world and it felt just so surreal. I looked up at Chhewang and he motioned for me to continue. I was now starting to tire, but I knew the summit was somewhere above us although it had disappeared from sight. There was one more section of fixed rope which started at the base of the final snow slope which I hauled myself onto with Chhewang in front and Rob right behind. As I clipped into this rope, I could see the summit only 100m ahead and a feeling of elation came over me. I knew that I could make it, perhaps for the first time ever, I let myself believe that actually, I could really do it, I would make the summit.

The fixed rope continued halfway up the snow slope where it came to a stop, anchored into the snow leaving the final section unprotected. I stumbled towards this anchor point but as I took each step, I could feel that the effort required to move was becoming more and more. I couldn't think why, I was confused. It had been a long day, I knew that, but still, I was now struggling to even stand up, let alone put one foot in front of the other. As I looked down, I grasped for the gauge on the oxygen line and realised that my cylinder had run out of oxygen. I couldn't believe it, it was the worst possible moment to run out of oxygen. I was only 50m from the top of the world, but very quickly, those 50m started to become 50 miles. I looked at Chhewang and pointed at my mask, and then collapsed to my knees. I physically couldn't hold myself up any more as a rush of emotions took over me. I was so close to the summit, and yet I hoped to God that Chhewang had a spare cylinder for me. I didn't know if I was meant to run out of oxygen here of all places, but I had, and I was too weak to do anything about it.

I knew deep down that if Chhewang had no spare oxygen, I could have stumbled blindly along the last 50m because it was the shock of running out and having to readjust to the oxygen-less world around me that was causing all my problems. There was still a trickle of oxygen flowing through my mask, but as soon as Chhewang unscrewed the cylinder, that meagre amount suddenly stopped and my mind started to spin. I could think of absolutely nothing, my mind was hazy and I suddenly felt very cold as hypoxia rapidly caught up with me. I knew that the Sherpas were ready for such situations, but due to the sudden stop of the flow of oxygen and the position I was in, I was caught completely off guard and the dramatic fall to my knees probably captured that quite well.

Oxygen is certainly a magic medicine up in the atmosphere, and almost as soon as Chhewang had turned my regulator back on with the new bottle, I felt as though nothing had happened and I almost wondered what I was doing down on my knees, as if what had happened had just played out in front of me on a fuzzy projector screen. This recovery was a matter of seconds which is quite a quick time to go from being as close to death as I would have liked, to being perfectly fine, given the circumstances, moments later. As soon as my oxygen supply had kicked in, I got back up, and with Chhewang, finally reached the end of the fixed ropes and unclipped. This final section was completely unprotected, and so any small mistake could quite easily lead to you sliding off the edge of the mountain.

As I climbed the final few metres, I became quite emotional as all of a sudden, every emotion that Everest had generated over so many years came flooding back. I thought of home and how proud Mum would be if she could see where I was standing, that I actually made it to the top of the world. The sense of relief was immense, as was the euphoria.

Chapter 57 – The Pinnacle of a Dream

Two more steps took me to the summit of Mount Everest. I couldn't even begin to describe each feeling, each memory or each emotion as I stood there gazing out at the world. At 6am on the 19th May 2012, I summited the world's highest mountain, standing 8,848m above the world below. My Sherpa, Chhewang Dorjee was standing right next to me, just as he had done for the whole climb, a fantastic and loyal Sherpa; we hugged each other and in that moment became brothers over an experience that was truly extraordinary. As I looked around Rob came up behind me and again it was a moment of true elation and I am sure satisfactory for him knowing that as his team, we had reached the summit. Becky, Valerie and Rick were also here, busy looking out at what we had achieved, but it was a view that was truly impossible to take in.

There were climbers standing the other side of the summit who had come up the north side of Everest from Tibet, and the summit itself was covered in Khata scarves and masses of prayer flags which flowed out into the wind dispensing the incantations across the Himalayas. After a bit of trying, I managed to free the zip of my down suit so I could grab my camera, and then started taking as many pictures as I could before the intense cold killed the battery. Chhewang took two pictures of me and then soon afterwards, the camera died altogether. This was a bit of a nightmare since I hadn't even taken a picture with my sponsor's flag which was still in the bottom of my rucksack, but any anxiety I had was replaced by the sweet happiness of gradual oxygen deprivation. I knew that Rob would take a picture for me before we started the descent, so I just stood and admired the view.

Whilst I was standing by the summit, I clipped into a random fixed rope just to secure myself in case I slipped. As I was looking at the edges of the summit snow fields, I could imagine the possibility of slipping and then struggling to arrest any motion once the slip turned into a fall. It was also whilst I stared out from the summit that I realised my misconceptions about the place I now found myself in. Quite morbidly, I had imagined that the summit would be a nice place to die, or at least as nice a place as anywhere else. I imagined it to be calming and relatively peaceful, the lack of oxygen making it easy to simply drift off unnoticed and forever lie at the top of the world with the best view going.

But there was a problem with my plan. The more I stood looking out at the world, the more I realised that I didn't want to die here, and more, I couldn't think of a worse place than atop this mountain. The environment was hostile and uninviting, completely the opposite to how I imagined the summit to be. The wind had a constant presence on the summit, continually gusting against climbers and the mountain like an icy breath. At the top, there was no feeling of safety, and there was a thought in the back of my mind that this really was the very limit, we were now on the edge and if something went wrong for example an oxygen cylinder running out prematurely, there would be no safety net, simply because help was thousands of meters down the mountain, and up here, we were completely self-reliant, constantly battling against the insurmountable forces of nature.

So instead of feeling content to stay on the summit for a while longer, I was in awe of everything I saw around me, and in that moment realised that was exactly how it should be. Everest had let us climb onto its icy summit for just a few short minutes, but that was enough, and to simply see such wonders as the curvature of the earth, and the world below under a blanket of cloud, that etched a memory in my mind that will last forever.

For the final few moments on the mountain, I took some photos for Rob, and then he repaid the favour, both of us gaining frosty fingers in the process. I managed to have a picture with Chhewang Dorjee and my sponsor's flag which finally took a significant weight off my shoulders, and the thought of going back home and going back into the boardroom to deliver the devastating news finally escaped my mind. We also wondered where Mollie had got to; had she gone back to her tent at camp four or even further down the mountain, or had she managed to carry on and was now somewhere battling the final snowfields and pitches of Everest? So far we hadn't had any word.

I knew that hypoxia wouldn't allow me to think of everything that I should have thought about on the summit, like all the previous years of training, the financial difficulties, the days spent with family and friends, not really knowing whether I would even get to Nepal, and then those final few days, perhaps even hours on the mountain where I didn't really know if I had what it took to reach the summit. But in the back of my mind, there was always a voice pushing me back down the mountain. The summit is only half way, and to fully achieve the goal and give full respect to the mountain, we had to make it back down alive which was about to turn out to be an epic in its own right.

We spent 30 minutes on that place atop of the world, the place where for many, the dream of a lifetime can be fulfilled. There is no place on earth quite like it, and whilst many mountain tops bear a resemblance, in the same way that no north face can match that of the Eiger, or no big wall can compare to El Capitan in Yosemite, no summit can truly compare to Everest's lofty peak. On that day, we were among the privileged few to visit one of the most inaccessible places on earth.

Chapter 58 – Rush Hour

But alas, after our 30 minutes of euphoric realisation, our team started to descend, and as Rob picked up his bag and Chhewang gave me the signal, I knew it was time to leave. It is strange that it takes so much effort and so many years of planning to finally realise this dream for 30 minutes on the summit. Still, this wasn't a place that anyone would want to linger, and in the footsteps of Chhewang, I unclipped from the fixed rope on the summit, and started down the summit snowfield. As I left the summit, I don't recall ever looking back; I knew that I would probably never attempt to climb Everest again, and so the 30 minutes of patchy memory from the summit was everything I needed, and now my attention was solely focussed on getting back down to sea level.

As we descended to the fixed rope halfway down the snowfield, I could see over to the South Summit where we had been gifted with our first glimpse of the summit. That was almost 2.5 hours ago and there had been no one else standing with our small group looking out at the view, but now, I could see climbers once again like ants down climbing from the South Summit, and crossing over to the Cornice Traverse. We couldn't see the route between the top of the Hillary Step and the Cornice Traverse though, so we had no idea how many people had already made the crossing. With Rob right behind once again, we just had to refresh our legs and keep down climbing as fast as we could, but from the top of the technical rock steps, even the South Summit felt like a long way away, so the South Col felt a million miles away and I just hoped that I would have the strength for the return journey.

As soon as we had descended the summit snow field, it wasn't long before we started to encounter hold-ups in the bottleneck areas around the more technical rock steps. There had been a few minutes with no one leaving the summit before I followed Chhewang down, and that meant we had no one to wait for in front of us, but all of the queuing was from a steady stream of people climbing the final sections to the summit. For the first few steps, we managed to just unclip and then grab the fixed line beyond the climber we had passed and then clip back in as soon as possible. At the start, this was fine since the climbers going up were often happy to clip around us meaning that we could stay clipped in, and the terrain here, although steep, was reasonably wide, and so two people could pass quite easily.

The further down we climbed, however, the harder it became to safely pass the oncoming climbers. As we got nearer to the top of the Hillary Step, it became a balancing act to try and move around these other climbers without falling off the side. Many of these climbers were in their own zones, they simply stood where they were, or just carried on climbing as if we weren't there, forcing us off the rope in order that they didn't pull us back up to the summit with them. The situation seemed to be crazy, a complete unorganized chaos with seemingly no ethics to dictate how many climbers could come up before someone let us down. We were always in a worse position, always the climbers closest to the edge, and since we were descending, we were inherently much less stable than those climbers who were still climbing up. Within five minutes of constantly leaving the fixed rope and then urgently clipping back on without making much progress, I realised my fears about there being too many people than the route could handle were probably true.

As we turned one corner, I recognised some of the logos on a climber's down suit and realised that Mollie had indeed been able to continue, but she had fallen behind and was consequently stuck behind slow and often incapable climbers. It was great news that she had been able to continue, and from her position, she was only 30 minutes from the summit, so she would surely make it. As Mollie was swept along with the crowd, it was time for us to concentrate on getting down the final rock section to the top of the Hillary Step, perhaps the most famous of bottlenecks on Everest. We struggled to even reach the top of the Hillary Step with climbers flooding upwards and blocking the way which was now only wide enough for one person at a squeeze. Some climbers seemed to appreciate the predicament that we were in and helped us to move around them as best we could, but many more seemed oblivious to our presence and only had the summit on their mind; they were drunk with sleep and oxygen deprivation.

Eventually with much climbing on the very edge of many rock ledges, we reached the top of the Hillary Step. The awkward rock which needed to be straddled and pirouetted upon was just in front of us, and due to the extreme lack of room, this time we made sure that we were the ones on the safe side of the drop with a bulk of rock forming the upper rock steps to our left, and the exposed southwest face to our right. As we crept around the corner, the route between our position and the South Summit opened up to us, and the sight was horrifying. There were climbers queued on every section of the route. There were no gaps along the whole section to be seen and every bit of space along the route was filled by hypoxic climbers all waiting in turn for their place on the summit. As soon as I saw this, I didn't quite know how we would get down, but perhaps some of the climbers ascending would let us past.

We waited at the top of the Hillary Step for at least ten minutes with climbers constantly climbing up the slab of rock which is only just big enough for one person at a time at most. After this ten minutes, Chhewang took matters into his own hands and climbed the awkward rock and then descended crampons first down the Hillary Step, trying to allow us some space so that we could start the descent before we ran out of oxygen altogether, but as soon as his feet hit the ground at the base of the step, people at the base started climbing once more, ignoring the fact that we were still trying to descend. Each time I went to climb over the awkward step, another climber's head would pop up from the slab, forcing me back around the corner to relative safety. Rob wanted me to go, but each time there was a space, another climber from below filled it, making descent simply impossible.

We had now waited over 30 minutes at the top of the step, and whilst Rob was starting to lose feeling in his feet, we were all losing precious oxygen. The situation showed no sign of improving, and the main problem was that we simply couldn't see the bottom of the step from our position so there was no way of stopping any more climbing up, but infuriatingly, all the climbers below knew that we were still waiting and they had seen how long we had been waiting for, but still they came.

Out of everyone that ascended, no one would let us past, and they didn't seem to understand the simple fact that if 100 people ascend and no one is allowed to descend, then how is anyone going to reach the summit, a place that only ten people can comfortably get to at any one time. These were the dangerous climbers that we had tried so hard to avoid, and up until this point, it had worked, but now, we were pinned in to a crevice in a rock face, hopelessly unable to move. The more we waited, the more we realised that not only do these climbers not care for our lives, they had no regard for their own, as each time they passed us, they unclipped from the fixed rope, and with no protection and a sheer drop below them, they casually plodded around us. A single slip at this point would undoubtedly be fatal.

Chhewang at the base of the step could do no more. He had tried to stop people coming up, but no one listened and still they climbed. There was nothing else that he could do, so he carried on to the safety of the South Summit where he could watch and wait for our eventual arrival. A further 15 minutes passed; we had now been waiting on the step for 45 minutes, and at that point we had had enough. We would tell the next climber to stop any more traffic, and then we would be descending no matter what. As the final climber came up, he complained of asthma and asked Rob to turn his oxygen flow rate up, but it was clear that his cylinder had run out, and the reason for his struggle was that he was breathing atmospheric air of 33% oxygen, and nothing else. Still, Rob turned the regulator up, and through the magic of the placebo effect, he felt the difference almost immediately, and proceeded to stop any more climbers from ascending after his Sherpa had joined him.

Finally, it was now our time to descend from this exposed spot that had been our home for far too long. We climbed over the awkward rock one by one; this time it was much more difficult than the opposite way, but I just about managed to get my legs over and to the top of the Hillary Step proper. From the top, I could see that the climbers below were still clipped into the new rope, but they wouldn't let go, forcing us onto the older tatty ropes that didn't look half as strong as they had a few hours earlier. I clipped in my karabiner, and then arm-wrapped as quickly as I could, before getting off the ropes and getting out the way so Rob could descend. There was still some tricky ground left to cover, but I knew that once we managed to get back to the South Summit, then we were safe. From there, it was simply a case of descending fixed ropes on much wider ground where bottlenecks would no longer be a problem.

The route ahead was still full of climbers, and so I motioned for Rob to go first, having more experience in the art of getting down through a queue of climbers. The selfishness seemed to continue again though, and still no one would let us down one particularly awkward piece of rock which was sloping down and off the side in the direction of the southwest face. The climbers still coming up could quite easily let us past if they waited, since there was nowhere for them to go until the base of the Hillary Step had been cleared of climbers, but they insisted in continuing their ascent. It was mind-blowing to think that either they had no concept of what was going on around them, or the extreme high altitude caused them to act in such a way; I wondered how these people towards the back of the queue ever expected to get down to the South Col in a reasonable period of time without running out of oxygen.

Somehow, we managed to descend across the glacial rock which didn't offer any traction at all, preventing the crampons from sticking, but allowing them to effortlessly glide uncontrollably across the surface. After this section, Rob went ahead with his Sherpa to a site of relative safety at the top of the Cornice Traverse, whilst I negotiated my way around more climbers, who this time were much more courteous, and at one point even did the unclipping part for me, although I didn't like the fact that they took it upon themselves to take me off the safety of the fixed rope, but still, it was better than them not helping at all and just standing with tunnel vision on the summit.

I joined Rob on a flat area of snow above the cornice traverse, and we looked at each other as if to say, was the nightmare that we just experienced really true? I also needed a pee at this point, and so this was as good a time as any to do my business and then have a quick drink for the first time in over 12 hours of climbing. I undid as many zips as I possibly could, and pulled down as many layers of clothes inside as I could reach before turning the pristine patch of snow in front of me into a dark gold colour. At first I didn't realise what was happening because I couldn't see below the goggles that I was now wearing to prevent any snow blindness from the intense light which was constantly bouncing off the snow all around us. But if I had have managed to look down, I would have seen that things weren't flowing quite as smoothly as I would have liked, given the type of clothes that I was wearing. Within a few seconds, I felt the warm comforting trickle down my leg and there was absolutely nothing I could do about it. I didn't have time or the energy to stop, reposition and try again, and the worse had already happened. So at around 8,750m, I uncontrollably wet myself, and could only feel amused at the nature and craziness of the situation I was in. Only on Everest could this happen, and indeed, we were still higher than any other mountain on earth.

I zipped myself back up, and gradually the legs of my down suit started to absorb the extra moisture. Rob went ahead again and managed to cross the Cornice Traverse before another group of climbers started the long traverse from the opposite side. As I got back down to the route, I was once again trapped, unable to move downwards due to the amount of climbers still ascending the incredibly narrow cornice which is only wide enough for one climber at a push. The bonus was that this wait gave me plenty of time to completely dry out, but now I was back into the game of trying to get past a whole group of climbers and this time on my own. I waited for 15 minutes, pleading and motioning to the climbers below to stop coming, so that I could get onto the traverse and leave the rest of the climb free for them. Even when they carried on, ignoring this message, they struggled to get past me, and very quickly the line was backed up right the way to the Hillary Step. There was nothing I could do, and Chhewang, looking on from the South Summit, decided to climb back past all of the impatient climbers, and across the cornice traverse without clipping on once to the fixed rope. He then got in front of me and, holding my karabiner, we free climbed the rest of the way across the Cornice Traverse which is something I never once thought I would have to do just to make it back down the mountain. One slip here by either of us, and we would have tumbled uncontrollably down the southwest face, but the snow under our feet was a good névé, compacted by the wind and stable to climb on. The climbers looking down at us from their perch on the traverse itself seemed horrified at the lengths we were going to just to get down to safety, but not realising for a second that they we part of the problem with only a small minority of climbers along the whole route back from the summit actually willing to help us pass, something that we were doing for the ascending climbers without a second thought.

We were now at the South Summit though, and free from all the dangers of bottlenecks and the risk of slipping whilst unclipped from the fixed rope. From here, we simply had to climb 5m up to the top of the South Summit, and then make the exhausting descent back to the South Col where the safety of our tents lay waiting for us. I started climbing whilst Chhewang got his bag from the base of the South Summit, and free from people climbing to the summit, we had an opportunity to get to the top. Ploughing through the deep snow at the side of the summit was tiring work, but I knew that if I managed to get to the top of the South Summit, I would be able to make camp four. My motivation for getting to the top of this snow mount was strong, and despite my weary legs, we made it to the top and were blessed with a view all the way down to The Balcony, hundreds of metres below where a half-filled tank of oxygen was waiting for me.

Chapter 59 – To the Col

Amazingly, there were still people ascending. It was unbelievable that it had taken them this long and still they hadn't even reached the South Summit. The fact that they couldn't even keep up with the tail end of climbers now waiting below the Hillary Step was a worrying sight, but they seemed determined to reach the summit, apparently at any cost. Perhaps they didn't realise how far the summit was, and maybe they thought it was just past the South Summit. Maybe in their haze of confusion compounded by severe hypoxia and dehydration they thought that the South Summit was in fact the true summit. They were clearly about to be disappointed if this was the case, but they had guides and Sherpas with them, so surely they knew what they were doing and the costly risks that they were now taking.

From the South Summit, the route was straightforward. It was simply a case of arm wrapping, a technique used to descend simply by holding the rope without the hassle and time required to use an abseil device. At the anchor end of each fixed rope, I took the time to get my breath back and to look around at the view. It was spectacular, but it was a very strange sense of déjà vu, firstly because the route resembled some of the descent from Baruntse, but mainly because I had already climbed up this section in the dark, and now seeing it in all its glory in the light was like adding colour to a black and white picture. I had already seen this place, but not in the vibrancy with which I was seeing it now. As we climbed down, we were blessed with a view for miles. We could see climbers negotiating the knife edge ridge of Nuptse, and I was sure that somewhere past Lhotse, I could see Makalu and Baruntse itself. We had spent so many hours slogging up the slope but looking only at our feet and the snow in front of us, and now, climbing down but looking out from the mountain, there was a spectacular view everywhere you looked, it was simply breathtaking.

I was just behind Chhewang for much of the descent to the Balcony, and Rob was ahead with his Sherpa. The arm wrapping technique meant that we could get down the mountain very quickly in comparison to the length of time that it had taken to ascend, and the method was also relatively safe, offsetting the increase in security with an abseil device against the length of time that the device would cause us to stay above 8,000m.

Just above The Balcony, to our shock, was a group of climbers still going up for the summit. They must have left so late, or indeed something must have happened for them to be such a long way from the summit this late in the morning, but whatever it was, it certainly wasn't a safe time to continue with the amount of traffic they would undoubtedly encounter if they reached the more technical sections after the South Summit.

We carried on descending, we were still at 8,400m and I was beginning to tire through the toll that the last few days had taken. I asked Chhewang if we could rest just for five minutes at The Balcony itself and thankfully he agreed. We sat on a small snow ledge, surrounded by oxygen cylinders. After making a radio call to base camp, Chhewang amazingly just looked at the pile of cylinders and then pulled mine out of the snow. After all this time high on the mountain, he still remembered exactly where he left it, which was even more impressive considering the pile that had built up since we were last here all those hours ago. I ate a few dextrose tablets, just as something to keep my energy ticking over since I knew that we weren't a million miles away from camp four, but I still had to remain focused and not take a single slip, even when close to the camp. I took my mask off for a second so that I could take a drink from my water bottle which had mostly frozen over, and as soon as the atmospheric air hit my lungs, I started gasping for air. I was so low on energy, and just taking the mask off for even a few seconds left me desperately fighting for oxygen.

It started to snow whilst we sat on the ledge, and very quickly, my gloves started to fill with the frozen powder. Chhewang motioned us to get going, he knew how much of the route we had left, and didn't want to spend any more time at this altitude than he had to, and so we stood up and shaking the snow from my gloves, I agonisingly slid my hands back in which felt like stroking a number of razor blades all at different angles but at the same time. Almost as soon as we had left the rocky outcrop of The Balcony, we could see the South Col, and on it, hundreds of tiny tents making up camp four. Right ahead, I could see Lhotse, and then the Lhotse Couloir which was the route Bonita and Bob were hoping to climb which was still not fixed after much of the Sherpas' efforts had been concentrated on Everest.

As we were now climbing in the light, the descent was simply a case of arm wrapping down the many fixed ropes, which were often interrupted by rock bands cutting across the face. I remembered this mixed section of climbing from the ascent as it was these bands of rock that necessitated large pull-ups, and now on the descent they required careful foot and crampon placement to maintain balance.

All the steps which had to be taken carefully required the legs to gently lower the body onto the next section which was incredibly demanding and after a few rock bands had passed, I was thoroughly exhausted. We eventually came to a section towards the bottom of these bare rock areas, and for the first time whilst climbing in the Himalayas, I saw two bodies lying in the snow. Numbed from the exhaustion and hypoxia, I wasn't immediately shocked by what I saw, even though I recognised what the figures were as soon as they came into view. Both the climbers were clothed and facing down into the snow which I was thankful for, but patches of their clothes were missing, exposing their flesh which had been preserved in the freezing temperatures, and bleached white by the constant exposure to the sun. However it wasn't the danger of seeing a face, or the sight of the skin which haunted me, it was the knowledge that after what we had seen all across the mountain, from the avalanches to the queues, any one of our team members could quite easily have joined these two bodies on the mountain. But strangely, the sight wasn't scary, but it instead evoked a sense of morbid fascination that I have never previously experienced. Here, as we walked past, were two human beings, lying in the snow, so peacefully they could have almost been asleep, and yet we knew they were dead. This situation never occurs in most parts of the world; when do you ever walk down the street past a dead body just lying on the pavement? This was so far removed and indescribable from anything I had experienced on the mountain, or indeed in life, and so to see it first hand, for the first time and in a place like this was overwhelming and at the same time, a very sobering sight. Thoughts of respect for these climbers and for the mountain entered my mind; in this game that we were playing, the margin for error was so small and yet the consequences of making a mistake or simply being unlucky were the costliest of all.

We carried on down the mountain, not wanting to wait near the bodies, and eventually came to a steeper snow slope which was free from the rock bands, making the slope seem much less stable. There was a small depression just ahead and we decided to have a quick breather before continuing all the way down to camp four which was right in front of us. As we sat, huge chunks of snow started to come down, knocked off their perch by descending climbers above, just the same as it had done in this section whilst we were on the ascent. Many of the pieces were far past us, but occasionally a large chunk the size of a football whizzed past our heads. Our rucksacks were hopefully high enough to stop anything hitting us in the head, and since we weren't wearing helmets, any impact to the head by a piece of compacted snow and ice of this size would likely leave quite a mess on the pristine snow around us. There was just as much chance of being hit whilst we were descending as there was if we stayed sat down, and so we enjoyed as much rest as we could before setting off for one long stretch down to camp four. In front, I could see a climber descending drunkenly. I pointed him out to Chhewang, and we both watched as the climber kept sitting down to rest, and then getting up to descend a bit further, before sitting down again. He didn't look too stable on his feet when he was climbing, and so we guessed he had most likely run out of oxygen. As we carried on observing, I noticed the climber was wearing big red gloves and a black down suit, both the same as Rob who was just ahead of us when we rested at The Balcony. Chhewang, insistent on staying with me right until we reached our tents at camp four wouldn't leave my side until he too realised that the climber stumbling about was Rob. I knew I was fine on the descent, despite the tiredness constantly creeping into my legs, and so I convinced Chhewang to get down to Rob where I would meet him when I caught him up.

Seeing a Sherpa move at their own pace on a mountain at high altitude is a phenomenal sight, so effortless, they were clearly born to climb mountains. Within minutes, Chhewang was down with Rob, but it would take me another 15 minutes to reach them. When I finally caught up, I saw it was indeed Rob who had run out of oxygen some time ago, and was in need of constant rest to get back to camp four. Chhewang didn't have any spare oxygen with him, and when I offered mine, we both knew that Rob would cope much better without the supplemental oxygen than I would, considering that the last time I ran out, I collapsed 50m from the summit. Then, just as we started moving down together, Chhewang's oxygen also ran out, and so all three of us separated, Chhewang going as quickly as he could to camp four, and even without oxygen, he was still far quicker than I was with it.

The final slope into camp four was almost pure ice, the same section that I had slipped on at the very beginning of the climb, and now in the light I could see why. The blue bullet-hard ice was almost impenetrable, even with a firm kick downwards with the crampons. Any half-hearted step on this ground just left the crampons skidding uncontrollably, but the effort to concentrate on every step was in short supply after such a long climb. Fortunately, the ice slope didn't last long, and after a few minutes of tentative climbing, I was on flat ground with just the boulder field to cross before I arrived at our tents. I looked back and saw Rob still coming down the mountain; Mollie too would be descending somewhere high on the mountain, but hopefully she wouldn't have to endure a long wait above the Hillary Step which certainly wouldn't be desirable after a long climb through the night.

As I arrived back at our tents, I just sat myself on the nearest pile of oxygen cylinders and stared in amazement at the route we had just climbed. Chhewang came out of one of the tents and helped me with my rucksack. I was so exhausted that once I had sat down, I could barely contemplate moving, let alone find the strength to act it out. I had felt good coming down on oxygen, but as soon as Chhewang turned my regulator off, my body went into a state of panic, desperately readjusting to draw enough oxygen back in to replace what I lost without the assistance of the supplementary oxygen. It was 12 noon, and the climb had taken 16 hours; ten to reach the summit, and a further 5.5 hours to get down which wasn't such a long time considering the queues that we encountered. In those 16 hours, I had taken a few sips of water, and eaten a whole pack of dextrose tablets, and nothing else. We had all now been awake for 30 hours, and in that time, we had climbed from camp three sitting at 7,470m to camp four at 7,900m, and then to the summit at 8,848m and finally back to camp four again which gives a total of 1,378m of ascent and a total of 2,326m for the amount of metres ascended and descended in that time. This is a fair amount of altitude gain and loss for any day out in the mountains, but when considering that most of this mileage was in the so called death zone, I felt I was rightly justified in wanting to keep my oxygen flowing for just a little longer.

It was tough to even maintain a seated position on the oxygen bottles as all I wanted to do was to lie down and close my eyes which were crying out for some rest. Somehow I managed to find some strength in reserve to pick myself up, and carry my bag and oxygen bottle to my tent where Rick was resting having left the summit just before Rob and me, but even Rick had got caught in the traffic which slowed his progress.

I could barely get down low enough to open the tent door, but when I did, I saw Rick's smile, and then just collapsed into the entrance, half inside with my legs sticking out the door. I was so exhausted I could barely move, but lying there, I was safe in the knowledge that I had just summited Everest.

Chapter 60 – The Summit Aftermath

Getting down from big summits is always difficult. On one hand there is the feeling of sheer elation, knowing that the summit has been achieved, but on the other, once the initial kick of adrenalin wears off there is the reality of needing to descend, this time over 2,600m just to get back to base camp. We wouldn't be pushing on downwards on this day though, we still had team mates on the mountain, and we would need to build our strength up and have a few hours of rest before we could even think about descending. As we both lay in the tent, we could hear other teams getting ready to go to the summit, having come up from camp three or having spent the night at camp four. Neither of us envied them, and we were both glad that we had taken the risk to go for the summit only four hours after arriving at camp four from camp three.

After two hours of lounging in the tent, Rob made it down to find Rick and me just lying there. I still hadn't moved from my half in half out position, and I still had my boots on, unable to find the strength to start undoing the complex system of Velcro and laces, but I would have to take them off eventually otherwise my saturated socks would very quickly lead to trench foot. At Rob's request, I did manage to prise my feet out of my boots and after a quick examination to make sure none of my toes were black with frostbite, I put on some relatively fresh socks and instantly felt them hugging my feet. It felt so strange being back in the tent, the place where we had left in such a hurry the previous night, but now, there was none of the anxious feelings or nerves associated with the summit push, only elation and extreme fatigue. When we could just about bear to take our masks off for a few seconds, Rick and I talked through what had happened. It was nice to actually talk to someone, the first time for hours, and we both felt the same, too tired to do anything except lie down and have the occasional Cherry Bakewell and some water to quench the severe dehydration. I even found it hard to kneel and pee in to my bottle through the cumbersome suit, this time making sure I didn't miss.

A few more hours went by and then we heard some footsteps by the tent. It was Mollie! It was good to have her back, and Rick and I waited patiently for her story; about why she had got separated and what happened on the descent. As we guessed, she had got caught behind slow climbers on the ascent, but kept going and reached the summit a few hours after we did. On the descent though, both Mollie and her Sherpa had got into serious trouble at the top of the Hillary Step and had been forced to wait in the same position for two hours, running out of oxygen at the same time. We couldn't believe she had had to wait there for so long, and was then faced with the descent of the step, and a long traverse before she could get a new cylinder of oxygen. But she had the scars to prove it; frostbite on her cheeks and under her chin gave away the length of time she had waited at altitude. Still, we were now all down at the safety of camp four, all feeling worse for wear, but alive and on the surface, well. But Mollie wasn't feeling too good after her arduous descent, and after a few minutes of being in the tent, things suddenly went from bad to worse, as she started to choke, and then faster than anyone has ever moved at camp four before, ran out of the tent in bare feet to find Rob's tent, frightened now for her life. It appears that through a combination of her time at altitude and the dryness of the air that we were breathing, her trachea lining was now damaged and she was literally choking on her own airway lining. Rob managed to calm her down and administer the appropriate medication, but it wasn't a great situation to be in, even with a doctor on hand, and we just hoped her condition would improve the following day so she could at least get down to base camp.

The harshness of the dry air, compounded by the even dryer supplementary oxygen that we were breathing, played havoc with all our airways, and a number of times I felt like I was in the process of choking on a lump of grunge in the back of my throat. All of this added to the impression that whilst we were back at camp four, we weren't really safe. Not until we reached our tents back at base camp would we be safe from the mountain, and we all still had to cross the Khumbu Icefall for one last time, so it really wasn't over by any stretch. Mollie would be spending the night under Rob's supervision in case another choking episode happened again, which left Rick and me in our tent for the night. We had sorted the tent out as best as we could under the circumstances. Our boots were outside along with our climbing gear, and inside, we tried to keep eating and drinking as much as we could in preparation for the next day. There is no way we could fully recover at this altitude, we were very slowly declining whilst lying in our tent in the death zone, and so by keeping the energy and fluid coming in, we just hoped that we could slow that process of decline as much as possible so we could make it to thicker air in the morning.

Just before we made a concerted effort to go to sleep, young Dorjee Sherpa came and gave us a bottle of oxygen for the night which would stop us from getting cold and would hopefully spare us some energy during the night which would make the descent to base camp the next morning slightly easier. Neither of us could remember what flow rate to use for the night, we were both physically and mentally drained, so we asked Dorjee what we should set the regulator to. He said 2L/min, and not being able to do the maths at this altitude, we just blindly followed, setting the regulator to a flow rate that would only last a few hours given the severe cold which would affect the performance of the cylinder, not realising that Dorjee hadn't quite understood what we were asking him.

We both tried to sleep, and with the high flow rate, we soon drifted off even though we were still in the so called death zone. At 2am, we both woke up feeling cold and out of breath, even though we had only been lying down asleep for the past four hours. I looked at the flow gauge on the oxygen line to my mask and after Rick checked his, we realised we had indeed run out. Within five minutes, I was absolutely freezing, despite the fact that I was sleeping in both a high altitude sleeping bag and still had my down suit on. The first bits to get cold were the extremities, especially the hands, and after reaching around to turn the metal regulator up, I could barely feel my fingers which quickly became useless. I found my spare summit mitts and put these on but even these didn't particularly help, and for three hours, we both lay in our sleeping bags absolutely freezing cold. At one point, I put the oxygen cylinder in my sleeping bag to try and warm it up a little and get some extra oxygen out, but this was no good either. We were both in a predicament, we knew that there was spare oxygen outside, but we couldn't even undo the zips on the tent to get out, so our chances of prising an oxygen bottle away from the pile and successfully reattaching the regulator and splitter didn't seem too likely. In our haze of confusion, we shouted in the general direction of our Sherpas' tent to see if they were awake, but in the storm winds that had built up seemingly from nowhere, we weren't having any luck, and so we tried to get as warm as possible, and then wait it out until the morning.

When 5am came round, Rick's Sherpa Chyang Jyabu Bhote managed to get out of the tent in blizzard conditions and gave us another bottle of oxygen. This was the best present we could have ever asked for, and after carefully screwing the regulator back on, we were blessed with an hour of warm, comforting sleep. As Chyang Jyabu Bhote had opened the door to the tent, we saw the amount of snow that had built up over night on the Col from a storm that was battering the mountain. Climbers had left the previous night and would still be battling their way to the summit if they had not done so already. We caught a glimpse of our boots which we had left in the front of the tent which wasn't particularly snow tight, and saw that they had been covered and most likely filled with snow too. We would have to deal with this at 6am when it was time to get ready to leave the Col, but for now, all we could think of to do was sleep.

Later in the morning, Mollie also joined us for a few hours after our time to leave the Col was pushed back to 9am. She was feeling worse for wear and unable to take supplementary oxygen due to her threaded throat lining, but she was also alive and able to descend which was the main thing.

Whilst Rick and I didn't have an organised female in the tent during the night, the floor space had become a dumping ground for all sorts of equipment and clothing which all had to be collected by the respective owners and taken down the mountain. Now with Mollie back in the tent, we could start to go through the mess piece by piece, but each time a new item was uncovered, it looked ten times worse than the previous item; for example Mollie's phone and camera had completely frozen together inside a cube of ice, and our boots didn't look much better. We brought our boots in for the final 30 minutes before leaving and attempted to thaw them just a bit, but even so, we still ended up sliding icy footwear onto our already battered and bruised feet.

At 9am, it was time to leave the wilderness of camp four. Drama was unfolding high on the mountain, but we wouldn't hear any of this until we reached base camp. Chhewang helped me with some of my kit, and then after gearing up with crampons, harness and a new cylinder of oxygen, I started the long climb down to base camp with Rick leading the way and Becky following. Unlike the summit, I gazed back at the South Col because I now had time and some more oxygen to take in some of the surroundings. I wanted to take in as much as possible since I would probably never visit the Col again, and as nowhere on earth is quite like it, I wanted as many memories as possible of this indescribable place. Managing to keep my camera a bit warmer this time too, I also took as many pictures as I could so if hypoxia did destroy my memory of the place, I would have some record of the views that I was seeing, views that without prior knowledge could only be taken from another world.

Chhewang and Rick's Sherpa were still helping up at camp four but Becky's Sherpa managed to meet her and helped her navigate the Geneva Spur and around the growing queue of descending climbers. Rick and I were on our own descending through some of the most spectacular scenery imaginable, none of which seemed to have any comprehensible scale; the grandeur of the mountains all around was breathtaking. As we descended, we passed all the anchors and ropes that we had climbed up only two days previously. It was a great feeling knowing that from now on, we would only be going downhill, and that not too far in the distant future we would be on the mostly flat streets of Kathmandu. Ahead, Sherpas were fixing the summit camp of Lhotse, and once we were over the technical mixed terrain of the Geneva Spur, we could see all the way down to camp three and down along the Western Cwm which was shrouded in cloud.

Just like another episode of déjà vu, Rick and I found ourselves once again stuck behind a queue of climbers who were clearly tired from the summit push the previous day. We had got over the Yellow Band, but were now slowed down to a crawl as the climbers in front even struggled to move downwards and clearly preferred the overused option of sitting down to the standing up and moving technique. This slow movement did, however, give Chhewang time to catch up after helping to clean up camp four, and soon enough we were on the move again, passing the stationary climbers and well on our way to camp three. On one particularly icy section which was a sheet of blue ice under a thin layer of snow; my crampons refused to bite and I slipped, only catching myself with one un-gloved hand, but I was now lying on my side tangled up with fixed ropes and oxygen lines and pinned down with a heavy rucksack. Each time I tried to get up, I found there was no purchase on the glacial surface, and so Chhewang had to help to get me upright. I knew I still had to be vigilant despite being on the descent, and so made the rest of my steps with purpose.

Chapter 61 – The Final Icefall

Instead of changing out of my suit at camp three, I think both Chhewang and I just wanted to be down and off the mountain as soon as possible so after collecting the kit and clothes that I had left in the tent perched high on the Lhotse Face under imposing seracs, we continued the descent, first reaching the steep ice wall section much earlier than we had expected, and then staggering over the rocky terrain at camp two in time for a large lunch and a surprise visit from our second summit team, Kenton, Roger, Ryan and Paul. The four climbers looked in great shape compared to their team mates who were descending from camp four to base camp, and so despite their delay in going for the summit push, we were sure that they would have a great chance.

Before leaving, various members of our small group who were descending had to radio their whereabouts to base camp and Rob who was still descending the Lhotse Face with Mollie who was suffering from her ordeal on the Hillary Step. Becky left for base camp first, and then after Chhewang had collected his rucksack to carry down to base camp which was 25kgs and only half full, we left for camp one with Rick following closely behind. We didn't stop at camp one, instead heading straight for the top of the icefall where we would have a quick rest and then continue as quickly as we could for base camp.

As we reached the flat ground at the top of the icefall, the safest place to stop before entering the craziness of the ice maze, for some reason, Chhewang wanted to trade crampons for the duration of the icefall. I couldn't understand why he wanted to do this since apart from the way our crampons attached to our boots, there were completely identical, or so I thought. I didn't argue with him as this gave me more time to rest and chew on more dextrose tablets which were the only things that were keeping me going after such a long time without proper rest or food. It took the best part of 20 minutes to change the length of both pairs of crampons so that they fit our boots, so I started to become interested in knowing what Chhewang's fascination was; perhaps they would completely revolutionise my climbing ability, although the icefall wasn't the most technical place to test out this ambiguous paradigm which would almost certainly rely on the placebo effect generated by a new pair of crampons causing an increase in performance.

We set off into the icefall for the final time. It was a privilege to be in such an environment, and I felt this emotion now stronger than ever. Except for the danger of being crushed by countless unstable ten-ton blocks of ice and perhaps the odd avalanche from Russell's Shoulder, I felt at ease, and with each step closer to base camp, a weight was lifted from my own shoulders. Whilst I was taking these steps, I could tell that something was different; something didn't feel the same as it had whilst descending the Western Cwm. I realised that something was different with Chhewang's crampons, and combined with my tired legs, I kept scuffing the front points into the snow. Even though both of our crampons were technically identical, as soon as I had a lapse of concentration, my boot would suddenly catch a hard area of snow and I would stumble forward desperately trying to grasp onto the nearest fixed line or ice wall. Fortunately I managed to catch myself from quite a few falls towards the top of the icefall, and slowly I started to adapt and tried not to overlook actually lifting my leg which seemed like a fundamental part of walking which I had clearly forgotten.

Further down the icefall, now becoming fully immersed in the world of ice around us, there were a number of fixed lines that had to be descended and then crossed at heavily loaded anchor points. Some of the anchors were long snow stakes which had melted out from the snow and were now flapping about uselessly, doing nothing to prevent a fall. The icefall had changed dramatically, becoming much straighter than the previous time, and I barely recognised any section of the route that we had climbed only five days previously. As we went through this section of fixed lines, some of the loose anchors made the fixed lines sit up at boot height above the surface of the snow, and right in the middle of the icefall, just as I went to unclip and step over the line, it sprang back up catching my crampons and I fell. I lost my grasp on the fixed rope that I had been holding, and fell face first down off the side of the route and onto a snowy depression, a perfect example of a snow bridge. There was nothing now protecting me from falling, and if the snow I was on turned out to be a weak snow bridge, there would be nothing preventing me from falling into the crevasse beneath it which could be anything from 5m deep to 90m+, a depth where at the base of the visible crevasse, there is only blackness. I just lay on my front, unable to move. I couldn't quite believe what had happened; every other time I had tripped, or slipped on any part of the mountain, I had been clipped in to some form of protection, but this time, I had made the worst mistake possible, and fallen in between changing protection, potentially a fatal mistake.

It is true that most accidents happen on the descent, and this was demonstrated perfectly by my fall. I had become complacent, thinking that because I had summited Everest and now I was nearly at the bottom of the icefall, I was free from danger and nothing could get me now. Just switching off for this split second could have cost me my life, and it was only Chhewang's loyalty and a bit of luck with a firm snow bridge that saved me. As soon as Chhewang stood in the depression to get me out, his foot started to sink, potentially breaking any strength that the snow had, and so at this point, I started to scramble out as fast as I possibly could. Chhewang grabbed my arm and began hauling too, and we both ended up on the snow, shaken from what happened on this occasion, but lucky. There was no more room for error and the fall had made me realise how easily things can go wrong, even when you think the ordeal is nearly over. Every step from now on was vigilant, and for the rest of the icefall, I wouldn't put a foot wrong. Chhewang deserved this much, since it wasn't just my life that was in danger; Chhewang would also risk his life to save me, just as he had to get me to the summit in the first place, so it wasn't fair to allow a lapse of concentration to endanger either of us again.

As far as descending the icefall goes, the rest went relatively quietly with the only highlight being Khumar from the kitchen who had travelled up into the icefall wearing only trainers and a handmade rope harness to protect him from the many crevasses he had crossed on his ascent. He had come to give us something to drink, but Chhewang told him not to venture into the icefall any further, and he should wait where he was until Rob came down. We enjoyed our drink though and then left Khumar who was quite a natural climber despite rarely venturing up into the mountains; we hoped Rob wouldn't be too long so Khumar didn't have to endure the penetrating cold that pulls energy from you so savagely.

Finally, we reached the end of the icefall. We had navigated the endless bottom section which was now full of lakes showing that the season was nearing its end and the sun was starting to gain an upper hand on the intense cold that grips the area each night. We crossed our final snow mound, and then descended and crossed the same river that had soaked Rob's trainers almost a month before. As we crossed over to the end of the ice plateau and onto the rocks of base camp where we would de-gear for the final time, Chhewang's mood completely changed almost instantly. Before he had been a reserved character, and not overly talkative, clearly wanting to get the job done. Whilst we had been on the summit push, he had been with me every step of the way, but he clearly had the weight of the world on his shoulders. I hadn't noticed this before, but it suddenly dawned on me whilst we sat there looking back up at the Khumbu Icefall. I realised that the weight he had been carrying around was me, and that he had been so focused on keeping me safe which, he couldn't afford any lapse of concentration like I had had. Whilst we were on the mountain, I was his sole responsibility, and upon realising this and what that responsibility meant to him, I felt so indebted to him. But now we were at base camp, his smile came back and finally we talked, free of stress and without the burden of the summit or the dangers of the mountain hanging over us. We were now talking as brothers and as equals, but after our comparatively short time together on the mountain, I would be humbled and always honoured to be in his company.

Walking through base camp, I couldn't help but feel a sense of pride at what we had achieved. We walked through many other teams' base camps and could also feel the excitement as some of their climbers also came back through the icefall from a successful summit push. On arriving back at our base camp, we were greeted by Kame Nuru Sherpa, our expedition Sirdar, who also looked like he had had a significant weight lifted off his shoulders. We all hugged, the only way that it was possible to convey the emotions of relief, happiness and euphoria that we had felt over the past two days after coming back from the summit.

Henry was waiting in the mess tent for our arrival, and it was great to finally be at base camp and give him the good news, although he had of course already heard the news days before, and I quietly wondered whether he already knew the outcome of our attempt before we had even reached the summit; whether he knew that with the position that we were in, and the reports from the Sherpas at The Balcony on summit day, whether he already knew what chance we stood of reaching the summit. Bonita, Bob and the new face of Hugo were also waiting for us at base camp. Bonita and Bob would be leaving base camp for camp two the following day, and from there would attempt to make the summit of Lhotse which was now in the process of being fixed all the way from the summit camp, right up the couloir to the summit.

I headed back to my tent once I had recovered just enough to contemplate moving, and then made the call back home which I had been waiting for days to make. I couldn't believe I was actually making this call, and despite thousands of miles between us and an awful phone reception, I could tell just how proud Mum was, and that she was smiling just as much as Bhim was that evening when he presented us with yet another cake for our summit.

Rob and Mollie also made it back to base camp in the evening and thus completed the team's success. We had a 100% success on the summit; however this just wouldn't sink in, and as much as I looked up towards the summit, I couldn't believe quite what we had done. I didn't know whether what we had accomplished would ever set in, but for now, we would just try to enjoy the time that we had left in base camp and slowly try to piece together the blur that had been the previous week spent on the mountain.

Utterly exhausted and unspeakably bewildered by what had unfolded on the mountain, I got into my sleeping bag and what followed was probably the best night's sleep that I have ever had on a mountain. I still wasn't home, but that would be the next goal, and I could plan that little journey in the morning.

Chapter 62 – Dark Clouds

It was only the following day when I was giving a series of radio interviews that I fully heard the news. I had done a number of interviews before I had left for Everest, and whilst they gradually got easier, there was always a sense that at any moment you could quite easily make a fool of yourself on national radio which I was keen to avoid. It was hard enough to do the interview in the same room as the interviewer, but when the delay that is encountered due to an international call being made starts to affect the flow of conversation, the interview becomes progressively worse, and at times, I imagined myself as a war correspondent feeding a story back to the BBC via sat phone. Base camp did resemble a war zone in some ways, and the phone reception which was often plagued with heavy interference only adding to the effect and difficulty in getting my answers across.

There was one question, however, that stopped me dead in my tracks and started to become a dark shadow over the efforts of so many on the mountain. Speaking to a broadcaster in London, I was asked about how I felt the expedition had gone, how my team mates were doing, what was the general life plan now that we had climbed Everest, and all the sorts of questions that make you feel that the interviewer really cares about you and finds what you had done remotely interesting. There is a point, however, when curiosity gets the better of an interviewer, and the question that followed had me stumped.

"What do you think about the deaths on Everest this year?"

Every interview I gave seemed to focus on the death toll of the Everest 2012 season, but this was the first time I had even heard such news. Could these be rumours? But how could these journalists have heard about anyone becoming lost on Everest before many climbers at base camp had even heard the news? Instead of the flow I was hoping for, I now became the interviewer trying to find out what had really happened on Everest.

For a day or so, a series of interviews cast dark clouds over the mountain, and instead of focussing on the positives regarding the many ascents of the mountain this year, the media immediately grasped onto the story that the death toll on Everest during the 2012 season was rising, eventually reaching a total of ten climbers and Sherpa deaths on the mountain.

The more that I heard about the tragedy unfolding high on the mountain, the more fascinated I became about what went so wrong for the people up high on the mountain, so wrong that they couldn't make it back to the South Col alive. I decided not to listen to any of the reports coming in from any of the media stations, since these were understandably not always accurate, so I listened to Henry and the news that was coming directly off the mountain.

The first piece of news alluding to the death of a climber whilst on summit day was that of Won-Bin Song from South Korea who had reportedly died on the mountain, perhaps at the South Summit or The Balcony, and early reports suggested that due to the climber not wearing any form of eye protection, Song had become snow blind and combined with HACE (High Altitude Cerebral Oedema), he had succumbed to injuries that he had received whilst descending the Hillary Step from the Summit. A similar story was that of Dr Ebehard Schaaf who climbed with Asian Trekking. Going with a company which didn't have the best reputation, Ebehard had been descending from the summit and had reached the South Summit when he eventually succumbed also to HACE.

These reports were shocking to hear from base camp. Our whole team had been at the summit, and due to the nature of HAPE and HACE, in all reality, any one of us could have been dealt this cruel hand. Indeed even with the best Sherpa and support team on the mountain, it would be very difficult to rescue any climber from above the South Summit, particularly above the Hillary Step, and so this could perhaps have happened to anyone, including my team, even myself. I did, however, feel confident in my team and that if I was made incapable of descending from the summit, if any team could have got me down to safety, it would have been the climbers and Sherpas who I had entrusted my life to. This made me wonder though; could these deaths have been prevented?

Of course some fatalities in mountains are pure 'roll of the dice', and just like the avalanche from Nuptse that flattened camp one, that could have been our time up if circumstances had been turned only slightly out of our favour. But there were many examples of deaths that occurred through easily preventable causes. Namgyal Tshering

Sherpa who fell into the crevasse at the top of the icefall wasn't clipped into any piece of protection, and so had he have clipped into the fixed ropes before making the crossing, only his pride would have been lost instead of his life.

There was one story that stood out from all the rest though. It was the one that the media concentrated their efforts on, and for me, it hit a note because it demonstrated how the perfect tragedy unfolds on Everest. The climber was Shriya Shah-Klorfine, a 33–year-old Nepali-born Canadian, and like Won-Bin Song and Dr Ebehard Schaaf, I would have unknowingly descended past Shriya during her climb to the top of the world. Shriya climbed with Utmost Adventures and died below The Balcony after her successful attempt to reach the summit.

As far as inexperience on Everest goes, Shriya was up there, having never climbed a mountain before in her life. She paid Utmost Adventures to teach her everything she would need to know about climbing the mountain before she set foot into the icefall, but even this simply demonstrates a worrying naivety about Everest and about mountains in general. It is true that Everest isn't the most technical mountain in the world, in fact far from it. There are many mountains all over the world with as yet unclimbed routes due to their remoteness and technicality, even the north face of Ben Nevis in Scotland has unclimbed routes which would far surpass any technical grade found on Everest, but it has to be remembered that Everest isn't attractive because of its technical nature. Climbers go to Everest because it is the highest, and with that comes challenges that go beyond your technical ability; exposure to extreme high altitude, the physiological limit to what humans can achieve, at least on earth. So having never climbed a single mountain before, let alone experienced the demands on high altitude, Shriya was among many climbers who venture to Everest who could be considered a danger to the climbers around her.

Luck may have been on her side, however. Had Shriya been with guides and Sherpas who were of the highest calibre on the mountain, she may never have reached the summit, but she would have stood a much greater chance of surviving the climb. It was the unfortunate combination of an inexperienced climber, and a dangerous tour operator that ultimately cost Shriya her life on Everest. Utmost Adventures were a start-up company and had never taken anyone to the summit of Everest before. This fact alone is worrying, however Shriya's safety was in the hands of two inexperienced Sherpas, and when she refused to descend, completely overpowered by summit fever, her guides seemed powerless to stop her ascent, and instead of ordering her down, she was given one final bottle of oxygen, enough to reach the summit, but not enough to get her back safely to camp four. Shriya descended to just below the balcony where she finally collapsed and died. Putting this into perspective, my climb and descent took ten hours, and most climbers take 12 hours maximum on summit day. When she died, Shriya had been climbing for 27 hours.

There were very mixed emotions at base camp on hearing this news. The first obvious reaction is sadness as a number of lives had been lost on the mountain, and simply the knowledge that many climbers would have passed the unfortunate climbers who didn't make it down at some stage on summit day is saddening. However, as we recalled the events on summit day, and the lack of any organisation between climbers who needed to pass each other on difficult sections such as the Hillary Step, I found my interviews becoming more and more focused on the attitudes of climbers high on the mountain, rather than thinking of a specific number when asked the question, 'Do you think there are too many climbers on the mountain?'

The obvious answer to this question would be to say yes, but through experience, the number of climbers is unlikely to change because the allure of climbing the world's highest mountain will always be there, and unless some drastic geographical change takes place, Everest is likely to stay as the world's highest mountain for some time. To me, the answer was simply to be courteous and understand that for every climber who wants to climb the Hillary Step, there is another that wants to come down; however this is only a temporary solution, and for a positive change to take place, climbers need to fully understand the risks that they are taking when entering the death zone.

Of course I was part of a lucky team that managed to get ahead of many other groups; however, we were still caught behind climbers who seemed to be being taught how to climb rock whilst ascending to The Balcony, and in the back of my mind, I wondered if one of these climbers was perhaps Shriya. Many other potential fatalities were avoided, however, as a number of climbers from experienced teams with experienced guides realised that once they were behind so many climbers, it was only a matter of time before the worst happened, and so they turned around back to the safety of camp four instead of risking a potentially life threatening wait below the Hillary Step before their chance came to reach the summit.

Deaths will always occur on the world's highest mountains, and even the world's smallest mountains, simply because this is the nature of climbing, and the human nature of pushing the boundaries will occasionally result in the boundaries being pushed too far, or indeed luck running out. Luck always plays a part in climbing, and it is always a calculated risk to head up into dangerous terrain; however when considering the fatalities on Everest in 2012, those that were not down to bad luck during the summit push were due to inexperienced climbers not knowing their limits, and not appreciating just how dangerous the mountain can truly be. Oxygen, or the lack of it is an invisible danger, and unlike the danger of a vertical rock face with thousands of metres of exposure, it is a danger that can be ignored, but one that often comes back to bite you when you are least prepared. The case of Shriya and the many similar cases on Everest in previous years should serve as a reminder that Everest is no place to learn how to climb. Everest is a mountain which demands respect, and if this deserved respect is not given, it does not matter whether you are a novice climber or one of the world's best alpinists, there is always a chance that you will pay the ultimate price.

In the pre-monsoon season of 2012 on Everest, it hadn't been the avalanche that Russell Brice's team had predicted and walked away from that had been so dangerous, but simply the threat of human error.

Chapter 63 – Clearing Skies

Despite hearing this news from the mountain, we had to focus on the positives from our own expedition and so in that respect there was plenty to celebrate.

The final few days on the mountain proved a great time to wind down before our imminent descent back to Lukla and then onto Kathmandu, but there was still much to be sorted such as kit to be transported back to the UK, and even before that, Becky who had sustained frostbite in her feet after the summit push was struggling to walk and would have to be taken down the valley on horseback to avoid further damage to the already damaged areas which would hopefully recover once thicker air was encountered at lower altitudes.

As soon as our first full day at base camp commenced, there was an overwhelming sense of freedom, almost as if Everest itself had let us away with our lives; now we were free of all the previous pressures from the unknown high on the mountain. We could walk around base camp and feel happy that we no longer had to make that dreaded trek up into the icefall, or wake up at 4am in the oppressively cold air, desperately waiting for the sun to rise and raise the ambient temperature above freezing. This was the also the time where we could actually start taking in the magnitude of what had happened, where we had been, and try to remember and paint a permanent picture in our minds of the otherworldly sights that we had gazed out at from the summit.

Instead of feeling the hostility of the environment we were in where avalanches and serac falls were an ever present danger just waiting to snuff out a life, we could now fully appreciate the beauty of the scene around us, and perhaps realise how privileged we had been to see nature at its rawest and most spectacular.

It is the Sherpas who live in these mountains, and perhaps they who fully appreciate the mix of beauty and danger that the highest mountains have to offer. For the Sherpas, the Himalayas are their office, where they earn money to live and feed their families. We had been surrounded by many Sherpas who were now getting ready to once again depart from base camp to go back up the mountain and help with the efforts of both our teams' second attempt on Everest and Bonita and Bob's attempt on Lhotse. The strength of the Sherpa people is truly inspirational and often described as having a third lung, they exude strength and efficiency whilst being among the most modest and humble people I have had the pleasure of meeting. During our final days at base camp, we had a chance to say thank you and goodbye not only to the Sherpas who were the reason for our success on the mountain, but also to the cooks and base camp staff who make 70-day expeditions run as smoothly as is humanly possible. To have the time to thank all these people was a privilege since they make up the fabric of an expedition; the ability to climb Everest in modern times, as in the 1950s, rests wholly upon the team of Sherpas and support staff, the masters of teamwork in every sense.

Alas, despite our love for the mountains, Everest was not truly home, and so on the 22nd May, only three days since standing on the summit, it was time to leave the mountain. Trekking out with Mollie, Becky and Rob, we made quick progress to Pangboche where we would rest for the evening. Becky was first to arrive thanks to her speedy horse which by all accounts galloped along the valleys and didn't particularly ease up even on the steepest descents. For the rest of us, the walk-out was slightly more taxing, but the prospect of an actual bed and good food kept our pace high, much to the anguish of Mollie who was in the process of coughing up most of her trachea lining.

There was a problem with our planned descent to Lukla the following day, however, as the horse which carried Becky to Pangboche wouldn't be able to navigate a number of very steep sections after Namche, and so evacuation by helicopter was the only option. I certainly didn't want to pay for yet another helicopter, and so spent the night dreading the ten-hour walk back to Lukla where it was still an unknown as to whether the weather would be kind enough to let us fly off the end of the cliff and back to Kathmandu. I woke up bemused at our surroundings the following morning. We were in a building which was warm and didn't look like it would fall down with a sudden gust of wind, but strangest of all, I had woken up in the dining room and then remembered that instead of requesting rooms for the night, we had all finished dinner the previous evening and then elected to sleep where we sat, too tired to contemplate moving to another room. Everest was in view out of the window, but it would soon be time to say goodbye to the mountain that had become such an important part of my life for so long. A phone call from Iswari in Kathmandu confirmed that Becky was able to travel back to Lukla by helicopter and then onwards to Kathmandu on a plane, but since her insurance was paying for the flight, there were three extra seats, and so quickly abandoning the idea of walking back to Lukla, we all joined Becky and cut down the journey time by a full nine hours 50 minutes. We had just climbed Everest after all, and so a bit of luxury wasn't such a bad thing. We would thank the insurance company for their clear act of generosity when we got home.

The final four days in Nepal flew by at a rate of knots. We had flown from Pangboche to Lukla, and then the following day we were blessed with blue skies which meant we could fly out of Lukla to Kathmandu. The flight was surprisingly smooth, and despite intentionally flying off the end of a cliff face, we had all become numb to danger as we had seen far worse on Everest, and so it was now only amusing to watch the captain reading the newspaper whilst the first officer took a relaxed approach to controlling the aircraft back to Nepal's chaotic capital.

Going back to the hustle and bustle of Kathmandu was a strange experience, mainly because we were now eager to get back home after having spent almost ten weeks away from the UK, the majority of which was spent sleeping in a tent with only the most basic of amenities. I longed for the simple things, such as being able to sit down on a toilet instead of having to perform a full set of endurance squats at high altitude, and the beauty of cold running water which was safe to drink, something we had all missed after having spent many weeks drinking hot water from our bottles.

The celebrations were in full swing in Kathmandu as many teams who had come down from varying peaks all through the Himalayas, including Everest, were converging on the bars and restaurants in the city to finally let their hair down and simply celebrate the fact that they had made it back to Kathmandu alive, regardless of the success of their expedition. Despite climbers converging from all corners of the Himalayas, the endless stories seemed to revolve around Everest which was still in the process of being climbed by teams who had opted to wait for a second weather window instead of becoming caught out behind the masses. It was amazing to hear the different stories of rumour and reality, and the tales of climbers who had been climbing on the Tibetan side of the mountain, just across the border from where we had been stationed at Everest base camp in Nepal. Despite being on the same mountain, just by being based in a different country brought additional challenges which ranged from political challenges of Tibet and China, to the challenges of the route to the summit of Everest. The southeast ridge route that is documented in this book is drastically different from the north ridge route starting in Tibet, with both routes having their own unique challenges such as windier conditions on the north side versus the threat of the Khumbu icefall on the south. To hear climbers' tales of both sides of the mountain was fascinating since over ten weeks, the mountain had become part of our lives and with each avalanche or change in the icefall, it seemed as though the mountain was alive and possessed a distinctive character, albeit a dangerous one. Through the stories of climbers from the north, we could begin to see the whole character of Everest, half of which was permanently out of view.

On the final day of our expedition, the 27th May 2012 marked the day which we had to return to the UK which brought mixed emotions. There was the thought of all that makes home so special, but there was also the longing to be back in the mountains, the allure of Everest making us want to see her impressive faces just once more. To distract us from our sadness at leaving Nepal, however, we had news which marked a successful end to the Everest and Lhotse expedition direct from Henry who was still at base camp having just wrapped up the 2012 season on Everest. The whole team had achieved great success on both Everest and Lhotse, and with every single member of the team, both climber and Sherpa returning home alive, the expedition was a success in every way.

On the 19th May 2012, Mollie, Becky and I became the youngest team to successfully climb Everest. Chhewang Dorjee made his 7th summit of the mountain whilst guiding me to the top, and then made his 8th summit only six days later whilst guiding Kenton Cool to his tenth summit which broke his own record whilst fulfilling the Olympic pledge with Arthur Wakefield's 1924 Olympic Gold Medal. Alongside Kenton were Paul, Roger and Keith who also battled their way to the summit despite their delay in going for the final push. On the 20th May, Leanna Shuttleworth became the youngest British female at 19 years old to summit Everest, a record which Bonita had held since her own summit attempt of 2010. Finally on the 27th May, a summit push was launched up the couloir of Lhotse where both Bonita and Bob made the summit of the fourth highest mountain in the world in great form.

Chapter 64– Blue Skies Part 1

Man sacrifices his health in order to make money. Then he sacrifices money to recuperate his health. And then he is so anxious about the future that he does not enjoy the present; the result being that he does not live in the present or the future; he lives as if he is never going to die, and then dies having never really lived. Anon.

Despite missing out on a first class upgrade and instead paying $700 to change my flight and $100 for excess baggage fees, I managed to make it home in the best possible shape considering the torture that all our bodies had just gone through. I had no evidence of frostbite and only small patches of frostnip on the tips of my fingers which felt numb to touch but would recover in a matter of days. I had also lost weight on the expedition, losing around a stone which was very quickly put back on even before I got back to the UK with many large meals in Kathmandu, and the largest possible McDonalds meal I could find in Abu Dhabi airport. Almost as soon as we had descended from the high altitude of the Himalayas, my appetite had been raging every day and this simply highlighted what ultra-high altitude environments exact from the body. For weeks, despite being able to eat as much food as we liked, the consumption of energy was vastly elevated just to keep our bodies working with deprived oxygen, and then once we reached the realms of 8,000m where the body is simply decaying, a debt of food, oxygen and everything in between is quickly being built up in the body.

As I landed in Heathrow, I stood in front of the double doors which I had become so familiar with. The first time I had walked back through them alone, I had failed in style on Peak Lenin, yet a mere four months later, I walked through the doors once more having not only been successful on Baruntse and Mera Peak, but having had the privilege of climbing with undoubtedly the best *team* that has ever ventured into the Himalayas; the proof of this being over the following year. Now standing at the doors, I felt like I had gone in a full cycle, with each previous time spent going through the doors becoming part of the overall plan which eventually led to Everest, and now that this expedition was coming to a close, there was a certain sense of satisfaction and almost disbelief at what a rollercoaster the previous two years had been. Walking through the double doors for me marked the end of the expedition and I was now home. I met Mum who had been patiently waiting for me at Terminal 4 for the past 60 days having taken up base in the Yotel constantly liaising between my sponsors and me to distribute the expedition updates, a step too far I thought and certainly the most dedicated PA I've met. She had seemingly gone through as much mental stress as I had on the mountain through constant worry. Outside, it was the first and last day of the UK's beautiful summer, and as the doors swung shut behind me, it felt truly great to be home.

Of course some wounds run deeper than a simple loss of muscle or cracked lips and skin. These wounds would heal quickly now that I was back in fully oxygenated air, and my weight loss was certainly taking care of itself; however, it was the mental scars that slowly began to show which gave me the full indication of what I had put myself through. Whilst on the mountain, there was never a moment where I wasn't aware of what was happening around me, I was always lucid and never felt I had reached the dream world which I had imagined about prior to going to extreme high altitude; however, despite remaining in control, minute by minute exposed to severe hypoxia, my brain cells were becoming damaged through severe oxygen deprivation. This process is part of the dark side of mountaineering and all climbers who venture up into extreme high altitudes start to kill off their brain cells in some fashion. Unless a critical level of brain damage is reached, there is another, perhaps more unpleasant cause of mental scarring which can rear its head even when safely back home.

There are many stresses to be found in life such as getting married and then realising it was all too fast and fraught with mistakes which usually results in a messy divorce. Coping with bereavement or even changing jobs after realising the position of Visual Clearance Expert wasn't quite as technical as expected, are also sources of common stress. The stressed faced on an expedition is up there with the most stressful events of life and can be compared with the analogy of buying a house, another extremely stressful life event.

When buying a house, there are many stresses to be overcome such as location, the size of property, perhaps the location, the age of property without overlooking the location, and also of some consideration, the cost; specifically, will you be able to pay the mortgage off before you reach 80 having evidently lost the fight against eroding sea cliffs some years earlier. Fortunately many of these stresses are encountered at different stages, and are only encountered together when at the end of the long journey when looking for the ideal abode, and even then, it is not always apparent what level of stress has been encountered until after the event has passed.

Strangely or not, this is a similar situation faced by expeditioners who have been gradually exposed to stresses over a period of many weeks, from the first signs of altitude sickness on the walk-in, to the fear and thrill of experiencing an avalanche at close quarters. All these stresses build up all the way to summit day where the biggest stress of all is usually found, the time where you are constantly battling against immeasurable forces of nature which have the power to stall a summit push or worse at a moment's notice. As a member of a climbing team, it is paramount that you are strong willed, and are mentally tough enough not to crumble under these pressures that build up. Of course unexpected stress such as seeing a team mate or any climber for that matter lose their life is enough for anyone to fall apart understandably, but with the general stress of an expedition, there is an importance placed upon keeping emotions in; after all, who wants to climb or be roped up with another climber who is an emotional wreck after a poor night's sleep at altitude and realising they are faced with the climb of the Lhotse Face the next morning. As such, throughout the course of an expedition, despite many different elements of stress at all different levels being gradually accumulated with no obvious escape, it is important to hold it together as much as possible where failure to do so would undoubtedly end up with the emotional climber being politely asked to 'man up', or as Paul put it, 'build a bridge and get over it'.

Being able to keep inside the stresses and emotion such as homesickness in and focussing wholly on the task at hand is an important skill, and when done successfully, built up stress goes almost unnoticed and it is only when back home that you can finally reflect on what has truly happened and as moments of the expedition start to sink in, the stress starts to leak out. So just as with the analogy of the house, the ordeal was now over, and at home, I was now beginning to reflect upon what had truly happened, free from the fog of hypoxia, and able to see clearly for the first time with adequate brain power to dissect events and try to piece together what happened on key events such as the summit push and descent.

Once home, it wasn't only the stress of the expedition that was leaving me, but it was also the anguish of the two previous years of not knowing whether I would get a chance to even set foot on Everest, let alone live up to the expectation of such a mountain.

As I managed to piece together the expedition and understand the story as a whole, I began to talk about my experiences. Public speaking never came naturally, however this time I was no longer speaking about a topic which I barely understood, I was now telling a story which I couldn't possibly forget, simply because it was my own. It is often hard to explain big expeditions or comparable events to people who have never shared the same experience though, and for a while, I struggled to find the right words with which to convey the experience and my message. I had been told, and began to tell others about the famous connection between Everest and business. After all, I had only been given the opportunity to climb Everest through what was essentially a business deal, and that sowed the seeds in explaining how Everest is really just a metaphor for business. Everything that is required for climbing Everest from the teamwork to taking calculated and vaguely justifiable risks is mirrored in modern day business. After one particular talk and a discussion which followed, I realised that in fact my climb, and indeed any climb of Everest is more than just a metaphor for business; Everest is a metaphor for life itself.

Take the Khumbu Icefall for example. This stretch of mountain exemplifies perfectly the need for luck in life. The Khumbu Icefall forces climbers to play a dangerous game of Russian roulette; often there is no warning of impending danger, and there is certainly no discrimination as both 'expert' and novice climbers can be caught out by any number of dangers in the frozen waterfall. The icefall simply emphasises the frailty of life, such that at one minute life can be flourishing, and then in another, it can be snuffed out in an instant. To be walking among giants and to see this power first hand simply stresses the overall lack of control we have on our own lives, and by virtue of this fact, accentuates the need to live and enjoy life at every available moment. Whilst the hallowed meaning of life isn't to be found on Everest, the mountain instead shows a unique perspective on the *value* of life through both the perception of time and the human nature to achieve. By its very nature, Everest and the mountains of the world eclipse all of human civilisation with their age; they were here before we arrived, and will be here long after we've gone, and this simply emphasises the need to use and enjoy the time that we have been given, no matter how short. And equally, Everest personifies achievement in every way, and so to climb on Everest, just as to climb in life, is to aspire to achieve.

The risk versus reward scenario found in the mountains is true not just in business, but in all walks of life. As mentioned previously, many of the greatest achievements have been made through much daring and calculated risk taking, and often after many previously failed attempts. The key is calculating that risk to generate the biggest rewards; however, with risk comes the danger of failing, never more apparent than on big mountains where the greatest danger of all is not coming home. At the beginning of 1953, Mount Everest was still unclimbed and many lives had been lost on varying attempts to reach the summit, notably Britain's George Mallory and Andrew Irvine. When Sir Edmund Hillary and Tenzing Norgay pitted themselves against the mountain, they were taking unimaginable risks; however, since they successfully summited and lived to tell the tale, they received the greatest reward. Nowadays, whilst Everest has been climbed by many climbers on many different routes, the fact remains that due to the nature of Everest, the mountain can never be truly conquered, and so whilst the rewards for climbing Everest are no longer recognition throughout the British Empire, the personal rewards are still just the same for many climbers as they were for Sir Edmund Hillary and Tenzing Norgay.

The reason that Everest is a powerful metaphor for life is not simply because it is only on the mountains itself that such events and thinking comes about, but instead, Everest is simply an exaggeration of every adjective, verb, metaphor and simile that is found throughout every walk of life. True, teamwork will help you along in life, but in the big mountains, it is a fundamental strategy for survival. Likewise risk, luck, strength, weakness, resilience, tenacity, cold and all other characteristics found in climbers and on the mountain are simply amplified.

This is why Everest is a metaphor for life, as is every mountain and expedition on earth where a human is tested to their absolute limit, the limit of enduring hardship where life is only clutched to by the thinnest of cords. And at that moment of reaching the summit and looking out at the world, perhaps for the first time it is possible to see the true beauty of life.

Chapter 65 – Blue Skies Part 2

What do you do after you have achieved your dream? For all its wisdom, not even Everest can tell you that for it only shows the value of life, not the meaning of it.

Uniquely, I had lived this particular dream at the comparably young age of 22; standing on the summit of Everest and taking in a view that was just as potent for me as it was for the climbers before me who have stood on that very spot no bigger than a kitchen table, looking down over the world. At 22, I was perhaps more impressionable than many older climbers who had given a number of their years in the pursuit of climbing the world's highest mountain, and so inevitably, I felt there was so much more to be gained from standing on the shoulders of a giant than simply the view.

From climbing in the Himalayas, I learnt more about myself as a person in a short space of time than I could have ever hoped to whilst at home, carefully wrapped up in the bubble of a safe environment. The ability to wake up in the morning without fear or to be able to go and see a doctor when you feel ill is often taken for granted. In this world we live in which is governed by health and safety with the sole aim of preserving life and where even computers are protected against so-called viruses, it is interesting to think of a situation where all of that support and safety is stripped away, where the excitement is not just in living, but in surviving.

Lenin, Mera, Baruntse and Everest, like all the biggest mountains in the world strip away that safety net, and by their very nature, they are unconquerable and hostile, no place for men or women to survive. Because these mountains strip away so much from the people who try and climb them both physically and mentally, you are given an opportunity to see yourself for the first time. Reinhold Messner, one of the greatest climbers in history said before a climb of Everest, "I am doing this for knowing myself". I think this is the best way to describe the mirror of the mountains, a mirror which at the hardest point of an adventure, where you are at your very limit, you can truly see yourself and understand what you are made of.

As I look back over all the work by myself and others which has brought me to this point, especially my very first diaries in which I tried to write a possible path to Everest, I find it interesting to see how my ideas and views have changed and evolved mostly influenced by time spent in the mountains. I think it would be a fair assumption to make that I started on this long journey as a boy, and then arrived back at Everest base camp from the summit as a man.

Of course this journey to the top of the world had to end somewhere, and fortunately with much relief, it has ended how I could have only dreamt it would. Not everyone who has tackled Everest has been so lucky though. Many have come back home empty handed, whilst many more have been lost to the mountain, providing a constant reminder of the power that these mountains have and the respect which they rightly command.

It would be hard to detail what specific outcome has been most rewarding over this whole experience since it is still a struggle to comprehend many of the wildest moments of the expeditions. I'm sure it will take many months, or even years to truly grasp just what experience I was a part of. Maybe the most rewarding outcome will not be a single point, but instead the inception, culmination and completion of the whole journey. However just as I noted after the expedition on Baruntse, perhaps the most special of outcomes has been the friendships gained and the existing relationships strengthened. After all, what use is it to get to the top of a mountain, to finish a journey or to succeed in your dream, no matter how big or small, if you have no one to share it with?

But, the question still remains, what *do* you do after you have achieved your dream? Well that is the beauty of life, for as long as you never stop daring to dream, there are always more adventures to be had. And so after Everest, I ventured back to the place where my dream really began, in the heart of the Lake District at the summit of Scafell Pike. Despite being worlds apart from Everest, Scafell Pike hadn't changed at all since I had last climbed it only a few months previously, and whilst I stood there looking out over the Irish Sea, I realised that whilst Everest and the mountains of the Greater Ranges had changed me in so many ways, at heart I was still the same.

It was almost fourteen years to the day since I had first climbed Scafell Pike and nothing had changed; there again I stood on its lofty peak, just a boy with a dream.

Glossary

ABSEILING (ABBING/ABBED) - To descend the rope using a *descender*.

ACCLIMATISATION – The slow process of allowing the body to adapt to increase in altitude, such as through an increase in red blood cell production.

ARÊTE – A narrow ridge

BELAY – To secure the climber to a projection/protection with the rope.

BERGSCHRUND – A large crevasse separating the upper slopes of a glacier from the steeper slopes of ice or rock above.

COL – A depression in a mountain chain, a pass.

CORNICE – Overhanging mass of snow or ice along a ridge generally formed by the prevailing wind.

CRAMPONS – Metal frame with spikes which attach to the bottom of the boot allowing movement across hard snow (*névé*) or ice.

CREVASSE – A fissure in a glacier, often of great depth.

CWM (also COIRE) – An enclosed valley on the flank of a hill.

DESCENDER – A friction device used when *abseiling*, such as a figure of eight or a belay plate.

FACE – A particular side of a mountain, mostly flat and separated by *ridges*. Often identified by compass/cardinal points, e.g. North Face.

FIXED ROPES - The practice of fixing in place bolted ropes to assist climbers in exposed mountain locations, usually found on commercial expeditions.

FROSTBITE – Localised damage to skin including cell destruction due to freezing which may require digit/limb amputation.

FROSTNIP – The initial stage of *frostbite* without cell destructtion.

GEAR – See PROTECTION

HACE – High Altitude Cerebral Oedema is fluid on the brain caused by exposure to high altitude often due to poor *acclimatisation*.

HAPE – High Altitude Pulmonary Oedema is fluid in the lungs with a similar cause as *HACE*.

HIMALAYA – A mountain range stretching for 1,500 miles across Asia, home to the highest mountains on Earth.

HYPOXIA – A deprivation of an adequate supply of oxygen, in this case due to high altitude.

ICEFALL – A frozen cascade of ice, often on a gigantic scale, created when a glacier passes over a change in angle or direction in the slope of the ground beneath.

ICE AXE – A handheld climbing tool which allows effective travel over snow and ice, usually paired with *Crampons* but not always used when *Fixed Ropes* are present.

JUMAR (JUMARED) – An ascending device used to climb fixed ropes (to ascend fixed ropes).

KARABINER – Usually a near oval shaped metal hoop with a spring loaded gate, used to attach a climber to a rope or *Protection*.

NÉVÉ – Firm compacted snow with exceptional climbing properties.

PORTER – Often confused with Sherpas. Porters carry supplies to the mountain, they do not climb.

PROTECTION (GEAR) – Various pieces of equipment used to secure climbers to a mountain, either through exploiting natural faults in a rock face, or by screwing into solid ice.

PUJA – A religious ceremony performed to give offering to various deities in exchange for safe passage on the mountain. Also commonplace in everyday life for Hindus and Buddhists.

RIDGE – An elevated crest on a mountain, often the separating feature of faces.

ROPING UP – To attach all members of the climbing party to the climbing rope.

SERAC – A tower or pinnacle of ice, often collapse in the Khumbu Icefall and can trigger avalanches.

SHERPA – An ethnic group from the high Himalaya with physiological adaptations to excel at high altitude.

SNOW BRIDGE – A layer of snow bridging a crevasse.

WALK-IN – The act of walking to the intended mountain prior to climbing.

YETI – The Abominable Snowman, often described as the Big Foot of the Himalaya.

###

About the author:

I expect that if you have managed to make it this far (a hearty congratulations for doing so), the last thing you will want to hear is more about the author. I will however leave you with thanks for purchasing and reading Dare to Dream, and also hope that it lived up to and surpassed your expectations. If however you would like to know more about the author, or for further inspiration for your own journeys, please visit the following websites:

www.matthewdthornton.com

www.twitter.com/mattdthornton

Finally for your amusement, here are some reviews of Dare to Dream by a number of inconspicuous publications:

The Mail on Tuesday
"A real page turner; the pages are 1.5% lighter, so light they almost turn themselves."

The Thursday Times
"We've seen all the words before, but never in this order."

The Dependant
"Avid readers of books will love this modern twist on 'the' book, still with just as many words waiting to be read..."

The Kiribati Post
"The author clearly has some grasp of the English language; if only he could speak Gilbertese this book would be of great use to our tiny nation."

News of the Sun
"The Harry Potter series is a must read, timeless classic collection of books which marked a historic point in British literature. This is also good."

The Parent
"This book will go down in history as one of the many books written in 2013."

The Daily Moon
"A great read. Keep your receipt."

The Weekly Mail
"Like the best novels ever written this book has a front cover, a back cover, and many words of varying lengths and meanings in between. This is a book in the truest sense of the word."

The Puffington Host
"This is a book."